MY LIFE IN THE LAW

PATRONS OF THE SOCIETY

Professor Constance Backhouse

Chernos, Flaherty, Svonkin, LLP

Gowling WLG

Hull & Hull LLP

Mr. Wayne Kerr

The Law Foundation of Ontario

McCarthy Tetrault

Osler, Hoskin & Harcourt LLP

Pape Chaudhury

Paliare Roland Rosenberg Rothstein LLP

The Hon. Robert Sharpe

Torys LLP

WeirFoulds LLP

The Osgoode Society is supported by a grant from
The Law Foundation of Ontario

The Law Foundation of Ontario
Building a better foundation for justice in Ontario

The Society also thanks The Law Society of Ontario
for its continuing support.

ROBERT J. SHARPE

My Life in the Law

Lawyer, Scholar, Judge

Published for the Osgoode Society for Canadian Legal History by
University of Toronto Press
Toronto Buffalo London

Toronto Buffalo London
utppublishing.com
Printed in Canada

ISBN 978-1-4875-6860-3 (cloth)
ISBN 978-1-4875-6876-4 (EPUB)
ISBN 978-1-4875-6862-7 (PDF)

Library and Archives Canada Cataloguing in Publication

Title: My life in the law : lawyer, scholar, judge / Robert J. Sharpe.
Names: Sharpe, Robert J., author |
Osgoode Society for Canadian Legal History, issuing body.
Series: Osgoode Society for Canadian Legal History series.
Description: Series statement: Osgoode Society for Canadian Legal History series |
Includes bibliographical references and index.
Identifiers: Canadiana (print) 20250220180 | Canadiana (ebook) 20250220210 |
ISBN 9781487568603 (cloth) | ISBN 9781487568627 (PDF) |
ISBN 9781487568764 (EPUB)
Subjects: LCSH: Sharpe, Robert J. | LCSH: Lawyers – Canada –
Biography. | LCSH: Judges – Canada – Biography. | LCSH: Scholars –
Canada – Biography. | LCGFT: Autobiographies.
Classification: LCC KE416.S53 A3 2025 |
LCC KF345.Z9 S53 2025 kfmod | DDC 340.092 – dc23

Cover design: Val Cooke
Cover image: Author portrait by Joanne Tod. Oil on canvas, 36″ x 28″.
Courtesy of the Faculty of Law, University of Toronto.

We wish to acknowledge the land on which the University of Toronto Press operates. This land is the traditional territory of the Wendat, the Anishnaabeg, the Haudenosaunee, the Métis, and the Mississaugas of the Credit First Nation.

University of Toronto Press acknowledges the financial support of the Government of Canada, the Canada Council for the Arts, and the Ontario Arts Council, an agency of the Government of Ontario, for its publishing activities.

Canada Council for the Arts | Conseil des Arts du Canada

ONTARIO ARTS COUNCIL
CONSEIL DES ARTS DE L'ONTARIO
an Ontario government agency
un organisme du gouvernement de l'Ontario

Funded by the Government of Canada | Financé par le gouvernement du Canada | Canada

FSC www.fsc.org MIX Paper | Supporting responsible forestry FSC® C016245

Contents

Foreword

As the title suggests, this book is a personal reflection on Robert Sharpe's long, varied, and influential career as a lawyer, scholar, and judge, which incudes a decade as the President of the Osgoode Society. After giving an account of his early life and education, Sharpe examines his time in the law starting with being a student in the late 1960s. In those years, and as a young lawyer in the early 1970s, Canadian law focused on legal doctrine, heavily influenced by English law. As a legal academic from the 1970s to the 1990s Sharpe participated in Canadian law's emergence from the shadow of narrow legalistic formalism, and then dealt with that evolution from the very different perspective of a judge and a legal history scholar during the first twenty-five years of this century.

Throughout the book, Sharpe writes about the people who influenced his trajectory. He articled and practised with a small firm, MacKinnon McTaggart, where he was exposed to several exceptional lawyers who later became judges. From his Oxford doctoral supervisors, Ian Brownlie and H.W.R. Wade, he learned how to tackle a major research project. As a University of Toronto law professor, he enjoyed the support of his colleagues who encouraged him to become an engaged scholar, which included starting the law school's constitutional litigation program. His three-year experience working as Chief Justice Brian Dickson's Executive Legal Officer prepared him for his twenty-five-year career as a judge, bearing the responsibility of passing judgment on one's fellow citizens and working as a judge in a collegial setting. Written in an engaging and accessible style, this memoir tells the story of a man fascinated by the law who actively participated in Canadian law's transformation over the last half century.

The purpose of the Osgoode Society for Canadian Legal History is to encourage research and writing in the history of Canadian law.

The Society, which was incorporated in 1979 and is registered as a charity, was founded at the initiative of the Honourable R. Roy McMurtry, formerly attorney general for Ontario and chief justice of the province, and officials of the then Law Society of Upper Canada. The Society seeks to stimulate the study of legal history in Canada by supporting researchers, collecting oral histories, and publishing volumes that contribute to legal-historical scholarship in Canada. This year's books bring the total published since 1981 to 129, in all fields of Canadian legal history – the courts, the judiciary, and the legal profession, as well as the history of crime and punishment, women and law, law and economy, the legal treatment of Indigenous peoples and ethnic minorities, and famous cases and significant trials in all areas of the law.

Current directors of the Osgoode Society for Canadian Legal History are Constance Backhouse, Heidi Bohaker, Brendan Brammall, Bevan Brooksbank, Shantona Chaudhury, Paul Davis, Doug Downer, Linda Silver Dranoff, Timothy Hill, Ian Hull, Mahmud Jamal, Rachel McMillan, Waleed Malik, Dana Peebles, Linda Plumpton, Paul Schabas, Robert Sharpe, Jonathan Silver, Alex Smith, Lorne Sossin, Michael Tulloch, Peter Wardle, and John Wilkinson.

Paul B. Schabas
President

Jim Phillips
Editor-in-Chief

Preface

This book focuses on my professional life in the law. My personal life – a supportive family, a long-term marriage, and three children and three grandchildren, of whom I am very proud – has been very happy. But beyond that, I will have little to say.

I started to write this book shortly after I retired from the judiciary in 2020. I had not planned to write a memoir. I felt that the exercise would be self-indulgent, but I undertook it because of several factors. First, coming to the end of my twenty-five years as a judge, after working for over fifty years in the law, caused me to reflect on what I had done with my life. Second, there was the task of dealing with all the files I had accumulated. As a sometime historian who had done archival research, I could not take the easy way out and send it all to the recycling bin. Going through my files, including items my mother had saved from the time I was a child, caused me to reflect on the sweep of my life and the variety of things I had done. Third, and perhaps most decisive, along came the COVID-19 pandemic and the lengthy period of isolation it imposed. That put an effective pause on my return to the Faculty of Law as a Judge in Residence and on my new work in the field of alternative dispute resolution. I had time on my hands and no other writing project on the go. And so, I started.

As will become apparent, I have lived a fortunate and essentially unplanned life. I do not come from a prominent family. I did not meet a lawyer until I was at university. Perhaps on account of my small-town upbringing, I suffer to some extent from impostor syndrome, genuinely amazed at my unexpected successes.

This book is based upon my recollections, supported by the material in my papers, where possible. I think it all happened as I describe it, and I have done my best to make this an accurate account. But, of course, memory is faulty. I am sure that I have forgotten events that were important at the time, and no doubt I have attributed importance to other events that did not seem as important when they occurred.

I want to thank several people who helped me write this book.

I owe a particular debt to Jim Phillips, Editor-in-Chief of the Osgoode Society for Canadian Legal History, who encouraged me to write the book and provided constant guidance and encouragement as I worked on it. Jim read the manuscript and made many helpful suggestions, as did Philip Girard, the Osgoode Society's Associate Editor.

I am also indebted to two anonymous reviewers. Their perceptive comments and suggestions made this a better book.

Several friends and colleagues read all or part of the manuscript. I thank Martin Friedland, Kent Roach, Arnold Weinrib and Patricia McMahon, and Claire and Geraldine Sharpe for their encouragement and assistance.

My summer research assistant, Benjamin Zolf, helped me pull the project together.

I am particularly indebted to Shirley Margolis who gave the manuscript a thorough edit and improved it immeasurably, just as she had done with my draft judgments when she served as my law clerk many years ago.

MY LIFE IN THE LAW

1
Beginnings

There is nothing remarkable about my origins or my early life. But that is where I begin this book, partly to follow the conventional start for a memoir and partly because the lessons I learned in my early life have strongly influenced me in my career as a lawyer, a scholar, and a judge.

I had a small-town upbringing, a loving and supportive family, and a happy, if uneventful, youth. No one in my family had ever gone to university, let alone law school. I did not meet a lawyer until I was at university. I learned from my family and early years the values of community, family, hard work, and decency to all, however humble their origins. Those have been my guiding principles.

My Birth

I was born on 4 December 1945, in Brantford, Ontario. My mother, Eleanor Jane Sharpe, turned twenty-five four days after I was born. She was the third of four children in her family. My father, Ira Sutherland Sharpe, had just turned twenty-seven at the time of my birth. He was the youngest in a family of nine.

The day I was born was my maternal grandmother's fifty-second birthday. I was her first grandchild. Annie Mae Cooper was such a warm, loving, and good-natured person that I am quite sure I would have been close to her even without the happy coincidence of our birthdays. But as a child I always felt it had somehow created a special bond between us.

My Father's Background

My father was serving in the Royal Canadian Air Force in western Canada when I was born. My mother had returned to her home in Brantford for the birth. My father did not serve overseas. He had been stationed in Brandon, Manitoba, and Weyburn, Saskatchewan, at flight-training depots. He worked as a bookkeeper and reached the rank of sergeant. Unlike many who served during the war, he never regarded the experience as a high point in his life. Instead, I think that he found it to be an unpleasant duty that had to be endured. While he was a highly disciplined person, he disliked military discipline and formality based, as he saw it, on nothing more than station and rank. He certainly passed that attitude on to me.

My father was raised in rural poverty. The youngest of nine children, he was born and grew up on a farm in Micksburg, a tiny one-store Ottawa Valley hamlet twenty kilometres south of Pembroke, Ontario. When I was about fourteen years old, I asked my father why his parents had so many children. He replied, "Ignorance," with no apparent thought that, but for that ignorance, he would not exist.

I know very little about my grandfather James Sharpe, who died of heart disease at the age of fifty-six in 1931 when my father was thirteen years old. James had worked as a barber before he married. He then worked as a carpenter and a subsistence farmer, struggling to feed his nine children. At the time of his marriage to Mary Ann Sutherland, James's name was spelled "Sharp," but within a few years, it became "Sharpe," apparently at the insistence of Mary Ann, who did not approve of some of the other Sharps who lived in the area. James was born in Canada as, so far as I can tell, was his father James, while my great-great grandfather, another James Sharp, immigrated to Canada from Ireland.[1] Ira spoke well enough of his father, but I never had the impression that he enjoyed a close relationship with him.

On the other hand, there was a strong bond between Ira and his mother, a remarkable woman who kept the family and the farm going after James's early death. Mary Ann Sutherland was born in the Micksburg area in 1880. She married James Sharpe when she was nineteen years old, and he was twenty-one.

Mary Ann's father, my great-grandfather, Daniel Sutherland, was born in Upper Canada in 1838. He was the child of parents who came to Canada in the early 1800s from Dornoch, Scotland, likely as a result of the Highland clearances. I have an oval framed photograph of Daniel and his wife, Jane Millar, which shows a magnificent rural couple looking their best for what must have been an extravagant gesture of having a formal portrait taken.

Jane immigrated to Canada as a child with her mother from Limerick, Ireland, to join her father, who had arrived the year before. Daniel's first wife, Jane's cousin, died after having two children. Daniel and Jane had nine children, of whom my grandmother, Mary Ann, was the eldest. My great-grandmother Jane Sutherland reminds me of Mary Ann, but that may be because my grandmother had the same style of clothing and hair, even up to the time of her death in the late 1950s.

My great-grandfather Daniel had a long grey beard and, but for that, I see a resemblance to my father. Daniel was a farmer and a beekeeper who also trapped and hunted. He met his end on a chilly November day in 1916 at the age of seventy-eight. Wearing a heavy coat, he decided to check his traps and perhaps do some duck hunting on the Snake River in a birchbark canoe. The canoe capsized and he drowned. His death haunted my grandmother. It left her with a phobia of boats and any activity on water, a fear she would express when my brother and I wanted to go boating or swimming.

Mary Ann had never set foot in Scotland, nor had her father, but she was extremely proud of being a Sutherland and, as she saw it, Scottish. I never heard her mention the fact that her mother was Irish, nor did I hear from her that her husband had Irish roots. She chose to ignore the family's Irish heritage in favour of her father's Scottish lineage. Mary Ann was a Presbyterian, as were the Sharps, although so far as I could tell, she was not particularly religious. I am not aware of her Irish mother having been a Catholic, but Mary Ann certainly seems to have been determined to distance her family from any suggestion of an Irish connection, probably succumbing to the commonly held anti-Irish feelings of the day. She had a very strong distinctive Ottawa Valley accent, with its mixture of Irish and Scottish influences. Her vocabulary and manner of speech sounded to me quaint and from a long-ago era. So too were many of her ideas about modern life. I remember how disturbed she was when the Russians announced they had sent the first man into space. That upset what she thought to be the natural order of things, which for her was to remain firmly on the ground, work hard, and look after one's family.

My father lacked a formal education. He attended the local one-room schoolhouse up to Grade 8, but there it ended. There were no school buses to take rural children into town to attend high school. He would have had to board in Pembroke to extend his education beyond primary school, but that was beyond the means of my widowed grandmother. I suspect that she was quite happy to have him, her youngest child, stay home on the farm with her, but he was very restless and determined to escape rural poverty.

Life on the farm was difficult and the depression had been slow to lift. The only source of income was derived from my grandmother's weekly trips to the farmers' market in Pembroke to sell a few chickens or whatever produce was available. There was no indoor plumbing and no electricity. The only source of heat in the uninsulated clapboard farmhouse was a large wood stove in the kitchen.

When he was about eighteen, Ira decided that he would head north to look for a job in mining. Fortunately, he was rescued from that perilous venture by his brother Ernie who was working in the car business in Brantford, Ontario. Ernie had just married. He and his wife, Mae, took my father into their home. Ernie paid for Ira to attend a private business college, where he learned the basic skills of bookkeeping. Ira then found a job at the same car dealership as his brother. Ira worked very hard for the rest of his life, but his success could be traced back to the extraordinary kindness and generosity of his brother Ernie and his sister-in-law Mae.

My Mother's Background

My mother's story was quite different, although she too had humble beginnings. Her father, Thomas Cooper, was born in England in the Liverpool area. He came to Canada as a young boy to work on a farm near Brantford. He came as either a "British Home Child" or "Barnardo Boy," both of which were social reform schemes designed to rescue disadvantaged English children from poverty and delinquency by sending them to work on farms in Canada and other parts of the British Empire. My grandfather complained of being ill-fed and ill-treated upon arrival in Canada, and it is now widely recognized that these child-rescue schemes, perhaps well intended, did lead to various forms of serious abuse.

My mother's maternal grandmother, Nel (Helen Hyam), was the daughter of domestics who worked at Buckingham Palace. My mother's grandfather, Frederick William Kerr, was born in Sligo, Ireland. He joined the British army and served with the Royal Horse Guards. He was involved in the Tel El Kebir engagement in the Anglo-Egyptian War in 1882 and in the relief of General Gordon's Khartoum expedition in 1884–85. He met Nel while serving with the Horse Guards in London in the 1890s. Frederick was several years older than Nel, who was still in her teens when, in what must have caused an enormous scandal, the couple eloped to Canada in 1893. They settled in Brantford. Frederick, a tall and imposing man, became a police officer, eventually the Chief Constable on the Six Nations Reserve near Brantford.

Although he was fifty-three years old when the 1914–18 War broke out, Frederick volunteered and served as Sergeant-Major of the 75th Battalion of the Canadian Expeditionary Force. He was wounded and returned to Canada in 1917 and then served as a Sergeant-Major of the flying corps. Frederick and Nel's son, and my grandmother's brother, William, known in the family as "Billy," enlisted at the age of nineteen. He was wounded in action, and my mother recalled that until he died at a relatively young age, he suffered from post-traumatic stress disorder, then known as "shell shock."

My grandfather, Thomas Cooper, enlisted at the age of twenty-one. There was, it seemed, no question that when England was at war, all able-bodied men, especially those with strong Anglophile leanings, had to enlist. In their wedding picture, my grandmother, Annie, appears as a very attractive young woman standing beside "Tommie" in his military uniform.

My mother was the only girl in her family. She had three brothers, two older, and one younger. To make for an even more male-dominated household, my grandmother's youngest brother, George, was only a few years older than her eldest son, and George became another older brother to my mother. When Frederick Kerr suddenly died in 1925 at the age of sixty-four, his widow, Nel, and their son, George, moved in with my grandmother and grandfather and their four children. Such living arrangements were common at the time, but as my mother grew older, she told me that she thought that generations living together was not ideal and that she would not repeat the mistake. She believed that Nel's dominating presence had caused problems in her parents' marriage.

Nel took a special interest in my mother, who always referred to her grandmother as "Mum." They shared a bed from the time my mother was a young girl until she moved from home to marry my father. I have a dim memory of Nel, who died when I was a young boy. She was an imposing woman who, according to family lore, often said "Don't argue with me because I know I am right." She retained her English accent and her English manners. She strongly influenced my mother, who was fascinated by the royal family and all things English. In 1936, Nel took my mother, then sixteen, on the "Vimy Pilgrimage," a partially subsidized trip to England and France organized by the Canadian Legion for veterans of the Great War and their family members for the commemoration of the Vimy Memorial by King Edward VIII.[2] That was the only trip Nel made to England after her elopement, and it certainly had a lasting impact on my mother. She visited distant relatives, including some who still worked at Buckingham Palace, and spoke in whispered tones about the coming scandal of the King's insistence upon marrying Wallis Simpson.

Despite her fascination and vicarious relationships with royalty through her forebears' domestic service at the palace, my mother was raised in a relatively humble working-class home. Her father, Thomas, worked first as a cigar maker and later at a brewery. As he suffered from alcohol use disorder – he blamed his disease on the abuse he had suffered as a child farm labourer – a brewery was perhaps not the best place for him to gain his livelihood. I recall him as a jovial Englishman, but he did not have a strong influence on me since he died when I was about ten years old.

My mother was a good student who enjoyed school, but after she finished Grade 11, she found a job in the office at the brewery where her father worked, and her formal education ended. As she explained it to me years later, the owner of the brewery liked her work and offered her a permanent job. It was the sort of job to which a woman with a high school education could aspire in those days. Her parents could see no reason for her not to quit school before matriculation. My mother knew that she would have enjoyed and benefited from an education. She was determined not to repeat for her children the mistake her family had made.

My mother's three brothers served overseas in the 1939–45 war, as did her uncle, George. I heard many tales of life in the army during the war from my uncles, one of whom was awarded the Military Cross. They certainly did not share my father's attitude towards the military. I could see that the war had left its mark on them. I often thought how the two wars had touched my grandmother, Annie, who had seen her husband, father, and brother off to fight in World War I and her brother and three sons off to fight in World War II. Miraculously, all returned more or less unscathed, save for poor Billie, who never returned to normal life.

I was close to both my grandmothers, and I felt the warmth of their love. I was fascinated by Mary Ann's quaintness and influenced by her example of hard work and frugality. Annie taught me the importance of maintaining a positive attitude and enjoying life in the face of adversity, in her case, Tommy's alcohol use disorder and early death and seeing her father, brother, husband, and sons go off to war.

Early Life

My father and mother met at an Anglican church dance. I am not sure how my father found himself at the dance, because he was not at all religious and certainly not an Anglican. My mother was a serious lifelong Anglican, so she belonged.

My father enlisted in the Air Force after the 1939–45 World War broke out. He returned to Brantford to be married in September 1942 and together my parents headed west to take up his posting.

After he was discharged, my father returned to work in the car business until his brother Ernie secured a Ford franchise in Sudbury, Ontario. My father accepted his brother's invitation to join him, and we moved to Sudbury. But the Sudbury adventure ended suddenly and tragically when my uncle Ernie died of a heart attack in 1947 at the age of forty-two. He left his widow, Mae, and his son, Jim, who was only six years old. Mae tried to persuade Ford to let her maintain the Sudbury franchise with my father's help, but the company could not imagine leaving an important dealership in the hands of a woman, and my father did not have the required financial wherewithal, so we returned to Brantford.

From the time he was a boy, my father followed his mother's example, scrimping and saving every penny. He was determined to build a better future and to run his own business. He was prepared to take risks, but his resources were limited. Ford offered him a franchise that had been abandoned by a bankrupt dealer in Picton, Ontario, a town 335 kilometres east of Brantford. I doubt that he was the company's first choice. Without ever having been to Picton, he accepted the challenge, and we settled in Prince Edward County long before it became a fashionable destination with wineries, restaurants, and cafés.

We first lived in the upper storey of a house on King Street, not far from the rather rundown garage my father took over from the bankrupt dealer. Our abode was very basic. Eventually we moved to a small rented house on Chapel Street.

My brother, John Ernest, named after my father's brother, was born in April 1949. I knew that my mother was going to have a new baby, and I very much wanted it to be a boy. One of my earliest memories is of my grandmother, Mary Ann, coming to get me up after my afternoon nap to tell me that I had a baby brother. I was thrilled. Children were not permitted to visit the local hospital, but my father and I climbed the fire escape to the window of my mother's room so that I could see her and baby Ernie. Ernie and I have always enjoyed a close relationship. Ernie is a gifted athlete and despite the difference in our ages, he had no trouble keeping up with me and my friends at hockey, golf, and other sports. After earning an MA in economics at Western, Ernie moved back to Picton and joined my father in the car business. After Ernie sold the car business, he became an investment adviser and provided me with some very welcome and sound financial advice.

My father worked very hard to build the business. Picton was an insular community. The locals were wary of newcomers. It took time and effort to break in, but gradually business improved. In the early 1950s, my father built a new garage and dealership at the edge of town and bought a large Victorian-era house on Centre Street, one of the nicest streets in town.

I have recounted this family history because I think that it says something about the lawyer, scholar, and judge that I became. I learned a great deal from my father's example and his rise, through sheer determination, hard work, and careful saving and planning, from rural poverty to a comfortable life. As the youngest of nine, he was a very family-oriented man. He got through some very tough times because of the resilience of his mother and the generosity of his brother. Through his example and by quite explicitly preaching the message to me, he did his best to ensure that I understood the values of hard work, frugality, and family. His determination to make a better life for himself and his family is an example I have always looked up to and admired. When I tackle a new project, I am guided by my father's determination to bring to a successful completion everything he took on.

My mother was a gentler soul and less driven, but she too had a very strong influence on me. In some ways, I think she understood me better than my father did. Like her, I have always been a reserved and essentially private person. My father was more outgoing, as he had to be to succeed in his business. He was often puzzled about why I would spend so much time quietly reading rather than engaging in play. My mother understood that side of my nature and interests. She enjoyed reading and she encouraged my interest in books. I am sure that I acquired my affinity for things English from my anglophile mother, but within me there is also a strong strain of Scots stalwart reserve and frugality inherited from my father.

My parents enjoyed a solid and long marriage. I grew up in a very happy home. We lived a comfortable life, benefiting from both my father's hard work and the good luck of the post war prosperity that helped elevate many rural and working-class Canadians to solid middle-class standing in the 1950s and 1960s. I did not suffer any of the deprivations my father had endured, but he made me aware of the fact that without hard work and careful saving, destitution was around the corner. My father enjoyed being the provider, and my mother was happy being a homemaker. An avid sewer, she made my clothes and those of my brother until we reached our teens. My father came home every day for lunch and, even when I was in high school, I did the same. This meant that my mother had three meals to prepare each day and that we were all regularly seated at the table discussing the affairs of the day. She assumed her household duties with joy and took satisfaction in making sure we were well fed, well clothed, and well loved.

As I have mentioned, neither my mother nor my father had much of an education. My father was acutely aware of that fact. I think that he was unduly sensitive about his lack of education. He was a highly intelligent, articulate man and quite engaging in conversation. But there was an inner and almost always hidden lack of confidence because of his educational deficit. No one from either the Sharpe or Cooper families had gone to university before my generation. My parents were determined that should end. My father may have been puzzled by my fascination with books, but he was determined that my brother and I would be educated. My mother fully shared that ambition. They left my brother and me with a strong message; there was never any doubt that we were expected to complete high school and go to university.

A County Upbringing

Picton is a county seat and the largest community in Prince Edward County. The County, as it is known to the locals, was a quiet, peaceful, and relatively insular community. In the 1950s and 1960s, the population of the County was about 18,000, of whom about 5,000 lived in Picton.

A stone cairn at Carrying Place, in the northwest corner of the County, marks the spot where in 1787, the opening negotiations for the "Gunshot Treaty" between the British Crown and the Mississauga Chiefs took place. Carrying Place was a portage route used by Indigenous Peoples to bring canoes from Lake Ontario to what is now called the Bay of Quinte. The Gunshot Treaty allowed the British to settle United Empire Loyalists, who fled the American Revolution, in the County and beyond. When I was growing up, the historic Indigenous presence in the County had largely disappeared, but not far away on the other side of the Bay of Quinte was the Tyendinaga Mohawk Territory reserve near Deseronto, northwest of Picton.

The economy was essentially agricultural. In those days, there was a very large canning industry with many local brands of tinned corn, peas, and tomatoes. There were several cheese factories, all making cheddar cheese, and quite a significant dairy industry. Two local dairies supplied milk, in reusable pint bottles and non-homogenized so that the cream rose to the top. In the early days, milk was delivered to our door from a horse-drawn wagon. Apple and cherry orchards were large and prosperous. Commercial fishers were active on Lake Ontario. Most of the catch was exported, but fresh fish was always available at what we called the "fish house." The fish house looked more like a garage than a food establishment, and when I was sent there to buy some fish, it seemed to me there was more drinking and gambling going on than fish processing.

Picton's Main Street had everything one needed. There were a couple of grocery stores, three hardware stores, two "five and ten cents" stores, two Chinese restaurants, two pool halls, a bowling alley and two seedy beer parlours, one of them in the since restored Royal Hotel. The Regent Theatre showed mostly B-grade films and almost always a western for Saturday matinee. The price of admission was in the ten- to fifteen-cent range. There were men's and ladies' clothing stores, barber shops and hairdresser salons, and, of course, the local branch of the LCBO. There was, and still is, a very good public library, and I was a regular user.

There was a surprisingly large Eaton's department store just across the street from its rather down-market local rival, Lipson's. If what we needed was not in the store, there was always Eaton's catalogue, as well as one from Simpson's, thick books of treasures that came in the mail two or three times a year. My mother was a frequent catalogue shopper. The clothing that I wore that she did not make herself almost always came from the catalogue. My father's Ford dealership competed with two garages selling General Motors vehicles and two selling Chrysler products, as well as Volkswagen and Rambler dealers.

The character of the County is strongly influenced by its geography. It was a peninsula jutting out into Lake Ontario but has been an island since the isthmus connecting the County to the mainland at Carrying Place, near Trenton, was severed by the construction of the Murray Canal in the 1880s. The County lies south of Belleville, about 200 kilometres east of Toronto and 85 kilometres west of Kingston. The land mass is approximately 380 square kilometres but with an irregular shape, so the County has a disproportionately long coastline. The lake is never far away, and the roads take many twists and turns.

There are several villages and hamlets. Wellington was and is a thriving community west of Picton with a very strong sense of community. Between Wellington and Picton lies Bloomfield, a quieter and more tranquil village. Other hamlets – Cherry Valley, Milford, Demorestville, Waupoos, and Consecon – all have their own identities and sense of place.

In the 1950s and 1960s, there were three ways to reach the mainland. One could cross a bridge over the Murray Canal at Carrying Place to go west, take the bridge to Belleville to go north, or take the Glenora Ferry to go east towards Kingston. The two bridges swung open to allow boats to pass, so one was never entirely sure how long it would take to leave the County. By the 1970s, the swing bridge at Belleville had been replaced by a taller structure, and another modern bridge was constructed near Northport to afford ready access to Highway 401 and eastwards.

When I was growing up, and to some extent still to this day, proximity to the water and relative isolation from the mainland produced what I would describe as an island mentality. There were many locals who rarely, if ever, left the County. The thought of moving away from the County was anathema, even for young people looking for work. Most people, it seemed to me, were born and raised in the County, went to the local schools, married other locals, worked, had families, and eventually would die as loyal County citizens.

Although my formative years were happily spent in the County, I never quite saw myself as a complete native. I was only three years old when we moved there, but somehow having been born elsewhere to parents who came from away made me different. My brother was born in Picton, but my mother used to say that the locals probably did not accept him as a native because he had been conceived elsewhere. I certainly did not resent the fact that my roots were slightly suspect, but it did make me think that, somehow, I was different.

When I was about twelve years old, my parents sent my brother and me to summer camp for a month. They wanted us to learn how to swim, a skill neither of them had. They sent us to Kilcoo Camp in Haliburton, an upmarket camp that my cousin Jim Sharpe attended. It was my first time away from home on my own. I was eager to go but I was also uncertain about how I would fare. My uncertainty was not so much that I would be away from my parents as a concern about how I would fit in. I knew from Jim that most campers came from Toronto, many from wealthy families, and quite a few attended private schools. This was not exactly the crowd I was used to. I worried that I would come across as a country bumpkin. But camp was a great leveller, and I thoroughly enjoyed the experience. I learned to swim, although I have never been particularly fond of swimming. I also learned to sail, canoe, make a fire, and go on a canoe trip. In my third year at the camp, I was picked to go on a ten-day canoe trip in nearby Algonquin Park. I loved the experience and eagerly pitched in with the portages, gathering firewood and making meals. Much to my surprise, I was picked as the person to give a report on the trip before the entire camp at the final dinner in the lodge. I was very proud to have been selected. It gave me great confidence to realize that I had not only survived being with all those fancy kids from Toronto but had been chosen ahead of them to speak on behalf of the ten-day trippers.

Sports, Politics, and Religion

As a young boy and teenager, I spent a great deal of time playing various sports. Much of my sporting activity was of the pick-up variety. A group of us would gather at the school yard and, depending upon the season, play a game of softball, baseball, or touch football.

We spent a lot of time playing ball hockey in our driveway. In the winter, the town was often slow to clear the streets of snow. As the road became packed down, we played on the street in our boots with a puck, making the surface even smoother. We knew one of the men who worked for the town spreading sand. When he saw us playing hockey, he would stop the sander and leave the slick surface for us to play on.

I also enjoyed playing golf, a game I still play, although I have never been better than an average golfer. My brother and I had junior memberships at the Picton Golf Club, and we could cycle out there to have a game with our friends. The course was established in 1907 and, although it has since been made into an eighteen-hole course, it retains some of its original charm. The nine-hole course I learned on was well-cared for by the club pro, Fred Purcell, a very genial Englishman who loved the game and loved being in charge of his own course. He welcomed young golfers. He gave me a lesson or two, but I learned the game more or less on my own with tips from friends and my father, who was a keen golfer. I still love getting out on the Picton links.

My father was a hockey fan. He took my brother and me to at least one game per year at Maple Leaf Gardens in Toronto. I can remember the thrill I felt when I first saw that fabled ice surface. The game between the Leafs and the New York Rangers ended in a 0–0 tie. No goals and, in those days, no regular season overtime. While the Leafs went on to win the Stanley Cup a number of times after that game – and, as a diehard fan, I am confident they will win it again – that first game symbolizes the frustration of being a Leafs fan. Exciting to be there, yes. Close, but not a win, and not even a goal against a team they should have beaten. But there is always the next game and the next season.

We were also regular spectators at the Belleville McFarlands Senior A games in the late 1950s. The level of hockey was very good. There were only six NHL teams. Several of the Belleville Macs went on to play in the NHL and many more would have reached that level had the league expanded earlier. The team won the Allan Cup, the national Senior A championship, in 1958. That made them Canada's representative at the 1959 World Ice Hockey Championship in Czechoslovakia. We listened to the games on the radio and were thrilled when our team, the beloved Macs, won the world title.

I started playing organized hockey when I was about twelve and the town got an artificial ice rink. I loved the game. I played on the town's competitive teams until I was in my final year of high school. For a few seasons, I proudly wore Gordie Howe's and Maurice Richard's number 9 with the "C" as the team captain. Our biggest rivalry was with the Wellington Dukes. We felt that the Wellington will to win sometimes went a little too far. I recall one game when, at a critical point, we scored a goal off the crossbar of the Wellington net. Unfortunately for us, the referee was the father of one of the Wellington players. He refused to count the goal by inventing a new rule: according to him, goals off the crossbar do not count. But I do admire the Wellington love of sports and competitive drive to win. Today, they have a Junior A team, the Dukes, a remarkable achievement for a town of that size.

In my final year of high school, I made Picton's Junior team but decided against playing because of all the travel and late nights. I was a decent hockey player, good enough to be invited to apply when I was in Grade 12 to play hockey at Brown University in Rhode Island. I was very interested in this prospect, wrote the SAT, and was accepted at Brown. But my father was not keen for me to go. Financial support would depend upon a means test and I would not qualify. I needed a reference from the principal of my school. He supplied the reference but suggested that it might be better for me to focus on academics. And deep down, I wondered if I was good enough to play hockey at the intercollegiate level. While the prospect of going to Brown was very attractive, in the end I decided, or was persuaded, against it.

My other experience with hockey was refereeing. The town's house league program started every Saturday morning at 8 a.m. From the time I was about fourteen, I would show up at 8 a.m. and spend the morning refereeing house league games. I graduated to refereeing at the competitive level and enjoyed it almost as much as playing the game. When I went to watch a hockey game, I would watch the referees as much as the players, studying where they positioned themselves and how they maintained order and kept the game moving along. Perhaps my interest in refereeing was an unconscious reflection of my latent interest in the law and judging.

As a boy, I took a lively interest in politics. I loved watching the election results. My first memory of politics was watching the results of the 1956 federal election when Conservative John Diefenbaker ended a long run of Liberal rule by securing a minority government and then, in 1958, a thumping majority. Unlike my father, a died-in-the-wool Conservative, I was not a Diefenbaker fan. This and subsequent Canadian political events led to some very lively debates around the dining room table, my father taking the side of the Conservatives and me, the Liberals.

I was a great admirer of Lester Pearson and thought him much superior to Diefenbaker. Dad thought that Dief was more a man of the people and that Pearson and the Liberals did not understand someone like him, who had worked hard to make it on his own. We enjoyed sparring and challenging each other's opinions. Our exchanges were heated but always in good fun, with one notable exception. At sixteen, I had a car from the garage to drive and I decided to fly the proposed new Canadian flag – the "Pearson Pennant" – from the aerial. My father did not want to be seen taking sides in that debate in conservative Prince Edward County, where the prevailing view strongly favoured retaining the Red Ensign. He was very annoyed with me, and I relented. After all, it was his car.

My father loved going on hunting and fishing trips with his buddies. He also regularly enjoyed having a few drinks with "the boys." He thought I was a bit too serious. I did go out with a few girls, and I had some friends with whom I would have the odd surreptitious beer, but on the whole, I led a very tame life. I was rather shy and quite happy to spend most of my time at home reading or watching TV. In my teens, my father encouraged me to get out and, as he put it, "have some fun." I was not quite sure what he meant by "fun," and he failed to nudge me out of my quiet, tame lifestyle.

My father's family was Presbyterian, but he had no interest in religion. My mother was a serious Anglican. She was an active participant in the activities of the church. I went to church regularly with my mother, attended Sunday school and went through the classes for my confirmation.

I no longer follow any religion, but my Christian upbringing has certainly been a strong influence. I can see this from the copy of the essay I wrote at age seventeen when asked to discuss this quotation: "Understand that a man is worth just so much as the things are worth about which he busies himself." I did not know it at the time, but this comes from the *Meditations* of Marcus Aurelius. In my essay, I demonstrate my Christian upbringing by starting with Jesus's parable of the talents and the reward received by the man who had used his talents and the reprimand given to the man who had hidden his. I conclude with what strikes me as a Christian message. We will, I say, be judged by our actions, not our intentions. We are morally bound to make use of the talents we have been given. I extoll the unequalled feeling of accomplishment of the person who writes a book. Our purpose in life, I say, is to be useful in the world and our prime goal should be accomplishment, not ease. Reading this essay, written when I was seventeen years old, I am struck by how much it reflects attitudes and beliefs that I retain to this day. I never would have predicted then that I actually would write a book, but I have since experienced the very feeling of accomplishment that I predicted.

Pride in Picton

I feel very fortunate to have grown up in Picton. We had the freedom to come and go and amble about as we pleased. It was a safe and welcoming community that had a great deal to offer. Small towns provide the comfort of a close-knit and, for the most part, caring community. But they also have their disadvantages. Everybody seemed to think they knew what everyone else was doing. There are conventions that cannot be broken. The community pride was admirable. But as I grew older, I started to resist what seemed to be smugness and unthinking self-satisfaction. The County certainly offered a great deal, but I could see that the world was a much bigger place. I was keen to get away to go to university.

While I was anxious to leave, I have always retained a profound fondness for the County, and I have always returned. When our children were young, we owned and greatly enjoyed a humble waterside cottage. Today, my wife and I own a house on a large woodlot between Bloomfield and Wellington. We manage to spend quite a bit of time there in the summer months. It is always good to go back home.

The County of today retains much of its original charm, but it has changed quite profoundly. The stores on Picton's Main Street have been transformed into art galleries, restaurants, and high-end shops catering to visitors. The wine industry has made the County a popular weekend destination. Every year new wineries pop up. There are excellent restaurants and cafés, jazz bars, stylish inns, and bed and breakfasts. There are music festivals, a lively creative arts community, and a summer theatre company. The Regent Theatre has been resurrected and refurbished. On Saturday afternoon, in place of the westerns I watched as a child, one can catch the regular HD broadcasts of the Metropolitan Opera. The Regent now shows some first-run and artsy films and hosts a variety of live events. I could not have imagined any of this when I was growing up in the County in the 1950s and 1960s.

2
Early Education

My early education was ordinary, but I did encounter some excellent teachers and professors who instilled in me a love of learning and intellectual enquiry. I have indelible memories of early lessons that influenced me for the rest of my life. It was at a very young age at university that I not only learned about Canadian history, political science and opera but met the woman who became my partner in life.

Primary School

My primary and secondary education was in the local public system. Just before we moved to our Victorian house on Centre Street in Picton, the high school located directly opposite burned down. In its place was built Queen Elizabeth Public School, and about a block in the other direction, a new high school was erected. I could never complain of having to walk far or take a bus to get to school. Both my primary school and my high school were minutes away. I was a good, but not spectacular, student. My marks were not what they could have been because I was sloppy and careless with my handwriting, and I refused to take the time to perfect my work. I was anxious to get my work done and move on to whatever came next. I resented a system that seemed to me to favour girls who had beautiful handwriting and placed an emphasis on neatness. But my resentment did not make me mend my ways.

I was a strong enough student to catch the attention of my Grade 3 teacher, Miss McAlpine, a very experienced teacher who read us stories from Greek mythology every Friday afternoon. She asked my mother to come to the school for an interview. The invitation alarmed my mother, who thought I must have done something bad. She was relieved when the teacher told her that I was a bright little boy and that my family should be planning to send me to university. She conveyed that message, she explained, because she had seen too many bright County children give up on education because their parents did not see the point of it. It was a message my mother did not need to hear given the strong belief she shared with my father that my brother and I would go on to university. But I think that conversation made her even more determined to see us succeed and to make sure we did not succumb to the self-satisfaction with County life and County ways that affected so many children.

I was also bright enough to be selected for skipping a grade when I reached Grade 4. This was very common at the time for above average students, perhaps a response to Ontario's insistence on having thirteen rather than twelve grades for reaching senior matriculation.

High School

When I entered Grade 9 at Prince Edward Collegiate Institute, there were eight Grade 9 classes. When I graduated from Grade 13, there was only one Grade 13 class. Each year, as students quit school, the number of classes declined. This was in part a product of the times. Most jobs available in the County did not require much of an education, and young people could not see the point of going on if they could get the job they wanted now. Graduation from Grade 12, called "junior matriculation," was seen as decent education. One could, for example, proceed from Grade 12 to teacher's college or training as a nurse, and it was all the education required for any of the trades or careers such as policing. But it was also in part a product of the attitude of many locals towards education that my Grade 3 teacher had warned my mother against. Many bright young men and women stopped their education long before they should have.

I enjoyed school, especially after I began high school. Prince Edward Collegiate Institute was a large school with over 1,000 students. It served the entire county and at least half of the student body arrived at school each day by bus. Some of my classmates had to be up very early to catch the bus, and they arrived back home very late in the afternoon.

The school catered to all interests and needs. I was in the academic stream, which meant that I took Latin and German as well as French, along with the usual mix of English, mathematics, history, and science. Other streams were "commercial," typing and bookkeeping, and industrial arts for those interested in joining the trades.

As in primary school, I was a strong student, but I probably did not live up to my potential. I was not good at bearing down on subjects that did not interest me, and I was still quite sloppy in my work habits. I did graduate with honours, but I was certainly not at the very top of my class. My father was not upset with my results, but he was concerned about my attitude, particularly when it came to sloughing off things I did not want to do. He sat me down and pointed out that he had to do quite a few things he would rather not do and that I had better get used to the idea. Until then, it had not occurred to me that his exceptionally strong work ethic was not just a product of his love of his work. He was a scrappy, hard-working survivor, determined to make something of himself and to provide a good life for his family.

I was fortunate to have several gifted teachers in high school and I have particularly fond memories of my English, physics, chemistry, and history teachers. Agnes Ross, my English teacher, was an amazing performer in the classroom. She loved Shakespeare and she literally performed the plays for us, acting, not just reading, the various parts. When she read Hamlet's soliloquy, it was as if Sir Laurence Olivier was visiting our class. Mrs. Ross was also an attractive woman, so some allowance has to be made for significant gender modification in her Hamlet performance. Her love for literature and the beauty of the English language was palpable. In retrospect, I have often wondered how she was able to maintain her enthusiasm in front of an audience of moody, sometimes loutish, teenagers. I was quite dismissive of Hamlet and his predicament. I could not understand why he did not just get on with whatever it was he thought he had to do. I expressed impatience with his indecision and procrastination. Mrs. Ross seemed to enjoy my challenge and to relish the prospect of trying to persuade me to develop a deeper and more sympathetic understanding of the profoundly human experience that she, Hamlet and Shakespeare were trying to convey. I distinctly remember her looking straight at me as she read from Hamlet "There are more things in heaven and earth, Horatio, than are dreamt of in your philosophy." The message was loud and clear. I had to beware of allowing my tendency to view everything in a strictly rational, analytic, and logical manner to unduly limit my outlook.

My other favourite teachers were a married couple, Jerome and Frances Rabnett. Mr. Rabnett taught us science, and one of my favourite courses was Grade 11 physics. We learned the building blocks of the material world: temperature, gravity, measurement, electricity, and the basics of atomic structures. Mr. Rabnett loved his subject and seemed to enjoy teaching it, and he mixed in a healthy dose of humour. I remember an experiment he had obviously spent the weekend devising to measure gravity. It involved a pendulum lined with carbon paper that was supposed to strike a falling ball. Despite valiant efforts, he could not make the pendulum hit the ball. "What," he asked, "does a physicist do in these circumstances? He improvises." Then, to our delight, he picked up the ball and flung it against the pendulum to make the desired mark. Another amusing lesson in science was learned in Mr. Malcolm Love's Grade 12 chemistry class. When he did experiments, his results were always perfect to two decimal points. Some of us were sceptical that he could achieve such precision in a high school lab. One of my classmates noticed that while one of his calculations was based on 300 millilitres of water, he was using a 250-millilitre beaker. When this was pointed out to Mr. Love, he looked horrified, but he soon dissolved into laughter with the rest of us, enjoying the fact that we had been astute enough to see through the deception he had practised to achieve a perfect result. These lessons did not shake my belief in science, but they did make me see that, done properly, science was a painstaking exercise that required enormous care, time, and patience.

Frances Rabnett gave me my first real introduction to history. Before her, I thought history was nothing more than an endless series of dates, events, and notable figures to be memorized. Mrs. Rabnett made me understand the contextual nature of history and that the events and great figures we studied had to be understood as products of their age. She made me see that history was very much a matter of interpretation. Different historians viewed the same events differently. The joy of the subject was to understand and engage with the various theories and interpretations.

At the end of Grade 11, I had a bit of a wake-up call. The school had a policy of exempting students with good marks from writing the final examinations. I had good marks and assumed I would be exempted. But exemption was discretionary, and, to my shock, I was not exempted. When my mother asked the school for an explanation, she was told that many of the teachers did not appreciate my attitude. They thought that I was too much of a smart aleck, deliberately asking questions that disrupted their classes for no other reason than to show off. When I thought about it, I had to agree that they had a point. It was an important lesson in how to get along. You are more likely to succeed if you make your point in a measured, respectful manner than if you seem to be trying to prove how clever you are.

Prince Edward Collegiate Institute was, for the most part, an ordinary district high school, but it had some extraordinary teachers, and I was very fortunate to be exposed to them. But I regard the ordinariness of the school as a significant part of my education. The student population was not racially or ethnically diverse – I can only recall one Indigenous student and no racialized students – but it was socially and economically diverse. Everyone from the community was there, rich and poor, children of professionals, farmers, labourers, and unemployed people. They came from every corner of the County, and they reflected a wide diversity of experience and lifestyles. I learned a great deal about life and its ups and downs from my fellow students and I also learned how important it was to treat every person from every level of society with dignity and respect.

Another important experience was working in my father's garage during holiday weeks and in the summer. I started doing this when I was fourteen or fifteen and continued until I started law school. I did not have an exalted position. I worked in the service station, washing cars, pumping gas, and keeping the used car lot in good shape. I think my father assigned me to these duties partly because I lacked the skill to do anything else and partly because he wanted me to see that one has to start at the bottom and work hard to ever hope to reach the top. It was important to me that the other employees not consider or treat me as the boss's son. I wanted to prove to them that I could work hard and contribute on my own. I am sure the boss's son mark could never be erased entirely, but I felt that I did gain their respect for what I was doing and not just for who I was. I came to know them very well and I learned a great deal from them about life. They obviously led more humble lives than my family, but they were decent, hard-working men who took great pride in what they did. They were interested in mechanical issues and understood engines in a way that I never could. Working with and getting to know them was an important part of my education.

In Grade 12, I was selected with two other students to represent the school on a TV high school quiz show, *Canadian Question Bee*. It was very exciting to be on television. We managed to beat two Kingston high schools before being knocked out in the final round. Another memorable Grade 12 experience was my participation in the Rotary Club's Adventure in Citizenship, which brought students from across Canada to Ottawa for several days to see the sights of the nation's capital and to talk about what it meant to be a Canadian. Given my interest in politics, it was a thrill to sit in the members' seats in the House of Commons, where we were presented with citizenship certificates.

In my final year of high school, I was elected president of the Student Council and, upon graduation, I was selected by the teachers to be the class valedictorian, an unexpected honour willingly accepted. I had very good grades, but I was certainly not the top student, so I was somewhat puzzled by my selection. It was redemption from my shame at having to write my Grade 11 exams, and I was happy to have regained the respect of my teachers.

In my valedictory address, I tried to summarize the "fundamental education" high school had given us. I concluded my remarks with these words: "We have a basic knowledge of several fields so that we can select our own particular area of interest. We have been taught to think in an organized manner, to set aside our prejudices, and to examine things in a rational manner. We have begun to think for ourselves."

I had begun to think for myself, and I was eager for more.

Choosing Western

When I was in my final year of high school, I began to think about where I should go to university. Having put the prospect of going to Brown University to one side, I saw three possibilities: Queen's, Toronto, or Western. I am not quite sure why universities like McGill or Dalhousie did not make the list. No one I knew had attended those universities, and I knew nothing about them. Universities did not recruit students in the same way as they do today, and the information available from the high school's guidance office was limited.

Queen's was the favoured university for County students, and I knew several people who had gone or were going there. I think I would have enjoyed Queen's, but it just seemed to be too close. The County students who went there tended to come home most weekends. I was determined to break away from the County pattern and, for that reason and that reason alone, I rejected Queen's.

The Vice-Principal of the high school, George Elson, had an MA from the University of Toronto. He was keen to promote U of T and he kindly took me and two or three of my classmates there for a visit. I was impressed by what I saw but somewhat overwhelmed by the size. I feared I would be lost in the crowd and thought U of T seemed like a better place for graduate work or a professional degree.

I knew very little about Western, then known as the University of Western Ontario. My cousin Jim, who would go on to become an accomplished neurologist, was studying medicine there. Western had a solid reputation, and the campus was described as quite attractive. The size of both the university and the city of London seemed right. So, more or less by default, I decided I would go to Western. I did not visit before applying or accepting the offer of admission, and the first time I saw Western was when I arrived in September 1963 to enrol in first year arts and science.

I endured the usual round of frosh parties, at which we were required to wear red ties and ridiculous purple beanies (purple being Western's colour). The outfits were not my style, but I guess something has to be done to break the ice and distract the minds of young people away from home for the first time.

Living in Sydenham Hall

For my three years at Western, I lived in Sydenham Hall, then a men's residence. I had a roommate in my first year and was then in a single room for my second and third years. Although I did not realize it at the time, Sydenham Hall resembled a small Oxford college. It had a grass quadrangle in the middle of four wings that were described as "houses" to create smaller groupings and a stronger sense of community for the residents. Dons, usually junior faculty members, occupied corner apartment suites and were often present and mingling with the students at mealtimes. Meals were served in the residence dining hall which catered exclusively to Sydenham residents. We lived in a truly collegial setting.

Sydenham Hall played no formal part in my education, but I could not help but learn from living there. Dinner would often lead to lengthy discussions over politics, religion, philosophy, history, literature, or science. Every discipline was represented. Ideas flowed freely. As one might expect from a group of keen undergraduates, some ideas were sound, many were adolescent, and quite a few were completely off the wall. I thoroughly enjoyed the spirit of our banter and debate. The residence gave me a digestible introduction to the collegial life of the academy. I attribute a significant part of my undergraduate education to what I learned within its walls.

I was a member of the Sydenham Residents' Council. At one of our meetings, we passed a resolution calling for the abolition of the monarchy. I have no idea how or why we thought we had a mandate to pass such a resolution. It likely was a continuation of one of our spirited dinner conversations. For some reason, this ill-considered and unauthorized resolution caught the media's attention. The university authorities were not pleased. Talk of abolishing the monarchy would not go down well with some of Western's conservative and wealthy donors. We were summoned to the office of the Dean of Men. He was clearly quite annoyed but, as I recall it, he handled the situation well. He did not come down with a heavy hand or demand that we repeal our resolution, but he did question both our mandate to pass it and its wisdom. We could hardly dispute his first point and, upon reflection, we could see that perhaps we had not given adequate thought before making what was then a very radical proposal. He asked us to think a little more carefully before making any other resolutions and let the matter rest there.

Studying Arts and Science

In the early 1960s, Western had about 10,000 students, one-third of its current size. The relatively small size of the university was, for me, a very positive feature. I had some large classes, but most had thirty to forty students. In my second and third years, I had several smaller seminars. I do not recall taking any course being taught by an adjunct professor or teaching assistant. The courses were, by and large, well taught. Some faculty members were well-respected scholars in their fields, and all the professors I encountered seemed to me to be competent and interested in what they were doing. We had regular writing assignments and tests, all of which were marked by the professor teaching the course. Western may not have been the best university in Canada, but it gave me a very solid undergraduate education.

I enrolled in the general arts and science program. While most courses were optional, to obtain a BA, one had to take a variety of courses in different subjects. To satisfy two of those requirements, in my first year I took French as my foreign language and chemistry as my science option. I also studied English, history, political science, and philosophy.

My political science course was taught by the Chair of the department, Henry Mayo, a Newfoundland Rhodes Scholar, who had published two books, *Introduction to Marxist Theory* and *Introduction to Democratic Theory*. At the time, he seemed to me to be elderly, but in fact he was only fifty-two years old. After Oxford, Mayo served in the Royal Canadian Air Force (RCAF) during the war and then returned to Oxford for his DPhil. He was recognized as a leading scholar in his field. His lectures were dry and hardly scintillating, but one could see his love for the subject and the depth and wisdom of his knowledge. He wrote about theory but taught, in the words of his obituary, "that politics should not be government based on idealistic theories but about citizens in open discussion, reconciling different interests, and agreeing on policies." That course and conversations with Robert Blackwood, a bright and keen second-year political science student at my residence, convinced me to enter the honours political science stream. That would take four years, rather than the three years required for a general BA. I had started to think about law school and knew that if I decided to pursue that route, I could still complete the general BA after three years.

In November of my first term in 1963, I was shocked by the assassination of US President John Kennedy. I recall returning to Sydenham Hall from classes and learning the news from a tearful Robert Blackwood. We spent the next few days glued to the television, watching the funeral and the murder of Kennedy's killer, Lee Harvey Oswald.

Kennedy had inspired people of my age and his liberal vision had been a factor in my decision to study political science.

In my second and third years, I took two political science courses in each year, two courses in history and English, and one in each of sociology, economics, philosophy, and music. My favourite courses were political science and history. I did reasonably well, but not brilliantly, at Western, achieving a sprinkling of A's, almost everything else B and, overall, a strong B average.

A few courses stand out as I recall my Western years. I enjoyed Peyton Lyon's course on international relations. Lyon was another Rhodes Scholar who had enlisted in the RCAF during the war and then obtained an Oxford DPhil. He served in the Canadian foreign service in West Germany before starting his academic career at Western. He had written a recent book on Canadian foreign policy, and he was an enthusiastic teacher. He gave me an enormous boost of confidence when I presented an essay at his seminar. He praised my presentation and encouraged me to make sure I participated in some sports and other extra-curricular activities, since that is what scholarship selection committees liked to see.

My favourite history course was on nineteenth century Canadian history, co-taught by several professors, including Bruce Hodgins and Fred Armstrong. Not only was the course interesting, but it was where I first encountered Geraldine, the woman to whom I have been happily married for over fifty-five years. As well as introducing me to my future wife, the course introduced me to the Family Compact, the 1837 rebellions, the rise of responsible government, and the union of Canada West and Canada East. Fred Armstrong was a kind man whom I got to know reasonably well. When he attended a conference in Prince Edward County during the summer of 1965 after I had taken his course, he dropped in for lunch, and in later years I would encounter him at the University of Toronto when he stayed at Massey College while doing archival research. Another favourite history professor was Jack Hyatt, a military historian who wrote a biography of Sir Arthur Currie, Commander of the Canadian Corps in World War I. I reconnected with Hyatt years later when writing my book on Currie's 1929 libel trial.

As I look back on the essays I wrote for my various courses, I can see that I was intellectually engaged in a very positive way. My essays were those of a raw undergraduate and they were certainly not brilliant, although I got good marks for many of them. They cover an impressive range of topics that reflects a suitably broadly based undergraduate education. In a popular philosophy course that combined the study of logic and philosophy of religion, we had regular biweekly writing assignments, all carefully marked by Professor Johnson. I wrote papers critiquing Pascal's treatment of reason and intuition, the logic of Aquinas's discussion of causation, and Hume's empiricism. I wrote papers in English on Ibsen's contribution to modern drama, Mark Twain's treatment of slavery and racism in *Huckleberry Finn* and a comparison between Sophocles's Oedipus Rex and Shakespeare's King Lear. In history courses, I examined the Canadian Federal Election of 1911, the failure of the radicals to gain popular support in Upper Canada in the 1830s, and North Vietnam and the Chinese world view. My political science essays ranged from the roles of ideology and nationalism in international affairs to a comparison of the political philosophies of Hobbes and Locke and Aristotle's concept of politics. I also wrote one essay on law for a course on American politics examining the United States Supreme Court's treatment of Sunday closing laws and freedom of religion. I preferred the dissenting opinion of Justice Douglas, who would have struck down the laws on a basis similar to that in the decision of the Supreme Court of Canada years later.[1]

I kept quite busy with extra-curricular activities, although this was before the era when an aspiring law student would have to consciously build an impressive résumé to gain admission to law school or a position with a choice firm thereafter. I enjoyed playing intramural hockey and watching the Leafs win the Stanley Cup in 1967. But my interest in playing hockey was fading and, given my positive academic experience at Western, I never regretted passing up on the Brown offer.

I was also involved in various forms of student politics. I was elected as a member of the Middlesex College Council, but I have no recollection that that involved anything very significant. I joined the Liberal Club and was an active member. We had meetings to discuss policy issues that I enjoyed, and we were involved in the university's model parliament. There was an election, we won, and I sat on the front bench as minister of foreign affairs. I was grilled quite vigorously and effectively by a radical NDP member who thought we should be taking a tougher stand on the unfolding American war in Vietnam. Western received a visit from future Prime Minister John Turner, then in his late thirties, soon to become Minister of Consumer and Corporate Affairs and even then, seen as the golden boy and potential future leader of the Liberal Party. I was amazed when, after being introduced to around ten members of the Liberal Club, Turner turned to an aide who just arrived and said, "Jim, I would like you to meet my new friends," and then proceeded to introduce each of us by name. It was a well-mastered trick that made me realize that I probably did not have it in me to become a politician.

Meeting Geraldine

As mentioned earlier, I first encountered Geraldine in a Canadian history class. I did not actually meet her, but I became quite infatuated just watching her in the class. She spent an inordinate amount of time fiddling with and filling her fountain pen from a bottle of ink she always seemed to have on hand.

She was a very attractive, slender young woman, quite elegant in her bearing. I had never worked up the nerve to talk to her, let alone ask her out. I was still very self-conscious about my small-town roots, and I suspected that she might think that I was not in her league. One evening at the residence, several of my friends were making plans to attend a "rush" party at one of the fraternities. One of them, Bob Weir, urged me to join them. I told him that I was not interested in joining a fraternity and that I did not have a girl to take. He urged me to reconsider and said surely there was someone I would like to go out with. I told him about Geraldine but pleaded I did not have the nerve to call her. I think I was afraid she would say no, and my illusion of getting to know her would be over. Bob said, no problem, I will ask her for you. He proceeded to look up her number in the student directory and call her and, identifying himself as me, invited her to the party. For reasons neither Geraldine nor I have ever been able to fathom, she accepted. She had no idea who I was, only that I was "some guy" in her history class.

When I went to pick her up from her basement apartment, she was hiding in the bedroom. I was greeted by Linda Webber, her flat mate, who, I could quickly see, was not someone to fool with. She grilled me about my identity and my intentions. Thankfully, she decided that I did not appear to be an axe murderer or a rapist. She retrieved Geraldine from the bedroom and off we went to the party. We spent the whole evening talking and I was smitten. We have been talking ever since and I am still smitten.

Some forty years after that first date with Geraldine, as I was waiting for the subway in Toronto, I heard someone roar from down the platform, "Hey buddy, want me to get you a hot date?" It was none other than Bob Weir with whom I had lost touch. I assured him that the one date he got me was quite enough.

Music Appreciation and Opera

My friends chided me for taking a course in music appreciation in my third year. It was considered a "bird course" and, indeed, despite my total lack of musical skill or aptitude, I did get an A. But for me, the course did much more than pad my transcript. It was taught by Professor Alfred Rosé, an Austrian composer and conductor who came from a very distinguished musical family. His uncle was Gustav Mahler. His father was Arnold Rosé a violinist, concertmaster of the Vienna Philharmonic, and founder of the famous Rosé Quartet.[2] Professor Rosé had been a solo coach and assistant conductor at the Vienna State Opera. He fled Austria to escape the Nazis. He recounted stories from his childhood about Richard Strauss, with whom his father had made music. He realized he had an audience of musical neophytes filling an open slot in their programs of study, but he made the most of the opportunity. He taught us the basics of the various forms of classical music and its history, but mostly how to listen to and enjoy music. Before I took the course, I had had no real exposure to classical music. Since taking it, I have spent countless happy hours listening to music and attending concerts and operas.

Prompted by Professor Rosé, Geraldine and I went to the Grand Theatre to see a production of Verdi's *La Traviata*, one of the most popular and regularly performed operas in the standard repertoire. It was a travelling production. The opera is written and almost always performed in Italian, but this production was sung in English. Alfredo, a young gentleman from a good family, falls in love with Violetta, a courtesan with a shady past who has become afflicted with tuberculosis or "consumption" as it was then known. Violetta tries to discourage Alfredo, but he persists, and they become lovers. Their bliss is disturbed by Alfredo's father who, in a very moving scene, persuades Violetta to abandon Alfredo to save his family's reputation and allow Alfredo's sister to marry. Violetta is persuaded that she must make the personal sacrifice and decides that she and Alfredo must part ways. Alfredo does not know the cause of the breakup and behaves very badly, causing his father to disown him. In the final scene, Alfredo and his father come to Violetta begging forgiveness and reconciliation as she takes her last breath, somehow managing to sing beautifully only seconds before expiring.

Alfredo and Violetta had strong voices. They sang in English with strong French-Canadian accents. The production was modest. There was no orchestra, only a piano to accompany the singers. But despite these shortcomings, I was completely captivated by the performance. The music was glorious, and while the plot was dated and implausible, it affected me at an unexpected emotional level. I found the combination of the superb music and the romantic, tragic theme powerful and memorable.

I think that the reason I love opera is that it takes me completely out of my usual world and leads me to explore an entirely different mental process. I am a very logical, linear thinker. That is my nature, reinforced by my work in the law. Legal reasoning tries to understand the influence of emotion on human actions but does its best to tame that element and to provide reasoned and rational answers. Opera, like other forms of drama, explores human experience at a different level. Emotion, feelings, and passion reign, rather than being suppressed. When I watch and listen to an opera, I find the music takes that exploration to a depth I do not otherwise often experience.

I have come to realize that opera is a very complex art form. It combines elements of drama, music, poetry, dance, and the visual arts. Since that first *Traviata*, I have seen many more. I am not a traditionalist who always wants to see the opera in its supposedly original form. I welcome new productions that give new shape and meaning to these classic pieces. The more times I see a classic opera in a new production, the more times I want to see another. In one *Traviata* production, Violetta was portrayed as suffering from mental illness. In another, she suffered from drug addiction. The second production was particularly brilliant. Giving Violetta a modern affliction made the production more meaningful, while the music, lyrics and plot retained a nineteenth-century flavour.

There is a moment in *La Traviata* that always brings me close to tears. It is when Alfredo comes upon Violetta as she is writing him the note to say they must part. Overcome with sadness, she proclaims her undying love in full soprano voice: "Amami, Alfredo, amami quant'io t'amo" – "Love me, Alfredo, love me as I love you" – and then rushes off. I realize that this depiction of a dying woman sacrificing her love on the altar of family honour is melodramatic and outdated, but every time I hear it, I am lost in the power of the music and the voice that makes the tragedy strikingly immediate and real.

My other favourite tear-jerking opera is Puccini's *La Bohème*, another story of young love and illness. Mimi, a humble seamstress, comes to the door of an artist's garret asking Rodolfo, a poet, to light her candle. Almost immediately, they fall in love and, although I have heard it hundreds of times, I always find their love duet "O soave fanciulla" – "Oh lovely girl" – very powerful and emotional. But, as in *La Traviata*, Mimi suffers from tuberculosis and their love is doomed by Rodolpho's senseless jealousy and very real fear that he will lose Mimi to her illness. They separate but reunite in the touching final scene proclaiming their love as Mimi expires in another tear-inducing scene, no matter how many times watched.

I continue to love these chestnuts, those of the bel canto period – Donizetti's *Lucia di Lammermoor*, in particular – and the other frequently performed pieces by Verdi and Puccini. I find the grace and elegance of Mozart operas delightful. My tastes have expanded to embrace the German repertoire and the works of Richard Strauss and Richard Wagner. Wagner took the art form to another level with his epic compositions that seem to take one to emotional and psychological levels one does not fully understand. I have seen only one live performance of the entire Ring Cycle. It was at the opening of the Four Seasons Centre in Toronto. It was courageous of Canadian Opera Company (COC) Director Richard Bradshaw to inaugurate our wonderful Toronto opera house in this manner and his gamble paid off.

I go to opera every chance I get. My wife and I have been COC subscribers for many years. We regularly go to the opera when we travel. My favourite opera venue is the Royal Opera House in London's Covent Garden. The productions are high quality, the house has an intimate and traditional feel, and the location in the midst of a bustling hive of restaurants and street performers is exciting. We also go as often as we can to New York's Metropolitan Opera and the Paris Opera, and we have been to many other famous opera houses in Berlin, Vienna, Prague, Barcelona, Zurich, Chicago, and San Francisco.

We are also regulars at the Met HD broadcasts, which offer ready access to the highest-quality productions featuring the great operatic singers of our time. The host always invites the audience to enjoy the HD performance but cautions that there is nothing like a live production at the Met or at your local opera house. I agree with that assessment, but the HD broadcasts have some attractive features not available in the theatre. The camera work is movie quality, providing a close-up view of the performance that cannot be replicated live. The interviews and commentaries reveal insights into the artists and the work of one of the world's greatest cultural operations. And it is wonderful to watch a performance live together with hundreds of thousands of people from all corners of the world.

So, my third-year "bird course" has had a lasting and profound effect on my appreciation of the arts.

A Liberal Arts Education

I never regretted my decision to attend university at Western. The size and style of the place suited me. I am sure I would have been happy at Queen's, but going to Western was a declaration of independence that I felt I had to make. My brother Ernie followed me there, and while he decided to return to Picton, he too enjoyed Western and, like me, he found his spouse and life partner while studying there.

At Western, and building on my high school experience, I had a liberal arts education. The courses I took were not designed to launch me on any particular career path upon graduation. They were an introduction to broadly based intellectual enquiry, aimed at equipping students to think and read critically and to develop sound writing and analytic skills. In my time, one could reasonably aspire to a well-paying job with a general degree. Studying the liberal arts is falling out of fashion, and perhaps the education I received is a luxury that many students can no longer afford. But it has stood me very well, both as a solid foundation for my legal career, and for my enjoyment of life.

Thinking about Law

While I thought that law might be a possible career, I was not at all sure. There were no lawyers in my family, nor did I know any lawyers. There were several law students living at Sydenham Hall and I became quite interested in listening to their conversations. The issues they were discussing sounded engaging. I was tempted to carry on with political science and pursue a graduate degree, but I was not sure where that would lead. Law appealed to me as a subject that had immediate practical application while also offering significant intellectual challenge.

Another influence was Geraldine's uncle, William R. Poole, QC. Bill was a prominent London criminal lawyer. He also taught at Western's law school and seemed to be a favourite of the law students at the residence. Bill and his wife, Nancy Geddes Poole, sometimes asked Geraldine to babysit their precocious daughter Andrea, then about five years old. I sometimes went along and, as a result, I got to know the Poole family. Nancy, a prominent member of the London arts community, was very welcoming and sometimes included me in her dinner parties. The conversation was lively and engaging. I was particularly taken with Bill's courtroom tales. He was the first lawyer I got to know. Listening to him certainly nudged me in the direction of a legal career.

I applied to Western's law school and was accepted. I had even arranged shared living accommodation with two other students. Then I started to wonder whether it was best to spend another three years at Western and started to think about other law schools. I decided to apply to the University of Toronto's law faculty. Law school admission was considerably simpler in the mid-1960s than it is today. There was no Law School Admission Test; that was introduced within a year or so, and I never had to write it. My strong B average was all I needed to gain admission to what I have always regarded as Canada's top law school.

Geraldine was returning to her parents' home in Montreal for the summer. I had had enough of service station work. I decided to see if I could find a summer job in Montreal. Her father and mother seemed highly dubious when I arrived and announced my plan. But miraculously, within a day or so, literally going door to door, I found a job with a building supply firm. I also secured a very nice and quite affordable apartment over the garage of a historic house in the Town of Mount Royal, near to where they lived. My surprising success won them over and we had a great summer in Montreal. In September, I started law school at the University of Toronto.

3
Law School

I entered law school in September 1966. The University of Toronto's Faculty of Law had a strong reputation, but I did not know what to expect. I was an uncertain law student. I had an interest in law but little idea of what it would be like to study the law. I knew no one in my class and nothing about any of the professors who would teach me. It did not take me long to realize that I had landed on the right subject at the right place.

Entering Law School

The first-year class was greeted by Dean Cecil Augustus Wright, known as "Caesar." As his nickname suggests, he was a formidable figure. Dean Wright greeted us with the legendary message he had heard as a student at Harvard Law School: "Look to your left and look to your right – at the end of three years only one of you will graduate." It was not difficult to gain admission to law school, and winnowing those aspiring to be lawyers took place after admission rather than before. At the end of our three years, there certainly was attrition, although I think the rate was less than one-third.

I quickly understood that, in Dean Wright's view, the law was not for dilettantes. A decade and a half earlier, he had fought to wrest control over legal education from the Law Society and to gain recognition for university-based law faculties. Until the mid-1950s, the only way to qualify as a lawyer in Ontario was to take the course offered by the Law Society at Osgoode Hall. Most classes were taught by practitioners, and the curriculum was heavily oriented towards the nuts and bolts of practice. There were classes at 9 a.m. and 4 p.m. and students spent the rest of their time articling in law offices. Wright taught at Osgoode and eventually became Dean, but when he could not persuade the benchers (directors) of the Law Society to adopt a more rigorously academic approach to legal education, he pulled up stakes and left.

Together with Bora Laskin, John Willis, and Stan Edwards, in 1949, he departed for the University of Toronto.[1] The university had a well-established undergraduate law program created and led by Dean W.P.M. Kennedy, an Elizabethan historian who had written a leading text on Canada's Constitution.[2] Wright took over as Dean. Determined to create a Harvard Law of the North on the campus of the University of Toronto, he abandoned Kennedy's combined law and arts degree and established a program designed to equip students for practice. But for almost 10 years, the Law Society refused full credit for U of T law graduates who were required to spend another two years at Osgoode to qualify. The U of T Law Faculty struggled to attract students. Those who came revelled in the small classes and proximity to their professors and many went on to become leaders in the profession and in the academy in the years to follow. By the late 1950s, the Law Society relented. U of T degrees were fully accredited, as were those of the newly established faculties at Queen's, Ottawa, and Western.

It was apparent that the struggle was still fresh in Dean Wright's mind as he explained how our legal education would teach us how to think about law, not just how to do law. One could not mistake the force of Wright's intellect, his fierce will, and his legendary determination to rescue legal education from narrow professionalism and make our law school the pre-eminent centre for legal study in Canada. This thinking permeated the faculty, proud to be members of an academic institution firmly rooted in the university and offering what they believed to be the best education for aspiring professionals.

I found the atmosphere at the law school to be very positive, but it was certainly quite different from that of today's law school. I have already mentioned the relatively relaxed admission standards. There was no sense of struggle to gain admission. Tuition fees were under $500 per year, which, even considering inflation, was a tiny fraction of the fees students now pay. The student body was strikingly male and white, entirely lacking in diversity. There was not a single racialized student in my first-year class and there were only four or five women. There were one or two mature students, but most of us were fresh from undergraduate study, some with only two years under their belts. We were expected to wear jackets and ties, a dress code that was not written down but rather enforced by habit and rumours that if Dean Wright found you in the library without a tie, he would send you home to get one. Before going to law school, I had heard stories about excessive competitiveness at U of T Law, but I did not experience any. The people

I associated with were cooperative and helpful. We operated on the basis that we were all in it together and everyone seemed willing to help if asked. I did not join a study group, although I knew they existed. I preferred to work my way through material on my own.

First-Year Professors

I was fortunate to have first-rate professors for my first-year classes.

I was taught criminal law by Martin Friedland, who would later become Dean and hire me at the faculty. I enjoyed Marty's somewhat quirky teaching style and admired his obvious commitment to scholarship. After I graduated, we became colleagues and friends and, for the rest of my career, Marty has been a mentor to whom I have regularly turned for advice.

In our class, Marty used the Stephen Truscott case to explain the criminal trial process and the very real risk of wrongful conviction, a risk that was not generally accepted by the profession. I already knew about the case. Truscott was about my age at the time of his arrest and trial. I had been shocked to learn that a fourteen-year-old boy had been accused of brutally raping and murdering a twelve-year-old girl. I had closely followed newspaper accounts of his trial and was even more shocked when Truscott was sentenced to hang. That sentence was commuted to one of life imprisonment, but the Truscott case did not go away. Isobel LeBourdais's book, *The Trial of Stephen Truscott*,[3] questioning the soundness of the conviction, was not well received by the legal profession, but it prompted the government to direct a reference to the Supreme Court of Canada to determine whether Truscott was properly convicted. That case was unfolding before the Supreme Court while I was learning criminal law in Marty's class. The Court's 8–1 decision upholding the conviction[4] was handed down as we were writing our final exams. Marty's use of the case was a brilliant teaching technique that showed me why the subject I was studying was vital and important. Several years later, I was a member of the court (but not the panel) that set aside the conviction and acquitted Truscott. A five-judge panel found that evidence that had come to light since the trial, when considered against the entire record, so seriously undermined the verdict that an acquittal would likely be the result if a new trial were ordered.[5]

My torts professor was Bruce Dunlop. A student favourite, Bruce coached the men's hockey team, which earned him the nickname "Punch" after the Leaf's famous coach, Punch Imlach. Torts was Dean Wright's subject and, although Wright was no longer teaching, Bruce invited him to give us a series of two or three lectures on the doctrine of *res ipsa loquitur* ("the thing speaks for itself"). The doctrine allowed the plaintiff to establish negligence from the fact that the defendant was in control of the situation in circumstances where the accident would not have occurred unless the defendant was somehow at fault. Dean Wright did not approve of the doctrine and, after listening to him demolish it, nobody in that class would have dared utter the phrase except to condemn it. It was finally put to rest by the Supreme Court of Canada in a judgment[6] written by Justice John Major, a Wright student who undoubtedly heard similar lectures in his time at the law school.

I vividly recall Bruce's torts class one morning in the spring term, the day after Dean Wright died suddenly at the age of sixty-two. Bruce had been very close to Dean Wright, and he was clearly shaken by his death. He made a short but eloquent tribute to the late Dean and then proceeded to teach the class since that, he assured us in an emotional voice, was exactly what Dean Wright would have wanted him to do.

Horace Krever taught us civil procedure. He was later appointed to the Supreme Court of Ontario and the Ontario Court of Appeal. Years later, we were briefly judicial colleagues when I joined the Court of Appeal for Ontario, just before Horace retired from the bench. I particularly enjoyed Horace's classes on the legal ethics of the adversary system. Legal ethics was not taught as a separate course, and Horace was determined to plug the gap with lessons about what it meant to be an ethical lawyer, resolutely arguing the client's case within the limits imposed by law and the rules of professional conduct.

My land law professor was Arnold Weinrib, then fresh out of Harvard and in his first year of teaching. He asked us to consider the puzzling question of when restrictive covenants run with the land. I had no idea what a restrictive covenant was or what it meant to "run with the land."[7] In the time-tested Harvard method, Arnie offered us no simple explanations. He left it to us to figure those things out by reading the cases and he expected us to be ready to delve into the intricacies in classroom discussion. Then, as now, Arnie had an acerbic wit. He has been beloved by his students in a teaching career extending over more than fifty years.

Richard Risk taught me contracts. He, too, practiced the Harvard Socratic method, although he was kind enough to end the class with a concise summary of what we had discussed, giving our halting answers far more credit than they deserved. Dick's scholarly interest was legal history, and when I joined the faculty and told him how much I had enjoyed his contracts class, he cringed. He clearly would rather have taught legal history, but as a student, I would never have guessed that his first love was not contracts.

We also had two half courses, one in each term. In the first term, personal property was taught by Gerald Morris, an international lawyer who had recently joined the faculty from working at the United Nations with Canada's Department of External Affairs. He started the first class by informing us that when Dean Wright asked him to teach it, he said, "But Dean Wright, I don't know anything about the law of personal property." According to Morris, Dean Wright's response was: "I know Morris, and it's time you learned something about the subject." Morris told this as a joke, but it hardly inspired confidence in what we were about to endure as we struggled together with our reluctant professor to unravel the intricacies of the law of personal property.

The other half course was agency, taught by Bradley Crawford. Brad was an enthusiastic teacher who took a real interest in his students. The course he taught us has long since disappeared from law school curricula. It dealt primarily with the legal authority of employees and agents to bind their principals, but Crawford used it to introduce us to concepts like unjust enrichment and fiduciary duties.

Learning the Law

All our classes were taught using the case method. We were given case books of the readings for the course and expected to read the cases assigned for each class and to be ready, when called upon by the professor, to state the key facts, identify the legal issues and offer our critical assessment of the court's decision. Most of the cases we read were so-called leading cases decided by appellate courts, but some were relatively obscure cases that raised novel or interesting points. From today's perspective, we read a disproportionate number of English decisions, particularly those of the House of Lords, a reflection of the dominance of English law that prevailed in Canada well into the 1960s. I do not recall any explanatory textbook being prescribed. We knew that texts existed but their use as a crutch was discouraged. Better, we were told, to struggle through the cases, to learn how to sort out the relevant from the irrelevant, and to build our own capacity to think critically and like a lawyer confronted with a difficult problem. Today's law schools put more emphasis on secondary writing and, even when I was a law student, I found relief from occasional bewilderment left by the cases by sneaking a look at a textbook.

The instruction focused on doctrinal legal problems, and there was little direct discussion of legal theory. On the other hand, it was apparent that we were not engaged in an exercise of rote learning. Together with our professors, we confronted legal problems on the basis of what has been called "mid-level" theory, looking beyond the black-letter rules and digging down to the underlying general principles that shape and structure the law as a whole.[8] Any belief we had that the law was clear and definite was quickly dispelled. There seemed to be far more questions than answers, and we never seemed to discuss an easy case.

Until Christmas, I was uncertain about how well I was faring or how long I would last. A few things persuaded me to keep going.

The first was my standing in the Christmas exams. I came to the law school one morning shortly after Christmas and saw many of my classmates clustered around the notice board. I had no idea what they were looking at. It turned out to be the results of our Christmas exams, posted for all to see. There were our names, every last one, ranked in order from first to last place. I started at the bottom and read up the list but could not find my name. I was astonished to finally see that I stood in fourth place, a result I could barely comprehend.

The second thing I did to test my commitment to studying law was to go down to the courthouse at 361 University Avenue and sit in on a trial. I came upon a grisly homicide case. The victim was a bootlegger who had been punched in the head by a customer, the accused, a man called "Moose." The victim, who had been drinking heavily, fell to the ground and choked to death on his own vomit. I was surprised to find that the trial judge was the same judge who had tried the Stephen Truscott case, Justice Robert Ferguson. He seemed to me to be old, crusty, and rather abrupt but for the most part quite fair. Moose's self-defence argument floundered under cross-examination, nor was he helped by his lengthy criminal record. The jury convicted him of manslaughter. The prosecutor was a senior Crown, and the defence counsel took an interest in the fact that I was attending and did his best to explain to me what was going on. I found the trial process fascinating, and I was very engaged to see some of the abstract ideas taught in the classroom come to life in practice.

I also participated in a moot court, where I made what I thought was quite an effective argument. One or two of my classmates agreed with me and seemed surprised that I had argued the case so effectively. Unfortunately, Marie Corbett, the second-year student who judged my moot, who years later became a judge, saw the case quite differently and I lost. It was a good lesson that would repeat itself when I practised law. Sometimes, faced with a difficult case, an advocate can shine yet still face a disappointing loss. Despite the loss, I enjoyed my mooting experience. Researching the law and preparing the argument gave me a taste of how engaging and challenging law could be.

It gradually dawned on me that the study of law was not about memorizing the rules and regurgitating them. Success certainly required a certain level of knowledge. But we were not always going to find an ideal cookie-cutter solution, especially not for the difficult cases. The real challenge was to understand all the dimensions of a problem and to grasp the subtlety and flexibility in legal principles that made them capable of producing just results.

Once I found my bearings, I enjoyed my first-year courses and found the reading and the classes intellectually stimulating. I was impressed by the first-rate minds of my classmates and my professors. I was especially interested in Marty Friedland's criminal law classes and the ethical dilemmas Horace Krever teased out in our civil procedure class. I admired the wisdom of Bruce Dunlop as we explored the difficult issues of tort law. I respected the elegance of Dick Risk's manner and appreciation of contract law. I enjoyed being taken along by Arnie Weinrib's razor-sharp mind to explore the concepts of property law. In his easy-going manner, Bradley Crawford's agency course provided me with a wonderful introduction to commercial law.

I started to believe that law was something I could do. I was taken with the fact that law was intellectually challenging and at the same time intensely practical. That combination captured my interest in the law as a first-year student and has sustained my interest in the more than fifty years that followed.

A Year in France

Towards the end of my first year, Geraldine announced that she was thinking of going to France for a year to improve her French. She planned to go to Caen, the city in Normandy where she and her sister, Liz, had spent a month in the summer a couple of years earlier learning French. Liz had remained in France and was now married to Yves Dat, a man she met on her summer travels, and was still living in Caen. I was not sure what to think. Geraldine was happy for me to come along but she had decided to go whether I came or not. I thought that if she spent a year away in the company of gallant young Frenchmen, the chances of her returning to me were not good.

But it was far from ideal for me to interrupt my legal studies in an era long before a term or year studying abroad had become accepted. I decided to discuss the matter with my torts professor, Bruce Dunlop, who was also Chair of the admissions committee. He explained that if I took the year off, he could not guarantee me a place in second year when I returned. I would be considered a transfer student, and the law school never knew how many spots there would be for transfers. He asked me why I wanted to take the year off, and I gave him a full explanation of my fondness for Geraldine and the fear that I would lose her if I did not go. I asked him what he would do in my situation. He paused and said, somewhat to my surprise, "If I were you, I would go." He was very sympathetic to the personal and romantic side to my story. My Christmas marks showed that I would be a strong candidate for readmission. A year away would be an adventure that would broaden my outlook, and a facility in French would be an asset for a career in law. This was the answer I was hoping for but not expecting. I decided to go. My parents were sceptical at first, but they liked Geraldine and could see that I was eager for the adventure. In the end, they fully supported my decision.

I have often thought how differently things might have turned out had Bruce taken a different view. The experience stuck with me in later years when students and law clerks would come to me for advice and made me realize how much wise counsel can mean to a young person finding their way in life.

I was mildly disappointed with my final results in first year, since I narrowly missed honours standing. I had a strong B average and stood 13th in my class. Ironically, the mark that deprived me of honours standing was a C in Bruce Dunlop's torts class. On balance, however, I was much more pleased with the advice he gave me about going to France than I was disappointed by the mark he gave me in torts.

I spent the summer in Picton working at the LCBO store and was able to extend my employment into October to earn some extra money for France. Geraldine spent the summer in Montreal. I travelled there several times to see her and to visit Expo '67, "Man and His World," Montreal's highly successful World's Fair that marked Canada's centenary. It was an event that symbolized Canada's highly positive outlook as we entered our second century. Those feelings were dampened by the rise of Quebec separatism, Western alienation, and the economic problems of the 1970s. People of my age look back on Expo '67 and its positive vibe with genuine feelings of nostalgia.

Geraldine and I arrived in Caen, France, in mid-October 1967. Caen is 200 km northwest of Paris, a short distance from the English Channel – "La Manche." Caen, a city of about 100,000 inhabitants, was heavily damaged during World War II. On D-Day, 6 June 1944, the allied forces landed on the nearby Normandy beaches. The allies bombarded Caen to drive out the occupying German forces. Only a few buildings survived, in particular, the eleventh-century castle and two churches, Abbaye aux Dames and Abbaye aux Hommes, all built at the time of

William the Conqueror. In the late 1960s, Caen was a pleasant and prosperous reconstructed modern city, but it clearly bore the legacy and memory of the war. Constant reminders of the war included the reconstructed city, the war cemeteries – prominent near the beaches and scattered throughout the countryside – and the German fortifications or "blockhouses" that had guarded the approach to Caen from the Channel coast. Canadians were welcomed because the Canadian contribution to the liberation of France was still very much in people's minds.

We each had a room in a new residence, one for men and the other for women. My room came equipped with a bidet, which seemed strange for a men's residence, but it proved to be useful for doing my laundry. The fees for residence and tuition registration were minimal. Residence was about fifteen dollars per month, and good meals could be had at the university restaurant, the "resto," for the equivalent of about thirty cents.

We were enrolled in a course on French language and civilization especially designed for foreigners. Our fellow students came from all over North America and Europe. There were a few Americans, several Scandinavians, one or two English students, and assorted other Europeans. The university had a large number of foreign students from former French colonies in Africa and the Middle East who were fluent in French and were studying other subjects. Like us, they benefited from the virtually free education and very cheap room and board provided by the French state. Extending the benefit of accessible education struck me as a wise policy. Most of these foreign students were the brightest and best from where they came and likely to return home to assume positions of prominence. Ensuring that these countries had Francophile and French-educated elites could only enhance France's international standing and influence.

Registration at the university and with the police to obtain my carte de séjour (residence permit) introduced me to French bureaucracy. Every activity required a card, and every card required at least one photograph and usually a second trip to fetch some additional document or additional information. I came equipped with 16 photos and had to obtain more. The officials came across as severe and annoyed by one's very presence, but I found if they were treated with respect and as if they were very important people, they could be quite pleasant and helpful.

We got to know several students. A Tunisian philosophy student named Hafid, a devout Muslim, had a Canadian girlfriend. Although the French were very welcoming to foreigners, the university restaurant made no attempt to satisfy diverse religious eating laws or habits. Hafid decided that he should do his best to eat halal meat when he could, so he went to the market and bought a live chicken that he intended to slaughter in the proper Halal manner. But when it came time to do the deed, he lost his nerve and asked me if I would chop the chicken's head off. I obliged and, somehow, by dispatching that unfortunate chicken, I had assisted my friend in observing Muslim dietary laws.

Our courses were not onerous. We were given a French proficiency test, and my high school training landed me in the middle group, not a beginner but not advanced. We had a very good French instructor who was clear and patient. Other courses dealt with French culture, very broadly defined, and were really intended to introduce foreigners to the French way of thinking and doing things. The method of teaching and learning took some getting used to, and I am not sure I ever mastered it. There was always one prescribed and correct method that had to be followed. No allowance was made for creative or intuitive thinking. An essay or an exam answer simply had to toe the line. There were rules for everything, and the rules had to be followed. At first, I found this frustrating, but gradually I accepted that it was the way things were done. I was in a foreign country on a sojourn to learn a different way of doing things. Even if I disagreed with the French method of education, I would gain more out of the experience if I did my best to understand and satisfy it. I could see that it provided a solid, structured program of learning and gave students a strong foundation of knowledge of the subject they were studying, considerably more concrete than the North American system that placed greater emphasis on creativity.

I found that within a reasonably short period of time my oral comprehension was quite good, but it took much longer to acquire a working facility in speaking French. That improved the more I forced myself to speak French, usually to other foreign students whose French was no better than mine. Our frequent contact with Liz and Yves and many of their friends gave our language skills a huge boost.

One of the most enjoyable and useful courses I took was French cooking. Food was considered a very important aspect of French culture. Much like the music course I took at Western, what seemed to be a frivolous course was highly engaging and added greatly to my enjoyment of life. I still prepare an excellent boeuf bourguignon using the method I learned in that class.

Our French-language and civilization course included bus excursions. We visited Arromanches, where the allies had created an artificial port to supply the invading forces. We also visited Bayeux to see the famous tapestry depicting the events leading up to the Norman invasion of Britain 900 years earlier, and the historic city of Rouen with its magnificent cathedral near the site where Joan of Arc was burned at the stake.

We were told that we could sign on to meet a French family, and I decided to give it a try. I was invited for a Sunday lunch by a couple who had two boys, the oldest of whom was slightly younger than me. The meal was extraordinary. It started at noon and did not end until 5 p.m. There were many courses and copious quantities of wine. I felt uneasy but enjoyed the experience until I noticed that there was something odd about the couple. As more wine was consumed, they started to express racist views about the "yellow peril" from Asia. I observed that they were displaying a portrait of Maréchal Phillipe Pétain, the World War I hero who collaborated with the Nazis in World War II. My gracious and generous hosts turned out to be adherents of the extreme right and to hold some nasty views.

Geraldine and I visited Paris with another Canadian student during the Christmas break. I was extremely impressed and made to feel like a bit of a country bumpkin by the beauty of the city and the magnificence of the Louvre, Notre-Dame, and the Opéra Garnier. On the other hand, the excessive nationalism exhibited by Napoleon's tomb at Les Invalides reassured me of the merit of Canadian modesty. At Easter, we took our bikes on the car ferry for a cycling and youth hostel trip to England. I adored towns like Winchester and Marlborough. We found a way to ship our bikes to Oxford and I fell in love right away with the city and the college buildings. On another trip, we visited Brittany, where we encountered women wearing traditional dress and speaking Breton and men working the fields with horse-drawn ploughs.

We spent a great deal of time with Geraldine's sister, Liz, and her husband, Yves. We visited Yves's parents and sister in Dieppe, and we got to know many of Yves's friends over meals and other gatherings. All of this was a huge help in learning the language and becoming acclimatized to a very different environment. Liz and Yves's first child was born at the end of December, and we were both fascinated by this amazing new life. Geraldine spent a great deal of time helping out with the baby. In the spring, we helped Liz and Yves move from their apartment in Caen to a house about five kilometres away in the country in a village called Cambes-en-Plaine.

I played field hockey with a team Yves belonged to. I was barely competent despite my ice hockey skills. The problem was that I played ice hockey shooting left, whereas in field hockey, one must play right-handed and not use the back of the stick to strike the ball. One of the advantages of being on the team was that we received better lunches at the "resto," served with beer. I never figured out why, especially why the beer? Was it a reward, or would it enhance our performance? I also played some tennis with a friend from the residence who, like me, was prepared to keep playing during the winter.

The most memorable feature of my French sojourn was the student uprising in May 1968. This happened just after I received my letter of acceptance to start second year at U of T in the fall. With examinations about three weeks away, French universities, and eventually most of France, were shut down by student protests. The precise cause of the student uprising that started in Nanterre was not entirely clear. It was in part a product of the times – the spirit of the anti-Vietnam protests in the United States, anti-authoritarian unrest in Germany and Czechoslovakia, and the push for sexual freedom. The rigid French education system was ripe for challenge. Students were expected to listen in silence to their professors and not question anything that they were being taught. University administration, like the rest of French public administration, was rigid and hierarchical and brooked no discussion. In early May, students occupied La Sorbonne in Paris, where they were supported by leftish intellectuals such as Jean-Paul Sartre. The police forced them out into the streets, and the barricades went up. Cars were burned, cobblestones were torn up and thrown at the police, and disorder prevailed. The dreaded CRS, Compagnies Républicaines de Securité, who wore full riot gear and were known for their toughness and brutality, were called in. Despite these violent confrontations, or perhaps because they appealed to the latent French revolutionary spirit, the students attracted a surprising amount of sympathy from the general population. On the other hand, the workers and the established left political forces distrusted the students and at first refused to become involved. Gradually, however, labour responded to the opportunity the students had created to demand improved wages and working conditions, and the entire country was shut down.

There were strikes and demonstrations in Caen but none of the violence that happened in Paris. The university was shut down and examinations were cancelled. I did venture out one day to observe a demonstration, where I had my one and only encounter with tear gas. I was not a participant in any protests, but I was very engaged by the unfolding events. I was glued to my radio listening to reports of the demonstrations and the pleas for order and restraint from President de Gaulle, who was clearly shaken by the disintegration of public order and his inability to control the situation. He was so worried that he disappeared for a few days to consult with the head of the French army, who was in Germany, to make sure he had the support of the military if the situation worsened. He eventually calmed things down by calling an election for June, which he won, but his authority and that of the established authorities was crumbling. The events of May 1968 failed to produce the revolution many of the students wanted, but they made it clear that things had to change.

I lived through a dramatic political crisis that shook France to its core. A powerful and well-established government led by the man who had saved France from humiliation during the war was severely threatened by an uprising of rowdy and disorganized students. I learned that one should never simply assume the justice of the status quo or think that things will not change. That element of instability was heightened by the assassinations of Martin Luther King Jr. in April and of Robert Kennedy in June 1968. They were men I revered and their loss, combined with news of student uprisings elsewhere and the turbulent events at the Democratic National Convention in Chicago in August, produced a feeling that the world was coming apart. As I was in France, I missed witnessing a profound change in Canada's political life, the selection of Pierre Elliot Trudeau as leader of the Liberal Party of Canada and Prime Minister in April 1968.

My year in France had a profound and lasting impact. I learned what it was like to live as a foreigner, completely immersed in another language and culture. I did my best to understand what was happening and to explain my own views. But, like many newcomers to Canada, I had to overcome barriers of language and culture. There was a French etiquette to learn and master, very different from the one I knew, about how to do routine things such as buying something in a store, ordering a meal, or dealing with a professor or someone acting in official capacity. I acquired a strong working facility in French, and I learned a great deal about a great nation with a rich cultural and intellectual tradition that had experienced both revolution and war. While there were things about France that I did not like or understand, I became a genuine Francophile. Although I would always be a foreigner, I feel strangely at home when I return to France to visit. I also saw that, from the perspective of distance and different experience, one gains a richer appreciation of home.

Back to Law School

I returned to the law school in September 1968. Geraldine and I were married in Montreal just as the term was starting. We settled into a small but comfortable apartment on Brunswick Avenue, a ten- to fifteen-minute walk from the law school. I was one of a very few married students in second year.

I had only been away for a year, but things had changed at the law school. There was a new Dean, Ronald St. John Macdonald, and while he was always meticulously turned out, a new dress code, or lack thereof, prevailed. Students were no longer wearing jackets and ties. Some even had long hair, wore blue jeans, and occasionally appeared to be high on pot. Apart from the variation in dress, the class was no more diverse and again there were only five or six women.

The curriculum was limited. In second year, we were required to take commercial law (sale of goods and bills and notes), company law, constitutional law, evidence, family law, real estate transactions, and income taxation. We then had to pick two optional courses, one from a list of commercial subjects and a second from a list that included comparative law, international law, the legal process, and the philosophy of law. I chose restitution from the first list and the philosophy of law from the second. It was only in third year that we were given more choice. Only administrative law and wills and trusts were mandatory.

This narrow curriculum was a product of the times. The Law Society of Upper Canada mandated a long list of compulsory courses until around the time I graduated. The faculty was relatively small, and the teaching program emphasized what were seen to be the essentials. It was assumed that while there might be a few students who would become academics or pursue other careers, the vast majority would practise law, and it was the job of the law school to prepare them accordingly. Law was studied, thought of, and taught primarily from the perspective of legal doctrine. There was very little emphasis on legal theory, and few professors were engaged in interdisciplinary studies. Canadian courts routinely cited and followed English decisions to an extent unimaginable today. The aspirations of Justices Bora Laskin and later Brian Dickson for a distinctively Canadian jurisprudence remained a dream. Our professors were certainly alive to these shortcomings. They prepared us for what was to come by criticizing the Supreme Court for being excessively legalistic and formalistic, mechanically applying rules without regard to the justice of the outcome and refusing to assume any responsibility for moving the law along to keep up with the times. So, while the faculty was small, the curriculum was limited and the legal education was very much a product of its times, I feel that I was given a solid preparation for what followed.

I did not find that my year away had impaired my ability or interest in the law. I had an entirely new group of classmates, whom I found to be congenial, and I made many lifelong friends.

Second-Year Classes and Experiences

My favourite second year courses were evidence, constitutional law, and restitution. Evidence was taught by Alan Mewett, who was a true performer in the classroom. He was highly entertaining but also highly effective at cutting through convoluted and sometimes contradictory decisions. Colin McNairn taught me constitutional law, a much dryer subject then since it only involved issues of federalism and the division of powers between the federal parliament and the provinces, but a subject that interested me greatly. Restitution, a relative newcomer to the law school curriculum, was taught by Bradley Crawford. I found it interesting since it seemed to cut across and fill gaps in the more traditional subjects of torts, contracts, and trusts. When I was in practice, I regularly encountered problems covered by restitutionary principles, which made me think it should have been a compulsory subject.

Although I was less interested in the more commercial subjects, I had outstanding professors for those courses. Commercial law was taught by Albert Abel, even then a law school legend. Albert came from Iowa and landed at U of T after he met Bora Laskin at Harvard. His office was at the top of a narrow, rickety staircase that served as the school's main thoroughfare from the first floor to the lockers and classrooms below. He always had his door open and always had a friendly smile for those passing by. Albert used the Harvard Socratic method, which did not make it easy for us to master the intricacies of the arcane law of bills and notes. For company law and income tax, I had two outstanding newcomers to the faculty, Frank Iacobucci and David Johnston. Both were well liked by their students, both were very effective in the classroom, and both went on to illustrious careers. Frank became Dean of the faculty after I joined it and went on to be Deputy Attorney General of Canada, Chief Justice of the Federal Court, and a Justice of the Supreme Court of Canada. Frank became a lifelong friend and mentor. David Johnston became Dean of Law at Western, Principal of McGill, President of the University of Waterloo and Governor General of Canada. They were both enthusiastic about their subjects and excellent professors. Frank began our first class by writing his name on the blackboard so we would know how to spell it and explained, "For you Old Testament fans, Iacobucci is Italian for Jacobson." His warm personality and amazing ability to connect with every one of us on a personal level won us over right from the start.

Although I have never been a theoretician, I enjoyed and learned a great deal about the law from my course in legal philosophy, taught by Angela Swan (then John Swan). Angela was fresh from Oxford, and she introduced us to the debate between the English legal philosopher H.L.A. Hart and the American theoretician Lon Fuller. Hart advanced a positivist theory of law, arguing that the law was a self-contained, integral discipline and that the force and validity of law did not depend upon external moral values. Fuller, on the other hand, argued that the validity of law depended upon an inner morality of principles, including respect, fairness, and predictability, and that failure to meet those principles rendered the law invalid. Angela was fully engaged by this debate. One could see that she was enticed by Fuller's theory and resisting the pull of her Hartian Oxford education. She became a colleague to whom I was quite close after I joined the faculty, and we have maintained a connection since we both left for other pursuits. I wrote an essay on criminal responsibility, examining the tension between ensuring justice and fairness on the one hand and the need for social protection and control on the other. Justice and fairness focus on the subjective moral blameworthiness of the accused. I explored situations in which justice and fairness concerns yielded to the interest of social control and imposed criminal liability on an objective standard. I strongly favoured justice and fairness concerns, arguing that the legal system could operate successfully only if it rested on a sound ethical and moral basis.

I also became involved in the law school's fledgling legal aid program. At first, it operated by having students volunteer to take on the odd case that had not qualified for the recently created government-run legal aid program. These were minor criminal cases, small claims files, and landlord and tenant disputes. There was no clinic or supervision, and the work was hit and miss. My classmate Roger Timms was determined to establish a proper law school clinic. I did my best to help, along with Jonathan Guss, a second-year student. Clinics were emerging at other law schools. Eventually, Roger, Jonathan, and I, with Professor Bernard Green's help, persuaded the cautious law school authorities to agree. By the time we graduated, plans for the clinic were in place. Roger went on to practise family law and serve as a lawyer at Osgoode's Parkdale Legal Clinic and eventually became a judge. We are still close friends. Clinics are now seen as essential aspects of a law school education and, as I will explain in Chapter 8, I returned to clinical legal education as a faculty member when I initiated the Constitutional Litigation Program.

I was not engaged politically as a student, apart from my Liberal activities at Western. I did not turn to "sex, drugs, and rock and roll" in the turbulent 1960s, nor was I caught up in the student radicalism of the late 1960s except as an outside observer in France in May 1968. I was opposed to the Vietnam War, but I struggled to imagine how I would have reacted had I been an American called up to serve my country. Although the invocation of the *War Measures Act* during the October Crisis in 1970 now seems to me to have been excessive, at the time I was prepared to accept the assurance of the Prime Minister that there was a real threat of violent insurrection. I do not think of myself as being a conservative but perhaps my reactions to these events indicate that I am, or was, more conservative than I think.

An unusual number of my classmates became judges. Most notably, Rosalie Silberman Abella made it to the Supreme Court of Canada. Several of us were appointed as trial judges. I made it to the Court of Appeal, where I joined John Laskin, who had been a classmate in my first year. Frank Marrocco became Associate Chief Justice of the Ontario Superior Court, and Ed Then served as Regional Senior Justice in Toronto. Other classmates who became judges include Tom Lofchik, Russell Otter, Roger Timms, and Brian Trafford. Others had distinguished and successful careers in practice, business, or government service. Neil Gold, who became Dean of Law at Windsor, was the only one who, like me, became an academic. We were, by and large, a collegial, cooperative, and happy group. We faced considerably less pressure than today's law students do. It was easier to get into law school and easier to find a job upon graduation.

At the end of second year, I improved my first-year marks and was on the honours list, standing sixth in my class. Again, it was a C, this time in income taxation, which prevented me from achieving a higher standing.

I was thrilled to receive a summer job as Dean Macdonald's research assistant. He was an enthusiastic scholar of international law who tried to push the faculty to look beyond our own borders and to see law in global terms. His career would later include a term as Dean of Dalhousie Law School and the remarkable distinction of being the only non-European to serve as a judge on the European Court of Human Rights.

Although it seemed very far away from his area of expertise, Dean Macdonald had agreed to prepare a study on the legal remedies available to the wife of an alcoholic. I spent the summer researching and writing a 100-page paper that surveyed all relevant aspects of family law. I interviewed lawyers, family court judges, and counsellors and tried to do an exhaustive search of the relevant case law and academic writing. While I was not particularly interested in the topic at the start, I enjoyed the research and the challenge of trying to write something of sufficient quality to satisfy the standards of my law school Dean. He was very easy to work for, always warm, friendly, and patient, and he seemed to be happy with my paper. I have no idea what he did with it, but he became very supportive of me and my career.

Rereading this paper more than fifty years after it was written, I am struck by the phenomenon I have already mentioned – namely, the dominance of English case law. Most of the authoritative statements I cite are from English cases. I am also interested to see how fundamentally many of the doctrines I canvassed – cruelty, desertion, alimony, and grounds for divorce – have either disappeared or changed.

My paper pointed out the shortcomings of looking to the law for a comprehensive solution. There is, I wrote, "infinitely more ... involved in the resolution of social issues than the formal results of the legal process, and this is especially true in the area of domestic relations." My recommendations included greater effort to coordinate between courts, counselling services, and treatment centres and to make both lawyers and social workers aware of the contribution each profession could make.

Third-Year Classes and Experiences

Many law students suffer from the "third-year blahs." I think I avoided that disease because of the break I had during my year away in France. As a third-year student, I enjoyed having greater choice for my courses. In addition to the compulsory subjects of administrative law and wills and trusts, I took courses in conflict of laws, land use controls, law and medicine, criminology, and insurance.

Both administrative law and wills and trusts were challenging, heavy courses, but both were very well taught. Colin McNairn taught me administrative law, and Ralph Scane taught me wills and trusts. Ralph was a lawyer's lawyer who had practised for several years and eschewed an overly academic approach. He was an engaging professor and very well liked by his students, with whom he regularly had coffee in the student lounge after class. My most terrifying exam was the one Ralph set us. He asked us to draft a will for a man who wanted to dispose of his property in ways that seemed to challenge or violate every rule in the book. I had never seen a will, and Ralph had never uttered a word in class about how to draft one. I had no idea how to respond and proceeded to discuss the pitfalls the testator faced. I came out of the exam shaken and thinking the best I could hope for would be a mark of about thirty per cent. I was astonished when I got my marks to see that Ralph had given me an A. When I saw him later that summer, I told him how pleased but surprised I was with my mark. He replied disdainfully, "You should have seen some of the other papers."

During my third year, I started to think that I might want to pursue graduate work in law. I was influenced in the direction of Oxford by some visiting lectures given by Peter Carter in my conflict of laws course taught by Derek Mendes da Costa. Carter, a long-time Fellow of Wadham College, had a reputation as a very demanding law don who was tough on his students. He was credited with having raised the standards of Oxford's graduate BCL degree.[9] He was very much a traditionalist with a wide knowledge of the law. I was impressed by the precision, elegance, and insight demonstrated by his lectures, and I started to think that Oxford might be the place for me.

The other Oxford-related element of my third year, although I did not know it at the time, was my choice of topic for my criminology course, taught by Bernard Green. I cannot recall why I decided to write an essay on the law of *habeas corpus*. What surprised me the most was that despite the importance of *habeas corpus* as a cornerstone constitutional principle, there was very little written about it. I did my best to explain the Canadian cases, and my project would come in very handy a couple of years later when I was looking for a suitable thesis topic at Oxford.

My third-year marks were the best I had ever achieved throughout my entire education. I obtained honours standing and came second in my class of approximately 130 students. At the time, there was no silver medal, but I was very pleased to be awarded the Butterworths Prize, given to the "student of the graduating year who, in the opinion of the Faculty, has been outstanding in (a) academic work; (b) participation in student activities, including athletics; and (c) who intends to engage in the practice of law." The prize consisted of a complete forty-volume set of *Halsbury's Laws of England*, the leading English encyclopaedic statement of English law. *Halsbury's* was a regularly used resource, yet another reflection of Canada's then-colonial legal status.[10]

Finding an Articling Position

After three years of law, I knew I had found my subject. I loved the intellectual challenge law posed. But I also wanted a subject that had immediate practical application, and law certainly had that too. My interest in graduate study had been sparked, but I decided that heading straight to graduate study would be a mistake. I wanted to experience first-hand how the law worked in practice. I decided that I would article and perhaps try practice for a year or two before pursuing graduate studies.

Despite my decision to article, I was slow to find a position. I interviewed at a few of the large firms most of my classmates wanted to join, but none of them impressed me as places I wanted to work. Nor, I think, did I impress the people who interviewed me. I had tried a few smaller firms with no success. One did mostly personal injury work, cases frequently tried before a jury. The partner who interviewed me, a man who became a trial judge and whom I would join years later as a colleague, told me that they were looking for the sort of person who would make himself the centre of attention telling jokes at a party. Both he and I knew that I was not the man he was looking for.

I wanted to do both civil and criminal work and was keen on finding a small firm. I applied to a firm that did both. My interviewer, again a partner who later became a judge and whom I would later join as a colleague, was preoccupied about knowing what kind of high school I had attended. Apart from that, I thought the interview had gone well and I was very disappointed when I did not get a job offer. When I told some of my friends, they said I had no chance with that firm since they would only hire a Roman Catholic. The high school question was a disguised method of determining my religious affiliation. It was well known that many large firms would not hire Jewish students, but until this experience, I had been unaware of any Protestant-Catholic divide.

Most of my classmates had articling jobs by the time classes started in the fall, but I was still at loose ends and unsure what to do about it. I bumped into Dean Macdonald, and he asked me if I had found a position. I told him that I had not. He replied, "Bob, I think I know just where you belong." He was right.

4
MacKinnon McTaggart

I only spent a short time in legal practice, but the experience had a profound impact on my career and on my legal perspective. I worked in a small firm that was home to a disproportionate number of outstanding lawyers. They took an interest in me, involved me in some fascinating cases, and became important mentors. Several of them became judges, a firm tradition that I was proud to follow later in my career. I look back fondly on my time with MacKinnon McTaggart. Its demise reflected the passage of an era when professionalism and the ideals of service to the public lost ground as the foundation of the practice of law.

My time at the firm was in two phases. I was an articling student first in 1970–71 and then, after my two years at Oxford, discussed in the next chapter, I was back at the firm in practice from 1973 to 1975. Despite the break in chronology, I will discuss both phases of my MacKinnon McTaggart experience together in this chapter.

Interviewing

In September 1969, as I began my third year, I went for an articling interview at MacKinnon McTaggart, the firm at which Dean Macdonald thought I belonged. I knew very little about the firm except that it had about a dozen lawyers and focused on civil litigation. I did not apply to the firm for an articling position. I was simply following Dean Macdonald's suggestion that I meet his friend Arthur Stone, a partner in the firm.

Arthur, a proud Cape Bretoner, greeted me warmly and told me about the firm. I quickly formed the impression that Dean Macdonald was right. Arthur was a warm, genuine person who exemplified integrity and commitment to high professional standards and ideals. He talked about the firm's history and philosophy. The firm, he told me, did not emphasize the "bottom line." The partners wanted to make a decent living, but they saw the practice of law as much more than a money-making exercise. Practising law was a form of public service. Integrity was central to the mission. The firm aspired not to maximize profits but to achieve professional excellence. Very shortly after the interview, I accepted Arthur's offer of an articling position.

The Firm

The firm, originally Wright McTaggart, was founded in 1952 by Peter Wright and Donald McTaggart.[1] Bert MacKinnon joined them a year later. When Peter Wright was appointed as a trial judge in 1969, the firm became MacKinnon McTaggart. The three original partners could hardly have been more different.

Wright came from a prominent Toronto legal family. Both his mother and his father were lawyers. His uncle was Newton Rowell, politician, and the leading counsel who argued the *Persons Case* in 1928 and later became Chief Justice of Ontario. Before World War II, Peter Wright had practised with McMillan Binch, where his father, Ward Wright, had been a founding member. After serving in the war as an officer in the Canadian Intelligence Corps, frustrated by his partners' refusal to allow him to become a director of an English bank, seen as a rival by the firm's major client, the Royal Bank, Wright left in 1952 to start his own firm with Donald McTaggart. He carried on a mixed practice that included corporate law, estate planning, and maritime law. Of the three founding partners, he was the only one with the sort of solid connections to the Toronto establishment that usually made for a successful practice, although Ian Binnie calls him "something of an anti-establishment establishment figure."[2]

Donald McTaggart grew up on a farm near Lake Simcoe. He qualified for practice by articling after high school matriculation and attending morning and evening classes at the Law Society's Osgoode Hall law school. He restricted his practice to real estate, wills, and estates. He was a thoroughly decent, quiet, modest, and unpretentious man. He did not have the blue-chip connections of Peter Wright, nor the brilliance of Bert MacKinnon, but he provided his clients with careful and reliable service.

Bert MacKinnon grew up in St. Eugene, near Van Kleek Hill in eastern Ontario, close to the Ottawa River and about halfway between Ottawa and Montreal. As he would frequently proclaim, he was the son of a poor beekeeper. He was a McMaster graduate who chose his university because of its connection with the Baptist Church, of which he was a proud member. He served in the Air Force during the war and later studied law at Exeter College, Oxford on a Rhodes Scholarship. He practised briefly in Ottawa and Toronto with other firms before joining forces with Wright and McTaggart.

The firm gradually added a diverse mix of partners and associates. Joe Potts, another World War II veteran, was a Cambridge law graduate who practised corporate commercial law and was actively engaged in Liberal Party politics as both a candidate and an organizer. Arthur Stone, who had earned an LLM at Harvard, taught maritime law at U of T and later wrote a well-regarded history of Nova Scotia's Admiralty Court,[3] had taken over Peter Wright's practice combining corporate commercial law with maritime law. Bill Herridge, a Harvard BA and LLB graduate, practised civil litigation, as did two other brilliant younger litigators, Edgar Sexton and Ian Binnie, another Cambridge graduate. Ian Binnie had taken a year away from the firm to work in Tanzania, and I only encountered him two years later, after I returned from Oxford. Tom Dunne, a very capable and tenacious litigator, joined the firm the year I articled.

The firm was unusual in many ways. It was more open than most to hiring women, and there were several women partners and associates during my time. An unusual number of partners and associates had graduate degrees in law. After Peter Wright's departure, the firm was entirely lacking in the sort of blue blood connections that the larger firms relied on to attract clients. All it had to offer was its formidable legal talent.

Because I was never a partner, I do not know the details of the firm's structure and governance, but a few things were clear. First, Bert MacKinnon was the leader. He was a brilliant lawyer possessed of the quickest legal mind I have ever encountered. He was quite casual about his personal appearance and clothing. It seemed to me that he wanted to distinguish himself from the Bay Street lawyer stereotype and preserve his image as a poor country boy who won a Rhodes Scholarship and who was succeeding purely on the strength of his wits and intellect. He was a teetotaller, and when we were working late and had to get dinner, Bert would lead us to his favourite restaurant, the Honey Dew, in the basement of Simpson's department store, a very ordinary cafeteria not frequented by any other leaders of the bar. By the time I articled, Bert was fifty years old and was recognized as one of Canada's top litigators. He was regularly in the Court of Appeal and the Supreme Court of Canada. Most of the cases he argued were referred to him as counsel by other lawyers. He invariably got into the office in the morning before everyone else and went through all the firm's mail to keep tabs on what everyone was doing.

The other significant feature of the firm was that there were no minimum hourly or billing targets for partners or associates. Everyone was expected to work reasonably hard, and everyone shared in the proceeds on a more or less equal basis, adjusted only to reflect seniority. The partners put achieving a healthy work-life balance ahead of maximizing profit. After MacKinnon's departure for the bench, without his strong leadership, this structure proved to be flawed, but it was delightful while it lasted. The firm's culture and philosophy suited me perfectly, although, as I will explain, in the end, the relaxed culture did not survive.

Articling: 1970–71

I started my articles in September 1970. There were two other articling students, Bob Peck, who later became a partner in the firm, and Eric Button, who joined his father's practice in Stouffville after articling. We shared a reasonably large windowless office that was better suited as a storage room than as an office. I worked on one side of a large, shared desk. On our first day, Donald McTaggart came to the office to welcome us and offer us some advice. Apparently, the previous year's articling students had been complainers. Mr. McTaggart wanted no repetition of that, and he instructed us accordingly: "Work hard and don't grumble." This sounded alarmingly gruff, but it did not take long for the three of us to realize that Don McTaggart was a very gentle and kindly man. He simply wanted everyone to be happy at the firm and he thought that would be achieved only if everyone rolled up their sleeves and got to work. He set the example by working steadily away in his corner office and regularly leaving for home in time to have dinner with his wife.

I could not have found a better place to article. We were not paid as much as students in the larger firms, but we were given a great education. The partners wanted us to gain a wide range of experience, and they considered it their duty to mentor us along the way to becoming fully fledged lawyers. If we worked on a file, we were always taken along to court for the argument. We were included in client meetings, and we were made to feel very involved with delivering high-quality advice and service. While civil litigation was the most prominent feature of the firm's practice, it did a full range of corporate commercial, real estate, and wills and estates work. As articling students, we rotated through each practice area, but I ended up spending at least half of my time doing civil litigation.

During my articling year, I worked closely with Bert MacKinnon, Arthur Stone, Bill Herridge, and Edgar Sexton. They were all wonderful mentors and teachers. Bert, Arthur, and Edgar followed the firm tradition established by Peter Wright of being appointed as judges. Bert MacKinnon was appointed to the Court of Appeal for Ontario in 1975, Arthur Stone to the Federal Court of Appeal in 1983, and Edgar Sexton also to the Federal Court of Appeal in 1998. Joe Potts was appointed to the Supreme Court of Ontario in 1981. Ian Binnie, who I first encountered after I was called to the bar, was appointed to the Supreme Court of Canada directly from practice in 1998, several years after the firm dissolved. I was proud to be part of this remarkable firm tradition when I was appointed to the trial bench in 1995.

I did work in all areas of the law. I searched titles, closed real estate deals, and worked on various corporate commercial matters. I prepared memos on a wide range of intriguing legal subjects. Did a stockbroker's failure to register allow a customer to claim the return of money invested? Could an investment broker reclaim money mistakenly paid to a client? Could a wrongdoer who had caused a death take property as an heir where the deceased died without a will? What did the doctrine of dependent relative revocation have to say about a testator who left a note saying "Other will destroyed by me. This is what I want"? Is the work of an accountant providing income tax advice protected by legal privilege? What use can be made of unopened road allowances? What is the nature and extent of the right of ships of all states to enjoy innocent passage through territorial waters? Are there exceptions to the non-deductibility of living expenses from income for tax purposes?

My memos on these subjects reflect what was expected of an articling student at the time. They were to be relatively short and to the point. There were no online resources. My research was based upon sources derived from leading texts and abridgements. The case law was reviewed, often focusing on old English cases. I avoided expressing strong opinions of my own. The research was very much geared to the needs of the client. Authority going against us was reviewed, but the emphasis was on finding law that would support the client's position. I did much of my work in the firm's library, which had all the basic resources, but I often had to venture to the Great Library at Osgoode Hall or up to the U of T law library, where I knew my way around.

Going to the Court of Appeal

I had enjoyed law school, but I was eager to learn the practical side of the law. I was quite surprised to find that the difference between theory and practice was not as great as I had expected. Shortly after I started, Bill Herridge, a litigation partner, dropped by the articling students' office and told us that he needed someone to prepare a detailed memo on the *Statute of Uses*, enacted in England in 1535. This sounded more like an arid law school assignment than something from the real world of practice, but for some reason I was intrigued, and I immediately volunteered to prepare the memo.

When Bill explained why he needed the memo, I was very glad that I had volunteered. He had been retained by a small municipality to argue an appeal in a case that would challenge a technique being used by land developers to circumvent land planning controls on the subdivision of lands. Under provincial legislation, without proper planning permission, the owner of land could not sever and sell smaller individual lots. Developers, eager to avoid the extra costs imposed by the planning authorities, devised various schemes that complied with the letter, but not the spirit, of provincial planning legislation. The scheme at issue in the case Bill would be arguing involved owning land by way of a "deed to uses," a conveyancing technique developed centuries earlier to transfer beneficial or equitable ownership, but not legal title, and thereby avoid payment of feudal fees. The *Statute of Uses* had been enacted to end the dodge but then conveyancing lawyers came up with a "use upon a use" to evade the statute. Ontario's *Planning Act* made it illegal for an owner to convey a parcel of land and retain the "fee" in abutting lands. The word "fee" was thought to connote legal title, so the developer argued that because he held only equitable title by way of a deed to uses, not legal title, he could convey the equitable title in abutting lands without planning permission.

The case posed a classic legal problem. Were the municipal planning authorities bound by the strict letter of the law, or could they insist that the developer comply with the spirit and underlying purpose of the law? At the time, the answer was less obvious than it might be today. The courts were reluctant to limit property rights without crystal-clear statutory language, and arguments about the spirit of the law tended to fall upon deaf judicial ears. I carefully researched the law and came up with a technical argument, based upon the *Statute of Uses*, that there was such a thing as an "equitable fee" and that, even on a strict reading of the legislation, the developer was caught.

I worked with Bill on the factum. The invariable practice of the firm, and one of the great benefits of articling there, was that students who worked on the factum were taken along to the Court of Appeal for the oral argument. Sadly, that tradition seems not to have survived with modern law firms and, years later when I sat on the Court as a judge, I saw few students accompanying senior counsel. I was there mostly to observe, and my duties were limited. Photocopied case books did not exist, and my job was to obtain the case reports we had cited in our factum from the Great Library so they would be available for reference during oral argument.

Bill faced a bench composed of Chief Justice Gale and Justices Schroeder and McGillivray. The Chief Justice was a stern but courteous judge. Justice Schroeder was a stickler for detail and, while he had a good legal mind, he also had a well-deserved reputation for nastiness. Justice McGillivray was old-school and at times could be quite severe. For most lawyers, appearing before the Court of Appeal was a terrifying experience. I sat behind Bill and in awe of the Court. Any thought that I would one day sit on that bench could not have been farther from my mind.

Bill made a very effective argument, and it seemed to me that the Court was with us. Judgment was reserved, and not long after we received the good news. In a judgment authored by Justice Schroeder, the Court ruled that "private property is not now immune from regulation essential for the public good," that the legislation has "for its object the prevention of the unrestricted subdivision of land," and that "[i]t is the substance rather than the form of the transaction which is relevant."[4] The developer's appeal to the Supreme Court of Canada, argued after I completed my articles, was dismissed in a short one-paragraph decision.[5]

My First Trial

I had my first solo trial during my articling year. One of the corporate lawyers in the firm acted for a car dealership. I was asked to take on a case in what was then called the Division Court (now the Small Claims Court) involving a customer who insisted that he was entitled to return a used car. The dealer refused, since the car had suffered an unusual amount of wear and tear. The customer was represented by a senior lawyer who had a QC but obviously had fallen on hard times. The trial took place before Judge Edra Ferguson, the mother of my classmate Dan Ferguson. Affectionately known as "Ma Ferguson," she was reputed to brook nonsense from no one. During the trial I stumbled on the fact that the customer had driven the car to Deseronto, near Picton. I knew that there was a drag racing strip in Deseronto, and I got the customer to admit that he used the car to do some drag racing. That was all Judge Ferguson needed to decide the case in my client's favour, and I returned to the firm triumphant with my first big win on my own, made possible more by local knowledge than by legal skills.

Practising Law: 1973–75

I returned to MacKinnon McTaggart as a fully fledged lawyer after my two years at Oxford, the subject of the next chapter. I first had to endure the dreary six-month bar admission course from September 1973 to February 1974, the Law Society's poorly taught attempt to equip law school graduates for practice, certainly the low point of my legal education.

In my first year at the firm, another exceptional lawyer, George Strathy, U of T Law's gold medallist, who combined legal brilliance with a mischievous sense of humour, came as an articling student. Years later he added to the firm's reputation as a factory for judges by being appointed to the Superior Court of Justice in 2007. He became a colleague on the Court of Appeal in 2013 and finally served as Chief Justice of Ontario from 2014 to 2022.

As a fully fledged but very junior lawyer, I continued to work as I had as an articling student with the senior lawyers in the firm, writing memos of law, drafting pleadings and factums, and attending in court when matters I had worked on were being argued. I gradually assumed more responsibility for these matters, conducting examinations for discovery and cross-examinations on affidavits and arguing motions, usually before a master but sometimes before a judge. I also acquired many files for which I assumed primary responsibility. I dealt with personal injury files, commercial matters, botched or aborted real estate deals and quite a few debt-collection files. I found it challenging to keep all these matters moving along, and I seemed to spend most of my time juggling to keep a list of about 100 matters on the rails.

I successfully took a case involving an aborted real estate deal to trial in what was then called the County Court. At Arthur Stone's request, I argued one case in the Court of Appeal on my own. We both knew that the case was very much an uphill battle and even though I lost, as expected, I considered my performance a success when the Court called upon the other side to respond.

Family Life

I worked hard but, in keeping with the firm's style and philosophy, I did not put in the punishingly long hours that most junior lawyers must now endure. I was home most evenings for dinner and did not go to the office on weekends, although I often worked at home during the evening and weekends. Geraldine and I had a busy life, getting together regularly with friends and family and going to concerts and the theatre. We had two children, Anne, born in Oxford in 1972 when I was a graduate student, and Claire, born in 1974 while I was in practice. While Geraldine bore the brunt of childcare duties, I was very involved with my daughters and took delight in seeing them grow and develop. Geraldine did part-time work, first for a news clipping service and later as a freelance translator. I was paid a decent, but relatively modest, salary. We managed to buy a three-bedroom house in North Toronto, a feat that would hardly be possible in today's market.

Criminal Cases

I remained interested in criminal law and the firm encouraged the junior lawyers to take on legal aid matters. I defended some paying clients charged with minor offences such as careless driving, and I also undertook a few impaired driving cases. I enjoyed this work, because I liked being in court and on my feet to make an oral argument. In one of the impaired driving cases involving a client who had too much green beer on St. Patrick's Day, I worked out an elaborate legal defence. However, I never had the chance to present it. When the prosecution closed its case, the judge dismissed the charge, since the Crown had failed to prove that my client was driving or had care and control of the vehicle. The client was relieved and grateful. I was also pleased that we achieved a positive result but a little disappointed that I was not able to present my argument which I thought was brilliant (but likely would have failed) about the admissibility of the breathalyser evidence.

I defended one young man I will call Tom who came from a very deprived background. He was charged with drug trafficking. I was a bit shaken when he was convicted and sentenced to a period of incarceration. I did not think that I could have done anything to prevent that from happening, because he really did not have a viable defence. However, the experience of seeing him carted off to jail upon being sentenced was unsettling. When Tom was released, he took up with an older man who was a career criminal. As winter was settling in, they concocted a scheme to rob a bank that they must have known would lead to their early detection and imprisonment. They acquired a shotgun and a hacksaw to saw off the barrel. They then left the end of the barrel and the saw in their dwelling. Using their own names, they rented a car and proceeded to hold up the bank where they cashed their welfare cheques. Within hours of the robbery, they were apprehended by the police, to whom they voluntarily made full confessions. Tom called me and asked me to represent him. I went to see him in the Don

Jail and was shocked by the conditions. It was overcrowded and noisy and the smell of antiseptic mingled with the stench of body odour and body waste was nauseating. Not surprisingly, Tom wanted to plead guilty, but he resisted my suggestion that we work on trying to get him a reformatory sentence of just under two years. He was determined to go to the penitentiary for at least five years. While that was a much more likely outcome than what I wanted to try for, it became clear to me that his older career criminal friend had convinced him that the pen was not such a bad place to be. There would be no worries about getting fed, finding a place to live, or keeping warm in the winter. When I resisted, Tom asked me to find him another lawyer to take on his case, which I eventually did. Tom must have had second thoughts about life in the penitentiary since he filed an in-person notice of appeal and applied for legal aid. He asked me to assist him, but his application for legal aid was refused. I offered to take his case without a fee and told him that he would have to bear the cost of disbursements but advised that it was unlikely that he would succeed in receiving a reduced sentence. He wrote me a carefully written and surprisingly articulate letter thanking me for what I had done, regretting that he did not keep me as his lawyer, and assuring me that he hoped I would act for him again should the need arise. That was the last I heard of Tom.

Tom's story has stuck in my mind all these years for several reasons. I could see that Tom was an intelligent young man who simply had no chance in life because of his deprived upbringing. He had done some very bad things, but he did not seem to me to be an inherently or irretrievably bad person. He had no family support and had fallen in with, and been strongly influenced by, a man who had adopted a criminal lifestyle and had become institutionalized, welcoming a return to prison. As I would later find as both a trial and appellate judge, many criminal cases involve accused persons who have hopeless stories like Tom's. They are criminals, and our criminal justice system treats them as such, acknowledging but failing to make sufficient allowance for the fact that they are often also the victims of deprived backgrounds, racism, poverty, mental illness, and addiction.

I was very concerned about what would become of Tom, and my inability to do anything to help him made me feel inadequate. I unburdened myself by telling Geraldine and our two daughters all about Tom and his plight. The children could hardly believe Tom's story and that he had no mother and father to guide him through life or resources for his education or well-being. For a long while after, they would say, "Dad, please tell us Tom's story again."

Family Law

I undertook a few family law matters involving divorce, child custody, and support. The *Divorce Act* of 1968 introduced the concept of marriage breakdown as a ground for divorce but retained fault based divorce for parties who had been separated for less than three years. Some judges did not like granting divorces for religious reasons and were sticklers for detail, but most treated the petitions as routine and managed to get through long lists in a single day. My most unusual divorce case involved the representation of a woman whose husband had come out to her as being gay. They loved each other but decided that they could not continue their relationship. While homosexual acts had been decriminalized in 1969, this was long before the era of acceptance of LGBTQ rights. The parties had been separated for less than three years, so to succeed, I had to fit the case into an established category of fault. I worried that if we ended up before a judge with conservative views, things might not go well. I thought that I had to put the details of the husband's sexuality and the sexual acts he engaged in before the court. Fortunately, the husband was very co-operative. I was impressed with the dignity he displayed in describing his sexuality and sexual practices when I examined him for discovery to provide a record that would justify granting a divorce under the law as it stood.

I found family cases in general, and custody battles in particular, to be wrenching and emotionally draining. I knew that family law was not going to be my métier. I developed a respect for those lawyers who are able to handle the emotional load of dealing with these cases in a properly detached and professional manner.

Arthur Stone

During my articling year and then in practice, I probably spent more time with Arthur Stone than any other partner. We worked well together. He appreciated my research and analytic skills, and I respected his high professional standards and his ability to render to his client thoughtful, careful, and wise advice. He had a remarkably varied practice that included maritime, administrative, and corporate law, and I enjoyed working with him.

One of the most interesting maritime files I worked on involved a ship that sank in the St. Lawrence Seaway. Within hours of the disaster, I travelled with Arthur to Alexandria Bay, Ontario, where the ship had gone down. There was no loss of life, but the captain and crew were visibly shaken. We took detailed statements to prepare for the inevitable claims and to deal with insurance issues on behalf of the owner.

I also spent a great deal of time with Arthur working on matters for the Institute of Chartered Accountants. This was extremely interesting work. We provided general legal advice on a wide range of issues. There were by-laws to draft and interpret, disciplinary proceedings to manage, and various legislative initiatives that required legal advice and lobbying. At the time, Institute members had the exclusive right to provide audit opinions. There was a long-running battle with the certified general accountants, who wanted to be recognized as capable of rendering such opinions. They mounted a concerted political campaign to have the legislation changed, and we assisted the Institute in resisting that change. I was also involved in the preparation of a brief on the class action legislation that emerged from an Ontario Law Reform Commission report. The Institute was concerned about the potential for virtually unlimited liability for audit opinions. Arthur and I wrote a strongly worded brief setting forth the Institute's position.

I spent a great deal of time dealing with Institute disciplinary matters. The Institute took a vigorous and proactive approach as part of its strategy to maintain the strong reputation of the CA brand in the audit field. Members who fell short of professional standards faced discipline. Arthur's mandate included assisting the discipline committee to conduct these proceedings, and I gradually took on more and more responsibility for this work. Our role was to serve as the discipline committee's legal adviser. The members of the committee were all accountants, and we provided legal advice when required. This was very interesting work. It required familiarity with administrative law principles, the rules of procedural fairness, and the rules of evidence. It required a delicate touch as we tried not to take over the proceedings and to intervene only when necessary. I had to respect the expertise of the accountants but ensure that the proceedings respected the procedural and legal rights of the member being disciplined. The senior lawyer who acted as prosecutor was quite aggressive and not above trying to slip in evidence of questionable admissibility. This was my introduction to running a trial, a challenge I would face many years later when I was appointed as a trial judge.

In keeping with its policy of vigorous protection of the CA "brand," the Institute prosecuted individuals who used the CA designation without being members. These prosecutions were brought under the Institute's incorporating statute as private prosecutions. I acted as the prosecutor for these cases, which got me on my feet in the criminal court in a very different and somewhat unusual role.

Arthur Stone was a wonderful mentor. He was a skilled and careful lawyer who also had an extensive corporate commercial practice. His practice covered an astonishingly wide swath of legal issues, and his knowledge and understanding of the law were impressive. He was a very patient and gentle man. It was a pleasure to serve as his junior. He was true to the message he gave me when I first met him for my articling interview. He saw the practice of law as a learned and noble calling. Integrity and professional excellence served as his standard and as his objective. Arthur was a proud native of Cape Breton, and he always exhibited a Maritimer's reserve and basic human decency. I think one of the reasons we got along as well as we did was that we shared a certain measure of common experience because of my small-town roots. Geraldine and I also developed a close connection with Arthur's large family, since we lived not far apart, and all but one of the eight Stone children served us as our regular babysitters.

Bert MacKinnon

During my articling year, I spent most of my time in the firm's library researching and writing legal memos. For reasons unclear to me, Bert MacKinnon often liked to work in the library rather than in his office. There was a phone in the library to which he had his calls forwarded. This was long before email, and most legal business was conducted on the phone. As I sat there quietly doing my work, I was treated to an inside look at how Bert conducted his practice. I heard how he dealt with clients, how he negotiated with opposing lawyers, and how he confronted issues involving the profession in his role as a bencher of the Law Society. It was a bit distracting, but it was a remarkable treat to be able to watch a great lawyer at the top of his game.

Bert was always open and friendly, but he was also quite intense, a bit restless, and, at times, impatient. I had to learn not to be intimidated by his quickness, his impressive knowledge of the law, and his sheer legal brilliance. What I liked most about him was that he was always completely straightforward, down to earth, and frank. He told you exactly what he thought, and you knew exactly where you stood in his eyes.

Bert argued his first appeal in the Supreme Court of Canada in 1950, before he joined the firm. He successfully represented a birth mother who had a change of heart and sought the return of the child she had given up for adoption.[6] The case was one of the last Canadian cases heard in the Judicial Committee of the Privy Council, where Bert succeeded in upholding the Supreme Court's decision.[7]

Bert taught constitutional law at the old Osgoode Hall law school as an adjunct professor. He argued over twenty appeals in the Supreme Court, and he made even more regular appearances in the Ontario Court of Appeal from the mid-1950s until his appointment to the Court in 1975. In the tradition of a leading counsel, he argued cases involving a wide range of legal subjects.

He represented the notorious union leader Hal Banks and persuaded the Court of Appeal that the *Globe and Mail* was not entitled to rely on qualified privilege to avoid liability for defaming Banks in an editorial alleging that he had abused his office and that his application for Canadian citizenship should be refused.[8] Bert argued two appeals for the Ontario Liberal Party concerning a commission of inquiry into improper interference with the investigation and prosecution of organized crime.[9] He argued two Indigenous rights cases before the Supreme Court of Canada, unfortunately in an era when the Court took a conservative view of such rights. He was unsuccessful in reversing the conviction of Mr. George, a member of the Chippewa Band residing on the Kettle Point Reserve, for illegal hunting under the *Migratory Birds Act*.[10] Bert also acted for the Native Council of Canada in the 1974 *Lavell* case dealing with the claim for restoration of Indian status by a woman who had lost her status when she married a non-Indian.[11] The court's dismissal of Ms. Lavell's claim that denial of Indian status constituted discrimination contrary to the *Canadian Bill of Rights* was heavily criticized and was later used by *Charter* proponents to secure a strongly worded section 15.

Bert won a significant victory when he persuaded the Supreme Court of Canada that a tavern serving a patron to the point of intoxication and then kicking him out knowing that he would be walking home along a busy road was liable for the injuries the patron suffered when he was hit by a car.[12] He secured a significant client for the firm when he represented the Christian Labour Association of Canada before Chief Justice McRuer in an application to set aside the Ontario Labour Relations Board's refusal to certify the union because it discriminated on grounds of "creed" by having a constitutional requirement that members must uphold "Christian and social principles as taught in the Bible." Bert, a staunch Baptist, convinced Chief Justice McRuer that requiring a member to uphold Christian and social principles taught in the Bible was not a requirement to subscribe to any doctrinal belief and that as the union's constitution precluded the refusal of membership by reason of creed, the union was not discriminating on the grounds of "creed."[13] In the years to follow, the firm represented the union or its offshoots in many interesting (although not particularly remunerative) cases, including the Marshall Crowe case that Ian Binnie and I later argued in the Supreme Court of Canada, discussed below in this chapter.

During my articling year, I worked with Bert and Tom Dunne on a fascinating case involving a contested union election. Our clients had narrowly lost the vote and complained of election irregularities. We moved for an interlocutory injunction, a pretrial remedy requiring a party to refrain from violating the right claimed pending trial. We were in court shortly after being retained. There was a great deal to do in a very short time. I helped Tom interview witnesses and prepare the factual record. I researched the law on how and when a court could intervene in the internal affairs of a union. We appeared in front of Justice Stark, facing Claude Thomson, a well-regarded litigator. Bert argued the case brilliantly and persuaded the judge to award our clients not only an interlocutory injunction but final judgment.[14] The case was a great experience. I had been involved from start to finish. I had the chance to deal directly with the client and the witnesses, and I had to engage with challenging legal issues, including the law of injunctions, which would later engage my interest as a legal scholar. I saw how Bert MacKinnon developed a strategy, put the case together in a relatively short time frame, and formulated and presented an effective and winning argument.

I learned an enormous amount from working with Bert MacKinnon. He was regularly in the Court of Appeal, and I assisted him as his junior on several matters. This was the era of the nasty Court of Appeal. Several judges were impatient and cantankerous. They relished reaming out lawyers who had difficult cases to argue or who they felt were wasting the Court's time. This did not appear to phase Bert in the slightest. He was fearless and always well prepared. He thought his cases through completely and he always focused on one or two points that he thought might carry the day. He was easily the intellectual equal of any member of the Court, and both he and the judges knew it. Most of his appellate practice was counsel work referred to him by other lawyers. It occurred to me that the nastiness of the Court of Appeal was good for Bert's business. Lawyers who did not appear regularly before the Court were so terrified to do so that they referred their appeals to counsel like Bert, who knew how to handle the heat.

Bert worked hard at finding the best way to present every case he argued. He would roam the office talking to his juniors and colleagues about his cases. It was as if he had to persuade himself of the justice of his client's case before he could attempt to persuade the Court. I recall one occasion when he was pressing what seemed to me to be an unlikely proposition in the most sincere and earnest fashion. Bert's client was the widow of a wealthy man whose will provided that his generous bequest to her would terminate if she remarried. The widow was living an extravagant lifestyle with a younger man to whom she was not married. Bert contrived the argument denouncing the deceased for forcing his widow to live in sin.[15] When I said to him, "I know that you have to argue that, but do you really believe it?" he gave me a scolding look and turned away without a word. I realized that by seeming to put personal views ahead of the client's interest, I had missed the point entirely. Bert was working to find the most persuasive argument possible and to find a way to present that argument as forcefully and with as much conviction as possible. Of course, he had to assess the likelihood of success. But whether he personally agreed with it was beside the point. The only questions were whether this was the best possible argument he could make for the client and whether he could argue it with conviction.

I also worked with Bert and Tom Dunne on the Pickering Airport Commission of Inquiry. The government had expropriated large tracts of land in the Pickering area in 1972 to establish a new international airport. There was strong opposition to the airport project from the expropriated owners who remained on their lands by agreement with the government and by other groups who raised environmental and other concerns. The Commission's mandate was to assess the government's decision that there was a need for a new international airport and that the airport should be located at Pickering. Bert was retained by the Government of Canada to defend the Pickering Airport decision. While the inquiry dealt with a number of interesting issues about projected volume of air traffic, airport noise, the development of new types of aircraft, the environmental impact of air traffic, and ground transportation, I could never understand why a Commission of Inquiry was the best way to assess and decide those issues. As it turned out, I was right. The Commission produced a thick report endorsing the government's decision to establish the Pickering International Airport. But in the end, that airport was never built. The Commission served to take the immediate heat off the government for having made a controversial decision, but eventually the political process prevailed. The federal government abandoned the project in 2025. Portions of the expropriated lands were leased for residential, commercial, and agricultural use with some of the expropriated owners becoming tenants, and it is now clear that the Pickering Airport will never be built.[16]

Many members of the firm thought that Bert was headed for the bench. In 1970, he had been asked if he wanted to be considered for an appointment to the Supreme Court of Canada. He declined because his wife and still-young family did not want to move to Ottawa. I do not know what Bert's chances were had he said yes. Several other prominent names were reported to be in the mix,[17] and in the end, Prime Minister Pierre Trudeau chose Justice Bora Laskin.

A few years later came another call, and this time he did not refuse. Towards the end of 1974, Bert was appointed to the Court of Appeal for Ontario. His appointment was part of a wave of appointments that would fundamentally change the nature and temperament of the Court. The Court was expanded from ten to fourteen judges, and the days of the nasty Court of Appeal ended. Bert was one of several highly regarded lawyers appointed directly from the bar to the Court of Appeal. His appointment was preceded by that of John Arnup in 1970 and Charles Dubin in 1973, both senior counsel. It was also preceded by the appointment of G. Arthur Martin, at the time, and in the minds of many still today, Canada's most distinguished criminal lawyer. Bert was appointed at the same time as three respected trial judges, Samuel Grange, Maurice Lacourcière, and Lloyd Houlden. They were soon followed by William Howland, a highly regarded solicitor. In the space of a few years, the character of the Court of Appeal was changed very much for the better.

Bert became the first Associate Chief Justice of the Court of Appeal in 1978, a position he filled until his death a few days short of his sixty-sixth birthday in 1987. I did not know it at the time, but Bert narrowly missed being appointed Chief Justice of Ontario in 1977 upon Chief Justice Gale's retirement. According to Ian Binnie,[18] Bert had cleared all the hurdles, and it was only at the last minute when the appointment went before cabinet that he lost out. John Turner, then at McMillan Binch but on his way back to politics, was able to persuade Minister of Justice Ron Basford to substitute McMillan Binch alumnus William Howland as Ontario's new Chief Justice.

Edgar Sexton

I enjoyed working on several matters with Edgar Sexton. He combined strong legal acumen with a remarkable ability to strategize. He loved tackling a tough case and turning what at first blush seemed to be a losing case into a winning one.

My favourite case with Ed involved MacLean and MacLean, a singing comedy group that performed in bars and taverns and often included lewd language in the lyrics for their songs. In the middle of an engagement in a tavern in London, Ontario, they were terminated after an inspector from the Liquor Licence Board threatened to cancel the tavern's licence if the group was permitted to perform again. We brought an action against the Board and its members for an injunction and damages for intentional interference with contractual relations, arguing that the licensing powers of the Board did not permit its members to censor entertainment in licensed premises.

Ed was a master at developing a winning strategy. Because of legislation restricting the availability of injunctive relief against the Crown or agents of the Crown, he decided to name the individual members of the Board as defendants. This brought the case squarely within the principle of the famous case of *Roncarelli v Duplessis*,[19] in which a Quebec restauranteur had successfully sued the Premier of Quebec for cancelling his liquor licence because he had provided bail to several co-religionists. That case is known to every law student as a beacon of the rule of law, and I was thrilled to be involved in a case where it applied. But we did have a problem: how could we prove that the members of the Board were directly involved in the decision to threaten cancellation of the tavern's licence? Sitting in the firm's board room with our client, Ed came up with a daring solution. He got the client, on the spot, to call the Board and ask to speak to the Chair. Miraculously, the receptionist put the call through. The client identified himself and asked the Chair to explain the Board's policy. The Chair replied that he and the other members of the Board would not tolerate obscene performances in licensed premises. That answer formed a prominent part of our client's affidavit filed in support of the injunction. Within a few days, we were before Justice Keith, who granted the injunction in a clear decision citing *Roncarelli v Duplessis* and ending the Liquor Licence Board's attempt to censor our client.[20]

Ian Binnie

Bert's appointment to the bench deprived me of an inspiring mentor with whom I could work. But that void was ably filled by Arthur Stone and Ian Binnie. Ian had taken a year off to work in Tanzania the year I articled, so I met him only when I returned to the firm from Oxford. Ian is well-known for his wit, and as soon as he met me and learned that I had a doctoral degree, he named me "Dr. Bob." That is how I was known at the firm thereafter, and that is what Ian still calls me.

As he departed for the bench, Bert advised me that if I wanted a career in litigation, Ian was the person with whom I should work. Although he was much younger than Bert and, at the time, less well established, Ian matched and perhaps even surpassed Bert's legal brilliance. He was then, as he is now, a great wit and an exceptionally hard worker. He has an unusual ability to size up a case quickly, to immediately see its strengths and weaknesses, and then to impose his own assessment as the proper solution. He sees the practical, real-world dimensions of every problem he confronts. It was a privilege to work with Ian Binnie.

I assisted Ian on several matters and went with him twice to the Supreme Court of Canada. The most memorable case was *Committee for Justice and Liberty v National Energy Board et al*,[21] challenging the proceedings before the National Energy Board for the approval of a $10 billion project to construct two pipelines in the Mackenzie Valley to bring natural gas south to serve both the Canadian and the American markets. The natural gas pipeline proposal, prompted by the discovery of significant fossil fuels in the Arctic in the 1960s, was controversial from the start because of significant environmental concerns and the impact the construction of the pipeline would have upon Indigenous communities along its route.

Our client, the Committee for Justice and Liberty (CJL), was a public interest group, an offshoot of the Christian Labour Association of Canada (CLAC), the union Bert MacKinnon represented when overcoming Ontario Labour Relations Board rulings that the union could not be certified because of religious discrimination. CLAC and CJL had limited resources, but both proved to be a terrific source for interesting cases. It was very much in the tradition of the firm to take on its cases despite the fact that the client could not pay anything approaching market rate legal fees. The CJL was led by Gerald Vandezande and John Olthuis, two committed Christian activists who had taken up the cause of the Dene Nation and other affected aboriginal groups who opposed the pipeline going through their traditional territories.[22]

CLAC challenged the proceedings before the National Energy Board in which the pipeline proponents sought a Certificate of Public Convenience and Necessity to authorize proceeding with construction. Before his appointment as Chair of the National Energy Board, Marshal Crowe held a senior position with one of the applicants before the Board. We were able to demonstrate that Crowe had taken part in meetings and significant decisions relating to the necessity, ownership, routing and financing of the pipeline, the very issues that he would be deciding as Chair of the National Energy Board. We argued that his association with the applicant and his active role in supporting the application disqualified him, because he had made a prior determination as to the merits of the proposal.

No doubt the oil and gas interests regarded the case as a "Hail Mary" attempt to block what appeared to be the inevitable approval and development of the MacKenzie Valley project. But our client was fighting hard before Justice Thomas Berger's Royal Commission. The commission was appointed in 1974 by the Trudeau minority government in response to concern raised by Indigenous and other groups regarding the environmental, cultural, social, and economic impacts of the proposed pipeline. Our client's strategy was to stop in its tracks the proceedings before the National Energy Board and delay the Energy Board's almost inevitable approval long enough to give Berger a chance to deliver his report.

The case began in the Federal Court of Appeal, where we faced a panel of five judges. Lined up against us was a long list of senior lawyers representing the energy and pipeline interests. Ian relished the David and Goliath challenge and, although he argued the case brilliantly, the five judges did not accept his submissions.[23] Justice Thurlow held that while Crowe's prior involvement "might give rise in a very sensitive or scrupulous conscience to the uneasy suspicion that he might be unconsciously biased, and therefore should not serve,"[24] that was not the proper legal test to apply. Rather, Justice Thurlow found, the issue was "what would an informed person, viewing the matter realistically and practically – and having thought the matter through – conclude. Would he think that it is more likely than not that Mr. Crowe, whether consciously or unconsciously, would not decide fairly?"[25] To that question the Court's answer was "no." Crowe held his positions with the applicant in his capacity as a director of the Canadian Development Corporation, which provided the applicant with financial backing. This meant that he was at the table as the representative of the Government of Canada, with no personal stake in the matter. According to the Federal Court of Appeal, the informed observer would consider that, since he had acted in the public interest and not his own, he would be able to approach the issue with an open mind.

We received leave to appeal to the Supreme Court of Canada and, again, faced a long line of distinguished counsel representing the energy and pipeline interests. For reasons I cannot recall, the panel comprised eight judges, in my experience a very unusual formation. We almost went down to seven judges when Justice Ritchie became disoriented in the courtroom. The hearing was adjourned, and Chief Justice Laskin called counsel into his chambers, a place I would revisit as the Court's Executive Legal Officer a little over ten years later. The Chief Justice explained that Justice Ritchie suffered from a war injury that caused him transient problems from time to time but that he was fine and that, with our consent, he would listen to the recording of the argument and participate in the decision. While Chief Justice Laskin asked for our consent, it was obvious that he wanted Justice Ritchie to continue hearing the case and, needless to say, all counsel consented.

The case took three days to argue, two or two and a half days longer than the Court would allow today. Once again, Ian was brilliant and, even better, this time our arguments carried the day by a majority of five judges to three. Our argument was not that Marshall Crowe had intentionally acted improperly but that a fair-minded observer would conclude that any decision he made would be influenced by his prior involvement with the corporate interests. Our factum reflects the more formal style of argument then in vogue. There are no flights of rhetoric, and almost all the cases we cited were decisions of the English courts. The only passage that reflected Ian Binnie's devastating wit is this one: "In his previous determination of these factual issues, Mr. Crowe may have been wearing [his corporate hat], but the informed, practical realistic [person] who has 'thought the matter through' would be more impressed by the fact that he used the same head."

The Court responded to the pipeline proponents' request for a quick decision by announcing the result the next morning with reasons to follow. It was obvious during the argument that the Court was divided. Chief Justice Laskin wrote the majority reasons. He emphasized that there was no question of actual bias and, contrary to the opinion of the Federal Court of Appeal, the fact that Crowe had nothing to gain or lose was irrelevant. The case is still cited as authority for the test for bias: "[T]he apprehension of bias must be a reasonable one, held by reasonable and right-minded persons, applying themselves to the question and obtaining thereon the required information … what would an informed person, viewing the matter realistically and practically – and having thought the matter through – conclude."[26]

The decision stopped a major energy project in its tracks and represented a huge victory for our client. It certainly shocked the proponents of the pipeline, including politicians, senior civil servants and the oil and gas industry. As our clients had hoped, Justice Berger tabled his report in 1977 recommending a ten-year moratorium on the pipeline to allow for further study and the settlement of Indigenous land claims. That process took more than ten years, and eventually the pipeline project was abandoned for financial reasons in 2017.

From a legal perspective, the case established an important principle, firmly rejecting the "old boy network" and "but he is a good chap" analysis of the Federal Court of Appeal. From a political perspective, the case represented a major victory for Indigenous groups and environmental activists joined in their opposition to a massive oil and gas project.

The Demise of MacKinnon McTaggart

Despite my departure for academe in 1976, I retained a connection to the firm until it folded. I continued to be listed on the firm's letterhead and I did a certain amount of legal work, mostly with Arthur Stone and Ian Binnie. Bert MacKinnon's departure for the bench in 1974 did not bode well for the firm. It led to a division and an exodus of some partners, including Edgar Sexton, whom I was very sorry to see depart, especially since his departure followed a failed takeover attempt led by Vic Seabrook and John McElwain, two commercial lawyers. The attempt to oust Don McTaggart, Joe Potts, Arthur Stone, Bill Herridge, and Ian Binnie from the firm's leadership was shameful, and I was very disappointed to learn that Ed was part of it. Because this all happened after I had decided to leave for an academic career, I was spared most of the bitterness.

The firm carried on, initially under the name McTaggart, Potts, Stone and Herridge, and then, after more departures for the bench, the firm reverted to its original name, Wright, McTaggart. But in 1986, the partners decided to go their separate ways, and the firm was dissolved in part because its financial structure was simply too loose and lacking in discipline.

Little did I know that the failed coup and the demise of the firm were an early sign of the profound changes that were to come in the legal profession. In the firm's heyday, loyalty to one's partners and associates prevailed over concerns about the bottom line. Joining a law firm was akin to getting married. There certainly were divorces, but departures for greener and more lucrative pastures were the exception rather than the rule. Lawyers expected to earn a decent livelihood, but few, if any, earned the million dollar-plus incomes that have become common today. The firm's demise preceded the era of national and global law firms, boutique litigation firms that are unable to avoid exponential growth, and small full-service law firms, like MacKinnon McTaggart that do not expand or merge with larger firms tend to fade away.

I am proud to have been a part of the firm, and I join its former members in revering its spirit. More than thirty years after the firm's demise, we still enjoy the traditional Christmas lobster lunch with baba au rum for dessert, where stories are told and reminiscences are shared.

5
Oxford

I did my graduate work at the University of Oxford. Guided by two excellent supervisors, I learned how to take on and complete a major writing project. I loved being in England and studying at one of its great universities. I participated in sports, enjoyed the collegial life of my college, took advantage of the proximity to France and Europe, and became a father. My time at Oxford was probably the most enjoyable period of my life.

Applying to Oxford

I enjoyed the exposure to practice gained in my articling year, but I had a lingering feeling that I wanted to do more academic study. I had thought about doing graduate work in political science when I was at Western, the seed having been planted by Professor Peyton Lyon. I had done well at law school, and Dean Macdonald encouraged me to think about graduate study. Geraldine and I had loved our year away in France. We were both keen to spend some time in England. Her Canadian parents had spent several years in England during the war, and she was born there. I had inherited my mother's Anglophilia.

Most of our friends were preoccupied with starting their careers and thinking about buying a house. They thought we were crazy to think about doing anything else. I decided to apply to Oxford and Cambridge and to see if I could get a scholarship. I was planning to do a course work degree. I thought that the Oxford BCL offered a stronger program than the Cambridge LLB (now called the LLM) and was delighted when I was accepted by the Oxford law faculty and Magdalen College.

Getting a scholarship proved to be more difficult. I applied for everything going but had a steady stream of rejections. Our last hope was the

Carswell, Sweet, and Maxwell Scholarship, but we heard nothing. The person administering the selection for that scholarship at Carswell was Boris Krivy, who later became a senior court administrator. As a joke, each day when I returned home from work, I asked Geraldine "Did Boris call?" and her answer was always "No call from Boris." One day when I posed the usual question, I got an unexpected answer: "No, but I called Boris. He said that if you want the scholarship, it is yours." They had offered the scholarship to someone else, who had left them dangling. I am not sure if their first choice had finally turned them down, or if Boris was simply tired of waiting. Nor am I sure what would have happened had Geraldine not made that nervy call to Boris. But I had the scholarship I needed to go to Oxford.

Magdalen College

We arrived in Oxford in mid-September 1971, a few weeks before the beginning of term. In my biased view, Magdalen College is the most beautiful college in Oxford with its magnificent fifteenth-century tower, chapel, and cloisters. There is a large, enclosed grove where deer roam, overlooked by the eighteenth-century Palladian style New Building. One can stroll on Addison's Walk along the Cherwell River, passing by the adjacent meadow. The only downside of Magdalen was that I could never pronounce its name ("MAWD-lin") the way the English do. My MAWD was simply too flat for the English ear. When asked the name of my college, I would do my best and, after about three tries, the person who asked would say, "Oh, you mean MAWD-lin!"

We had secured a flat in the Waynflete Building located near the college across Magdalen Bridge. The Waynflete was a men's residence – the college did not yet admit women – but it had three flats on the fourth floor for married graduate students. It was a nondescript modern building, then only a few years old, quite out of keeping with the college's historic buildings. The College Fellows regarded it as an embarrassment. However, we were happy to be there in a relatively large and reasonably well-equipped one-bedroom furnished flat, close to the college and to the law library. Even the rent was reasonable – 35 pounds a month. It needed a coat of paint, and the college agreed to supply us with the necessary equipment if we were prepared to do the work. One curious feature that cut down on the painting job was that the living room walls were covered with Styrofoam, apparently applied because of a condensation problem. We found that it provided a welcoming surface for pictures and posters, and we ignored the fact that it presented a serious risk of fire.

The first official event was the Matriculation Ceremony for incoming students. We had to wear "sub fusc," the academic attire required for all official University events, including examinations, consisting of an academic gown, dark suit and socks, black shoes, white shirt, and formal white bow tie. We assembled at the college and then proceeded as a group, along with streams of new students from all the other colleges, through the streets of Oxford to the Sheldonian Theatre, where we were formally made members of the University. The whole exercise seemed a little ridiculous, but the English have a wonderful way of pulling off such traditions with a sense of occasion and not taking things too seriously. There were sherry parties to welcome us to the college, and we were invited to meet the President, James Griffiths, in his college lodging. While most of the incoming students were young undergraduates, Magdalen had a large number of graduate students who formed our circle of friends and acquaintances. We seemed to have a natural rapport with the Australians. Our neighbours at the Waynflete were American, both lawyers. We also connected with a delightful couple from Chile.

I met the college's law tutors, John Morris, Colin Tapper, and John Feltham. They were very welcoming. As the BCL is a graduate course, I would not receive college tutorials, in which one or two students meet with a tutor to discuss an essay, but rather would simply attend the university's BCL lectures and seminars. By the time I returned to Oxford as a visiting professor years later, that had changed and I found myself giving tutorials rather than receiving them.

I became a regular attender of the Middle Common Room, available to the college's graduate students. My first visit was discouraging. When I entered, there was only one person there. He was reading a newspaper. I went over to introduce myself and he looked up and, without telling me who he was, replied coldly, "You are new, aren't you," and went back to his newspaper. I learned that the only way to become accepted was to quietly sit in a corner until you became like a familiar piece of furniture. I became very aware that it was not easy to fit into an institution heavily populated with privately educated students imbued with British class-consciousness, although because I was a "colonial," my faux pas were more readily overlooked or forgiven than had I been of middle- or lower-class British stock. My integration was greatly assisted by the arrival of the Australian and American graduate students, who were considerably less formal and class-conscious. Denis Galligan, years later Oxford's Professor of Socio-Legal Studies, and Kevin Pose, who went on to teach taxation at Monash University, became good friends.

A Change in Direction: DPhil and *Habeas Corpus*

In the first term, I was taking evidence, conflict of laws, and restitution, all courses I had taken at law school. I discovered that none of these courses were offered at the undergraduate level and that most BCL students would be encountering them for the first time. I attended a few lectures. They were interesting but not significantly different from or better than what I had experienced at U of T Law. I also realized that I had already spent six years attending lectures and I began to wonder if two more years of BCL lectures were the right fit for me. I had intended to write a short thesis to complete the BCL, but it struck me that perhaps I should think about switching to the DPhil, Oxford's thesis-based doctoral degree.

A chance conversation with Mark Aronson, an Australian who was working on a DPhil, helped me make up my mind. Mark, who would go on to an academic career at the University of New South Wales as a leading administrative law scholar, explained how the DPhil worked. One had to have a topic approved and then write a thesis under the rather loose supervision of a senior faculty member. I told him I did not have a specific topic in mind but that I would like to research something in the area of public or constitutional law. He said that his supervisor, Professor H.W.R. Wade, a prominent administrative and constitutional law scholar, had been trying to find someone to write a thesis on *habeas corpus*. I knew from the paper I had written in law school that very little scholarly work had been done on the topic and that it was something I could take on and complete in a reasonable amount of time.

As the entry I would write years later for *The New Oxford Companion to Law*[1] explains, *habeas corpus* is the common law's famous remedy allowing anyone illegally imprisoned to petition the court for immediate release. The writ of *habeas corpus* ("have the body") commands the jailer to bring the prisoner immediately before the court and to explain the reason for the imprisonment. If the judge finds the imprisonment to be unlawful, the prisoner is entitled to immediate release. *Habeas corpus* is a cornerstone of the rule of law and a fundamental common law constitutional guarantee to ensure the liberty of the subject.

Habeas corpus has deep roots in the common law tradition, and its origins can be traced to medieval court records. The modern form of the writ was established by the late sixteenth century, when *habeas corpus* was used to challenge executive orders committing prisoners deemed to be enemies of the state. *Habeas corpus* played a significant role in the early seventeenth century in the constitutional struggle between the Stuart Kings and Parliament. *Habeas corpus* has been used in a wide variety of situations to protect personal liberty. In *Somerset's Case* (1772), *habeas corpus* was used to secure the release of an enslaved person held on a ship.[2] *Habeas corpus* is now protected by the *Charter*[3] and remains available in times of national crisis to challenge internment or executive detention orders, although this right has sometimes been effectively suspended by emergency legislation authorizing extraordinary powers of detention. *Habeas corpus* has also been used in civil cases to rescue a child from unlawful custody, or to release patients unlawfully committed to psychiatric hospitals or other institutions. While *habeas corpus* has now been superseded in many areas by more specific statutory appeals and other means of review, it remains a fundamentally important constitutional principle. Astonishingly, despite its importance, there was no comprehensive scholarly account of its development or use.

H.W.R. Wade

I decided to seek an appointment with Professor Wade to see if he would be prepared to take me on as a doctoral student. I wrote him a note and shortly thereafter he welcomed me to his rooms in St. John's College. He thought that *habeas corpus* would be an ideal thesis topic and he was prepared to be my supervisor if I could get the necessary permission from my college and from the university to switch to the DPhil from the BCL.

I was very pleased to have Wade's positive response. He was one of England's leading public law scholars. His book *Administrative Law*, first published in 1961, was an accepted authoritative source in England and Canada. He had written a long list of crystal-clear and often trenchant periodical articles in which he often took issue with judicial decisions. Wade was just as well known for his work as co-author of the leading text on real property law, *Megarry & Wade's Law of Real Property*, first published in 1957, and regularly used as a text in Canadian law schools well into the 1990s. He was a Cambridge graduate and taught there until his appointment to an Oxford Chair in English Law in 1961. He believed that the courts had an important role to play in controlling government actors and that a relatively strong dose of judicial intervention was required to maintain the rule of law. I believe that Wade's approach provided a valid and enduring platform for the study of *habeas corpus* and the judicial protection of personal liberty.[4] I also became imbued with his idea that "the task of the academic was to search for and identify the fundamental principles upon which a coherent legal structure and system could rest."[5]

The DPhil was a strictly research degree with no course requirements of any kind, distinguishing it from PhD programs in other universities that include a significant element of course work and qualifying examinations to screen candidates. An Oxford DPhil candidate was initially admitted to read for the BLitt degree. Candidates were then required to submit evidence of sufficient progress after a few terms to warrant full admission to work towards the DPhil. This was not a high hurdle and nothing like the typical PhD comprehensive examinations.

The BCL was, without question, the graduate degree preferred by most of Oxford's law faculty. Few law faculty members had a doctoral degree, and most seemed to be dubious about the worth of the DPhil. I explained my situation to John Feltham, a law tutor at Magdalen with a BCL who favoured that degree, but who was a kind and sympathetic man. He certainly would not stand in my way but explained that I would have to receive permission from the college's senior law tutor, John Morris, a conflict of laws scholar who had been a central figure in establishing the BCL on a firm modern footing.

I arranged to see Dr. Morris in his rooms in the New Building. Morris was an imposing figure. He sternly warned that I was making a terrible mistake, that I would be strictly on my own with the DPhil, and that I would have nothing to show at the end if I did not manage to produce a satisfactory thesis. I decided to hold my ground and, when he could see that I was quite determined to make the switch, he reluctantly agreed to give me the required approval.

I also encountered some resistance from Bert MacKinnon. He was a proud BCL graduate and, when I wrote to tell him of my plan to switch to the DPhil, he expressed his disappointment. He told me that he had discussed the topic of *habeas corpus* with Ed Sexton and that they both thought it was too narrow to be of any use in practice. Bert and Ed advised me to think about doing something in the area of wills and trusts, where there was a dearth of litigation expertise. I appreciated the advice but stuck with my plan. I pointed out that *habeas corpus* was an interesting topic I could pull off in two years that "really gets to the guts of English Constitutional law and history." I do not doubt that Bert and Ed were right if my purpose was to carve out an attractive niche for practice. But deep down, I knew that was not my purpose and I could not resist the opportunity to tackle a fundamental issue of constitutional law that had strangely been ignored by legal scholars.

The Oxford DPhil has changed since my time as a student at Oxford. A significant number of faculty members now hold doctoral degrees, and there is now a large contingent of DPhil students in law. It remains a research-only degree, but there is a more structured and supportive approach than there was in my time, when many DPhil students floundered for a year or more trying to identify a suitable topic and then sank under the weight of the research and writing. I saw exactly what John Morris had warned me about.

Habeas corpus was an ideal topic. It was well defined, and there was not a mountain of writing on the topic with which I would have to compete. It was simply a matter of thoroughly reviewing the case law and the history and providing a coherent, unified account of an ancient and vitally important legal concept. In a statement of proposed treatment of my subject that I submitted to the faculty, I defined my task as follows: "I propose to present an exposition of the remedy of *Habeas Corpus* in English law. This involves a thorough examination of the relevant English and Commonwealth authorities. Considerable attention will be paid to historical development. My aim is to present a complete description of the law of *Habeas Corpus*, critical discussion of its use and efficacy as a remedy, and hopefully, some suggestions for its improvement." I had planned to be in Oxford for no more than two years and thought that, if I worked steadily, I could pull it off.

Professor Wade urged me not to approach the task of writing the thesis by spending a year or two on the research and then writing it up. Better, he advised, to start with a key area and write a chapter as soon as possible. He made it clear to me that we would work best together if we only met to discuss something I had written, even if it was only part of a chapter. He also made it clear that he did not think it would be productive for us to meet otherwise. He suggested that I start with the problematic area of determining contested questions of fact on *habeas corpus*. It was an excellent suggestion, a definable chunk that went to the heart of one of the most contentious aspects of *habeas corpus*.

Professor Wade had clear and strong views about my subject, but he left me to work my way through the thicket of cases, providing me with his provocative and quite definite thoughts on what I wrote. He encouraged me to question what appeared to be accepted wisdom, but only if I could back up my analysis with well-honed and well-supported arguments.

He was a very formal man who never let his guard down with me, even in the comfort of his own office. He always addressed me, both in person and in writing, as "Sharpe." I once greeted him with a "good morning" as we passed in the law library, and he walked by me without responding. I learned that he was not to be bothered except if I wrote to request a meeting, to which he invariably responded promptly and positively. At our meetings, he was friendly and encouraging, but had no time for small talk and immediately turned to a discussion of the draft I had asked him to read.

It was only several years later that I saw a different side of Professor Wade. I had joined the faculty at the University of Toronto, and by that time Professor Wade had moved from Oxford to Cambridge as Master of Gonville and Caius College. He later succeeded Glanville Williams as Rouse Ball Professor of English Law. I wrote to let him know that I would be in Cambridge for a conference. He immediately replied with an invitation to dinner at his college, where he warmly received me as a full academic colleague. He could not have been more friendly and welcoming.

Ian Brownlie

After one term, Professor Wade went away on a sabbatical, and I was advised by the faculty that Dr. Ian Brownlie would be my supervisor in his place. Wade had launched me on the right path, for which I will always be grateful, but I often thought that the change of supervisors was healthy. Brownlie, as I will explain, was an excellent supervisor, less directive, and more willing to let me find my own way with the material. Although I basically agreed with Professor Wade's views, I wanted the thesis to be mine, not his. Ian Brownlie gave me the freedom and latitude I needed.

Ian Brownlie was a fellow of Wadham College and about forty years old when I first met him. He was a brilliant, hard-working scholar and certainly not the typical Oxford don. He came from Liverpool, was not privately educated and retained a distinct northern burr in his accent. He had briefly been a member of the Communist Party and, despite his departure from the party after the Soviet invasion of Czechoslovakia in 1968, that history had made him suspect in government and establishment circles for quite some time. As a college tutor, he taught many subjects, and he had a remarkably wide-ranging knowledge of the law. He had spent some time arguing mainly public law cases as a barrister and had published a book in 1968, *The Law Relating to Public Order*, dealing with the law relating to public meetings, freedom of assembly, and other related topics. That may have identified him as someone who could be my supervisor. His principal scholarly interest, however, was international law and, as his *Times* obituary put it, eventually he became "unarguably the British doyen of international law both in practice and as an academic."[6]

Brownlie was a remarkably productive scholar. His Oxford DPhil thesis, *International Law and the Use of Force between States*, was published in 1963, soon to be followed by his major work, *Principles of Public International Law*, in 1966. Many editions of that book followed. It was translated into several languages, and it is widely accepted as an authoritative source.

At our first meeting, Brownlie made it clear that he thought that virtually all doctoral candidates spent far too long producing a thesis and that he was convinced that the job could be done in two years. I told him that two years was all I had for this project, so we quickly formed an alliance. Like Professor Wade, he suggested that we should meet only when I had some written work to show. He stressed the importance of writing early, even if that meant that a first draft would have to be changed as the research progressed. After a few meetings, I could tell that he was pleased with the progress I was making, although more from the absence of negative comments than from any effusive praise. It was when I showed him that a case comment I had written on an interesting *habeas corpus* case had been published[7] that he started to become more visibly enthusiastic about my work. I knew I had his confidence when he told me to be sure to think about my project as both a thesis and a book. Essentially, he made it clear that I was on my own. I did not keep track of how many times we met, but it was not more often than two or three times during each of the eight-week terms for which he was my supervisor.

Significantly for me, Brownlie implanted in me what I call the "fifteen-minute rule." He explained that he had to squeeze his writing into a busy schedule consumed by student tutorials and other college duties. He had learned to make use of short periods of time to write a sentence or two, check a reference or complete a footnote. That was the only way, he explained, to bring a large project to completion. The other lesson he implanted was the "one brick at a time" principle. Pointing out the window to a large brick wall, he observed that approaching writing the thesis from the perspective of having to build that entire wall would be daunting. By seeing my task as laying one brick at a time, I was much more likely to succeed. Aim to lay a brick today and another tomorrow and soon the wall will be built. These lessons left an indelible mark and, for the rest of my career, I have followed both the fifteen-minute rule and the one brick at a time principle in my scholarly and judicial writing.

Ian Brownlie was an excellent supervisor. He was encouraging but also demanding. He trusted me with the details but insisted that arguments be soundly based on principle and authority. He often pointed out where I might benefit from considering principles from other related areas of law, and I certainly benefited from his wide knowledge. As Phillipe Sands reported in the obituary he wrote for the *Guardian*, "a distinguished former doctoral student [Sands does not say who, but my guess was Professor James Crawford] describes Brownlie as a 'formidable supervisor … striking exactly the right balance between care and allowing the student to get on with it.'"[8]

Not long after I worked under his supervision, Brownlie left Oxford to assume a Chair in international law at the London School of Economics. He then returned to Oxford in 1990 as the Chichele Professor of Public International Law and gradually shifted his attention to what became a flourishing practice, regularly arguing cases before the International Court of Justice. He was known to follow the "cab rank" principle, accepting briefs if he was available, even if the client was unpopular or not in tune with his own political beliefs. He achieved a notable success arguing in the House of Lords that the Chilean dictator Augusto Pinochet could be extradited to Spain for crimes committed during his time as the country's president.[9] Brownlie continued to write and argue cases until the end, when he was tragically killed at the age of 77 in a traffic accident while on vacation in Egypt.

Writing a Doctoral Thesis

By today's standards, *habeas corpus*, or at least the way I approached it, would perhaps lack the theoretical component expected of most doctoral theses, although my research did have a significant historical component. I was confronted with that criticism only by David Lawson, a fellow Magdalen DPhil student from the United States. He was working on conflict of laws, and we agreed to read each other's work as we progressed. Our idea was that we wanted our work to be comprehensible to a non-specialist. It was a fruitful relationship and, since I was interested in conflicts, I enjoyed reading his work. David was a very perceptive and helpful reader, but from time to time he would ask me if what I was doing really amounted to a thesis. I recognized that he had a point, but because my supervisors did not seem to share his concern, I carried on. I am very glad that I did. The historical perspective may not yield neat theoretical answers as history rarely conforms to a single theme. But history does help us understand the law from a broader perspective and, as I will explain in later chapters, later in my career I became a devotee of legal history.

My thesis had no single theme or theory, but it did take considerable intellectual effort to provide coherent structure that would comprehensively rationalize and explain centuries of common law development. There were hundreds of cases to be read, digested, understood in their historical context, and organized into sensible categories that were, at best, implicit when I began my work. As with almost every writing project I have taken on, I constantly wondered whether anyone would be interested in what I was producing. The work was, at times, tedious and frustrating, but I persevered until I convinced myself that I was producing something worthwhile.

Life in Oxford

I loved the Oxford atmosphere of learning, scholarship, and toleration for eccentricity. The college provided a wonderful interdisciplinary environment. I regularly had lunch at the college, Geraldine and I went for the occasional college dinner, and we often enjoyed Middle Common Room dinners catered by the college and provided in a private meeting room. I attended a few lectures, the most memorable being those given by historian A.J.P. Taylor about World War II and a series delivered by Ronald Dworkin. Dworkin, appointed as Professor of Jurisprudence in 1969, was previewing his famous book, *Taking Rights Seriously*, published in 1977.[10] He was a brilliant lecturer, probably the best I have ever heard. His lectures were engaging and entertaining, and he made his theory seem self-evident.

Working on the thesis kept me busy, but I did not let it overwhelm me. I decided to approach it as a 9-to-5 job, working steadily but also taking time off for other activities. I joined the college field hockey team and greatly enjoyed playing. I was not very good at the game, but that did not seem to matter, and it was great exercise. Magdalen had a very fine sports ground not far from the college with a gorgeous grass pitch and a nice pavilion. After the game, both teams would gather in the pavilion for a glass of "shanty" and polite conversation about the game. I reached the pinnacle of my field hockey career when I managed to score a goal in a game that ended in a 2–2 tie. I played one game of cricket with little success, but considerable enjoyment, when a local village team challenged the Magdalen MCR to a match. I made a catch but was bowled out on the first ball I faced.

I was also a proud member of the Oxford ice hockey club, in the tradition of Bert MacKinnon and a long list of other Canadians. We had a South African goalie. He was not a good skater, but he had terrific reflexes and instincts for stopping the puck, derived from his experience as a cricket wicketkeeper. My teammates included Hugh Arnold, who later served as Dean of U of T's business school when I was Dean of Law, and Herman Wilton-Siegel, who became a good friend and a judge after a successful career practising corporate commercial law. There was no ice rink in Oxford, so we had to travel for all of our games. One team member was an Englishman, vital to the team not for his hockey skills but because he owned a car. We won our first game, played in Birmingham, 5–3. We were ahead 4–3 when we thought the game had ended, but play went on, it seemed to us, because our opponents thought we were getting tired, and they would be able to tie the score. We scored another goal, and the game promptly ended. We also played in Southampton, where we lost to a better team, and in Bristol, where we were amazed to have a large crowd watch us lose to the local Redwings. Our planned Varsity match with Cambridge was threatened by the power cuts resulting from the coal miners' strike that paralysed Britain, but we finally managed to play it in Blackpool. We trounced Cambridge 9–0 in a rink with right angle corners at one end and at the other end shaped like the narrow end of an egg. The puck rebounded at surprising angles at both ends. The game was reported in the *Globe and Mail* with an amusing account written by Cambridge's goalie.[11] We prevailed again the next year 8–2 in a game in Billingham, Teesside, about 400 kilometres north of Oxford. We were fortunate to win, since several members of our team arrived about halfway through the game, having mistakenly driven to the wrong town. Playing on a line with our captain, Herman Wilton-Siegel, and perhaps because of the extra ice time required by the late arrival of our teammates, I scored three goals. I quickly decided to end my hockey career on that high note.

Geraldine and I managed to travel to France a few times to see her sister and brother-in-law and their growing family. We went skiing in Austria and attended a course on the European Convention on Human Rights in Strasbourg in the summer. We made several trips to London, where we saw Rudolph Nureyev and Margot Fonteyn in a ballet, Kiri Te Kanawa, the New Zealand soprano, as the Countess in Mozart's *Marriage of Figaro* at the Royal Opera House, and Alec Guinness in a West End play. We visited Stratford to see Shakespearean plays and went to the steeplechase races at Cheltenham. Quite how we managed to do all this on my rather modest scholarship is now a mystery, but I did receive some generous additional support from my parents. After I had transferred into the DPhil stream, I was able to apply for a Canada Council Doctoral Fellowship, which carried us through for the second year.

We were struck by the almost total absence of Canadian news in the UK media. Before the internet era, our only source of Canadian news was the Saturday *Globe and Mail*, sent to us every week by my parents. I have always regretted that I missed the legendary Canada–Soviet Union Summit Series in September 1972. The *Times* gave only the scores, and I did not experience the thrill of seeing Paul Henderson score his famous goal that won the series.

We lived through an interesting time in English politics. We arrived at the time of decimalisation for British coinage and the UK's entry into the European Common Market. The "Troubles" in Northern Ireland led to the collapse of the Stormont parliament and UK government's introduction of interment without trial, a rejection of the principle of *habeas corpus*. Conservative Prime Minister Edward Heath's attempt to reform trade unionism and deregulate the economy was proving divisive. A prolonged coal-miner's strike and resulting blackouts in 1972 ultimately ended with substantial pay increases for the miners.

Parenthood

The most important event to occur during my time in Oxford was the birth of our first child, daughter Anne Elizabeth, on 24 December 1972. It was easily the most moving and memorable experience of my life to that point. We had a midwife who visited us each day until Anne was 14 days old – a marvellous service to calm the nerves of anxious first-time parents unsure of how best to cope with a new baby. Babies were an unfamiliar feature of life in the Waynflete Building. We were unsettled when we received a note from the college home bursar telling us that the birth of our daughter meant that we would have to vacate our flat. The threatened eviction would have been a serious disruption to our lives and to the completion of my thesis. Once again, John Feltham came to my rescue. He understood our plight and spoke to the home bursar, and the eviction notice was rescinded.

Anne was not a difficult child and, despite some anxiety about our ability to cope with the unfamiliar task of caring for a tiny infant, we were thrilled to have her. I continued to work most days from 9 a.m. to 5 p.m. at the library, but the flexibility of student life gave me the freedom to spend time with this precious new life. The added responsibility of parenthood forced me to bring even greater focus to completing the thesis, since getting it done and finding gainful employment had become a matter of immediate concern.

Thinking about the Future

As I worked away on my thesis, I had two overtures for teaching positions in Canada. Ronald Macdonald, by then Dean of Dalhousie's law school, wrote to ask if I had any interest in an academic appointment. I received another overture from Donald Carter, a fellow Picton native, who was teaching at Queen's. After I returned to Canada, I received another from David Johnston, then Dean of Law at Western. I was tempted by the prospect of an academic career but decided that I should practise law for a couple of years, because I was convinced that a dose of real-world experience would make me a better scholar and teacher.

We enjoyed living in England so much that I toyed with the idea of trying to find a job there. Ian Brownlie told me he thought I would be an attractive candidate for an academic position. I also thought about practice at the bar. I wrote to the Council of Legal Education to see what credit I would be given for my U of T law degree. The response was very discouraging. The more we thought about it, the more we realized that, although we loved England, we would never be fully accepted, and we realized that we really belonged in Canada.

We had many visitors, both family and friends. Several members of the MacKinnon McTaggart firm dropped in to see us, including Bert MacKinnon, Arthur Stone, Edgar Sexton, Bob Peck, and Tom Dunne. When Bert and his wife, Joan, visited us in May, we made the final arrangements for me to return to the firm after I completed the bar admission course. I was to be paid $12,000 per year, which seemed astronomical at the time.

Finishing the Thesis

Ian Brownlie, ever determined that I should complete my thesis within two years, asked me to give him a complete draft of what I had in May 1973 so that he could assess my overall progress and provide me with comments. He seemed pleased with what I gave him, and I proceeded with the seemingly endless task that confronts me with all my writing: when I think I am done and just need to tidy up a few things, I realize that there is still another large hill to climb. Parts of the thesis had to be cleaned up, citations had to be checked, and the entire document needed to be retyped, copied, and bound. I realized that it would not be ready for formal submission before we left Oxford at the end of August 1973.

With enormous help from Geraldine as typist, proofreader, and grammar critic, I did manage to complete everything not long after we returned to Canada. I put the finishing touches on the thesis while attending the bar admission course. In late November, I sent off three bound copies of the thesis, requesting that examiners be appointed and that the oral examination, known in Oxford as the "viva," be arranged. This, I am proud to say, allowed Ian Brownlie to proclaim to those who succeeded me as his DPhil students (as several have complained to me) that a DPhil thesis can be written in two years. He immediately went to work on having my thesis published using his connections with Oxford

University Press (OUP). I felt obliged to send the thesis to Sweet and Maxwell on account of the scholarship. I was relieved when Mr. Maxwell politely replied that he did not think there would be sufficient demand for the book to make it economically possible for his company to publish it, leaving me free to pursue publication with the academically prestigious OUP.

David Bentley, Christ Church Oxford, and Professor S.A. de Smith from Cambridge were appointed as my examiners. De Smith was the author of a leading text, *Judicial Review of Administrative Action*, and certainly one of England's leading public law scholars. After the date for the viva had been set, I learned that de Smith had died. The University moved quickly and replaced de Smith with Professor J.A.G. Griffith from London School of Economics and Political Science. At the time, I knew little about Griffith, but I learned that he was a decidedly leftish legal scholar who challenged liberal orthodoxy and the idea that judges were neutral arbiters unaffected by their political views. Perhaps he was not the ideal person from my perspective, since my thesis did rest on the proposition that the protection of personal liberty depended upon a strong judicial role. Fortunately, I had qualified my faith in the judges, recognizing that they could not always be trusted and that, in times of crisis, they sometimes failed to put the law ahead of political considerations.

The viva was a very interesting experience. Bentley was a more conservative public lawyer, and most of the two-hour session was spent with the two examiners facing off against each other rather than grilling me. At the end, they thanked me and told me they had to report to the faculty before announcing their decision but asked if I had made any arrangements for publication. This, I thought, was a very positive sign. I eventually received a letter from Ian Brownlie telling me that, while the final decision was for the Faculty Board, the examiners were recommending that I be awarded the degree. His note concluded with characteristic reserve and understatement. "I am very pleased," he wrote, "and offer my congratulations on a good piece of work." "Good work" seemed to be rather faint praise, but then he added: "The Clarendon Press has been in touch and I have given strong support for publication."

My thesis was accepted for publication and appeared in print in 1976. Not long after, Professor Griffith published his important and controversial book, *The Politics of the Judiciary*, in which he quoted a lengthy passage from my thesis and book, criticizing wartime internment decisions for ignoring legal considerations and deciding cases on the basis of politics.[12] So maybe there was more legal theory in my book than I thought.

I was delighted to have several very positive reviews by some distinguished public lawyers. Mark Aronson,[13] the fellow student who put me on to Professor Wade and his interest in the topic, reviewed the book for the *Law Quarterly Review*, and Graham Zellick, who later visited the law school and became a good friend, did the same for the *Times Literary Supplement*.[14]

I prepared a second edition of the book, published in 1989, and a third edition, published with an English barrister, now a High Court Judge, Judith Farbey, in 2010. I also contributed a paper on *habeas corpus* to a Festschrift of Ian Brownlie[15] and gathered with about twenty of his former graduate students at Wadham College, Oxford, to celebrate his career upon his retirement in 1999.

Returning to Oxford

I have returned to Oxford many times since completing my thesis. As I will explain in the next chapter, my family returned for a sabbatical year in 1981–82 and spent summers there. I also went back as a visiting professor for short periods from 2011 to 2021.

Oxford has changed since my time as a student. The faculty now includes many more international scholars and students. The university has made a significant effort to attract and admit more publicly educated students to its undergraduate programs. The DPhil program now occupies a prominent place in the life of the Law Faculty, and theoretical and interdisciplinary work is emphasized to a greater degree than it was during my time as a student. But the place looks and feels the same. I will never tire of walking the grounds of Magdalen College, visiting Blackwell's bookstore, and strolling the streets in the early evening bustle as professors and students make their way back to college for dinner.

6
Law Professor

In 1976, after two and one-half years of practice as described in Chapter 4, I decided that I should give teaching a try. I enjoyed practice but I started to wonder if perhaps I was not better suited temperamentally and intellectually for the academy. I could see that in practice one had to slog through whatever came along and that it would take some time before I could hope to build an interesting practice of my own. The freedom to be able to research and write on topics that interested me held great appeal and certainly trumped the possibility of a higher income in practice.

Applying to Teach at U of T

I called Dean Marty Friedland to see if I could undertake some part-time teaching. My timing seemed to be ideal, since Horace Krever, my civil procedure professor in first year, had been appointed to the bench, and the faculty needed someone to teach the subject. My time in practice, together with my academic credentials, qualified me for that role.

I was disappointed when Marty seemed lukewarm to the idea of a sessional appointment. Civil procedure was a core first-year subject and, while the law school had used sessional instructors to teach it in the past, there was a strong preference for having first-year courses taught by full-time academics.

But then Marty asked me about my Oxford thesis. I told him that it had been accepted for publication by Oxford University Press and that I was currently reviewing the page proofs. His attitude quickly changed. Marty is a committed scholar. He was impressed by the fact that, just as he had done with *Double Jeopardy*,[1] I had been able to turn my thesis into a book to be published by the same highly reputed scholarly press. He also knew that teaching a course as a sessional lecturer would give me a one-sided and incomplete idea about academic life. If I really wanted to try it, he told me, I should think about coming for a full year and immersing myself in the world of teaching and scholarship.

I was hesitant at first, but as I reflected, I could see that Marty's suggestion provided me with an ideal opportunity. I thought that I would be able to maintain my relationship with the firm and return if I decided that I would be happier in practice after all. Marty suggested that I come for what was then known as "Friday lunch," when several members of the faculty gathered at the Hart House Gallery restaurant for informal discussion on ongoing research or a topic of general interest. He suggested that I come prepared to say something about a recent proposal for court reform. This was a very low-key version of the far more formalized hiring process that evolved after I joined the faculty, but it was all that I had to endure. I did not have to present a written paper, and the discussion was quite informal. The lunch seemed to go well. I enjoyed talking to many of my old professors and meeting some newer faculty members. Marty asked me for a copy of the page proofs for my book. He said that he would take a look and leave proofs in the faculty common room for perusal by other faculty members.

Not long after the lunch, Marty called to offer me a job. I could come for the year and teach civil procedure, criminal law, and an upper-year course that we could discuss. We eventually agreed that I could offer a course in remedies, one that had not been previously offered and that I would have to design. I later learned that he had obtained appraisals of my work from both Ian Brownlie and my DPhil examiner J.A.G. Griffiths, from Bert MacKinnon as to my abilities as a litigator, and from recent graduates George Strathy and John Gregory as to my potential as a law teacher.

This offer presented me with a wonderful opportunity. I was reasonably confident about my ability to teach civil procedure, and teaching criminal law would give me the opportunity to develop my long-standing interest in that subject, something I had struggled to do in practice. I was also keen to take on the challenge of designing a course in remedies.

After a rather awkward discussion with Arthur Stone, I accepted Marty's offer. Arthur was clearly disappointed to see me go, but he was also very understanding and accommodating. I worked out an arrangement with him and the law school that would allow me to maintain a connection with the firm. I would remain listed on the firm's letterhead and continue to take on some work, provided that I complied with the law school's "moonlighting" rules of spending no more than one day per week doing outside work.

As we sealed the deal, almost as an aside, Marty said, "By the way, I have made your appointment tenure stream." My preliminary offer to teach a course as a sessional instructor had quickly evolved into an amazing and, as it turned out, career-changing opportunity. If I did not enjoy the academy, I could return to practice after a year. But if I did like it, I had the option to remain in the tenure stream as a full-time professor.

I have often thought about how different my situation was from that of aspiring academics who came after me. I did not have to compete for the job, and the application and hiring process was informal and flexible. I enjoyed a seller's market. Shortly after I joined the faculty, the job market for academics tightened. There were many highly qualified candidates competing for few positions. The hiring process became much more rigorous. Candidates were expected to present polished and sophisticated research to demonstrate mature intellectual prowess. Only the most committed young scholars were hired. Had it been necessary for me to go through the process that exists now, I am not sure that I ever would have applied for an academic position. My ambivalence about whether my long-term goal was to devote myself to scholarship and teaching or return to practice would likely now be perceived as a fatal flaw. I agree that law professors should devote themselves to full time academic work, but I worry about a tendency on the part of some legal academics to distain practice. After all, without the world of legal practice, they would have few students and little to teach. Academics and practitioners have shared interest in mutual respect and collaboration.[2]

Teaching

I quickly learned that teaching is hard work. Even when I taught the same subject year after year, I found that I had to devote significant time to preparation to ensure that I had a firm grasp of the material and would not be caught off guard by a question from the students. Facing an audience of seventy razor-sharp minds was always daunting, even if I knew that not all of those razor-sharp minds had engaged with the readings as much as I would have liked.

The best part of teaching was the intellectual challenge of dealing with interesting and cutting-edge legal issues before an audience of intelligent aspiring lawyers, eager to master the craft of legal reasoning. That was a genuine privilege. My approach was to do my best to understand, explain, and rationalize the legal principles used and articulated by the courts and considered by legal scholars.

I never adopted an overtly theoretical approach. On the other hand, I tried to explain the law at a level of principle and to conceive of the law, to the extent possible, as a coherent regime based on certain fundamental principles of justice. This meant digging below the black letter rules to the underlying principles that structure the legal system as a whole. I adopted what is sometimes called a "mid-level," "operative," or "interpretive" theory[3] approach and urged my students to do the same. I tried to approach legal materials and judicial pronouncements in a critical fashion, always on the lookout for improvement in keeping with the lofty ideals of justice but with a healthy respect for the difficulty of the pursuit of justice in the real world.

In my first year of teaching, I was fortunate to have Yoram Dinstein, an experienced and hard-nosed visiting Israeli academic, in an office across from mine. Yoram had clear and strong views on most things and would regularly come into my office after he had overheard a conversation I was having with a student. He did not hesitate to tell me when he thought I should have been tougher on the student. Very often, I had to agree with his assessment. He gave me an excellent piece of advice: "There is only one thing to remember about your first-year of teaching – it will soon be over." I later communicated with Yoram when I was on sabbatical and living in Boar's Hill near Oxford. In his reply, he asked, "What is a nice Jewish boy doing on Boar's Hill? It sounds very non-kosher to me." I considered it to be a badge of honour that this deeply committed Israeli thought that I was Jewish.

Civil Procedure

Civil procedure was a teaching challenge, but I was interested in the subject and my experience in practice made me reasonably confident about my ability to present it competently. The other first-year courses – contracts, torts, property, and criminal law – dealt with substantive law. Substantive law defines the rights and duties of citizens in their relations with each other and with the state. Substantive law tells people what they can and cannot do and what happens if they fail to comply. First-year students could readily relate to and see the importance of what they were studying in those courses. For most people and most situations, substantive law is all that is required.

Procedural law comes into play when there is a dispute that cannot be resolved by agreement and the courts are called upon to pronounce on the rights involved and the legal sanction that should be applied. Procedural law is conceptually more difficult to pin down than substantive law. The status of procedural law is often relegated to that of "the handmaid of justice."[4] Procedural law is about the process of adjudication and dispute resolution, in particular the framework and operation of the institutions devised by society to determine the facts of the dispute and to decide how the law applies to those facts. The question is what is the fairest and most efficient way to move cases along from commencement to judgment.

The objective of procedural justice is to devise techniques that will allow decision makers to arrive at the truth in a way that is perceived to be fair. It is difficult to pin down how best to decide factual issues. We are dealing with uncertainties created by fallible human memory and affected by emotion, passion, and self-interest. There is no metric to decide the truth, and the objective of determining the truth must be balanced with other goals. The decision will only be accepted if it is the product of a process perceived by the parties and the public to be fair. Litigants are entitled to their day in court, and the fairer and more even-handed the rules of civil procedure seem, the greater the likelihood that the litigation process will be respected. Fairness must take into account the principle of proportionality. Fair procedures are time consuming and costly. Pretrial oral and documentary discovery procedures are seen as being essential to preventing "trial by ambush" and ensuring fairness, but they are also very expensive. If the cost and delay of achieving fairness puts dispute resolution out of the reach of ordinary citizens, the objective of fairness becomes self-defeating. Efficiency should not trump justice, but without efficiency, there will be no justice.

I saw the problem of access to justice as a central issue and a significant failure of our system of justice when I was teaching civil procedure, and the problem became even worse in the years that followed. The need to provide an efficient and accessible system of justice that will produce proper decisions in a fair manner continues to be one of the most pressing issues our legal system faces. I regret that, after fifty years of teaching and working as a judge, I have not done more to find a solution.

I thought that the importance of procedural law was obvious, but I had to work hard to convince my students that they could not assume justice would somehow automatically flow from nothing more than a proper application of the substantive rules. Just results cannot be arbitrarily imposed; they must be the result of both just rules and a fair fact-finding process that respects the right to be heard in an open court by an impartial tribunal. I also had to try to convince them and, it must be said, many of my colleagues, that the study of procedure was a worthy intellectual exercise and not just a series of boring rules that would be better taught in the bar admission course. Civil procedure continues to struggle to maintain its place as a core first-year course. Sadly, this battle is being lost in many law schools, including my own.

I started teaching well before the ages of PowerPoint and other visual aids, but I came up with an innovation in my second year of teaching that helped make the subject more accessible. I thought that the significance and importance of some of the details of procedure would be easier to grasp if, at the start of the course, the students were given an overview of a civil action, from beginning to end. With the help of the university's media centre, I created a five-hour video that did just that. I wrote an outline based on a case Bert MacKinnon had argued in the Supreme Court of Canada, previously described in Chapter 4.[5] It involved the liability of a bar for personal injuries sustained by an intoxicated patron who had been served too much to drink and was put out of the bar and then struck by a car while walking along the road. We had a professional actor play the leading role of the patron, and I found a psychiatrist to provide an expert opinion on a controversial aspect of the injury. Three excellent civil litigators, David Stockwood, Edgar Sexton, and Tom Dunne, acted as counsel. The video started with the first meeting between the injured party and his lawyer and proceeded through a preliminary motion, discovery, and trial. Master Stuart McBride heard the preliminary motion. Justice John Morden, then a member of the High Court and later Associate Chief Justice of Ontario, presided at the trial. I created the pleadings and other documents that would be found in the court file and counsels' files. I enjoyed putting the production together and learned how much work goes into making a film or documentary. I was pleased with the result and used the video every year thereafter to introduce the subject to my classes. The video was also taken up by several other law schools.

When I started teaching civil procedure in the late 1970s, the subject dealt almost entirely with private disputes. That gradually changed, and the subject became more interesting as the horizon of the civil justice system broadened with the advent of class actions, the *Charter of Rights and Freedoms* and public interest litigation. These were American-inspired developments that started to push courts and judges into a more public and controversial role,[6] a development that made the prospect of teaching civil procedure more attractive. In retrospect, I probably did not give adequate attention to that aspect of civil procedure,[7] although class actions were in their infancy when I taught the subject and, as explained in Chapter 8, I used a clinical model to explore *Charter* litigation.

Another area that was underdeveloped and unexplored by my teaching was alternative dispute resolution (ADR), although the significance of ADR has grown considerably since I taught the subject. I did explore the settlement of disputes and the impact of procedural rules, particularly cost rules, on achieving settlement. But my approach was to focus on civil litigation and the settlement of disputes within the framework of court-based proceedings. I mentioned, but barely touched on, the role of negotiation, mediation, arbitration, and less adversarial administrative law processes for the efficient resolution of disputes. Were I teaching the subject today, I would have to include consideration of online dispute resolution and the use of artificial intelligence to provide cost-efficient justice.

My first-year torts professor, Bruce Dunlop, served as the editor of the *Ontario Law Reports* and *Dominion Law Reports*. Because of my work in civil procedure, Bruce arranged for me to become one of several associate editors. My job was to focus on procedural cases so that even in the pre-internet age, I was always on top of current developments in the subject. This greatly assisted me in teaching the course. While it did not amount to scholarly work, the task of reading many cases and composing a "headnote" or pithy summary to be published with the report of the case, digesting a large amount of information, and distilling it down to the essentials was excellent training in writing. Another advantage was that the publisher paid a monthly stipend that helped in paying some of the bills.

Family Life

Our family had grown to three children with the arrival of Stephen in 1979. Geraldine gave priority to her childcare duties, but she managed to supplement our income with her part-time work as a freelance translator. I did my best to balance work with family responsibilities. I almost always made it home in time for dinner, and I genuinely enjoyed our children. They accuse me of skipping pages when I read them bedtime stories. I plead guilty to that charge. I often succumbed to the pressure I felt to get back to my desk to do some work. In mitigation, I say that, after all, I had read them those same stories many times before.

Adversary System and Legal Ethics

In teaching civil procedure, I decided to follow Horace Krever's example and devote a significant amount of time to discussing the theory of the adversary system and related issues of legal ethics. I found this to be the most interesting part of the course to teach. It raised difficult moral and philosophical issues, and the issues went to the heart of the subject.

The adversary system structures our system of civil procedure. While many of the rough edges have been knocked off the adversary system, we still adhere to the basics. The judge is a neutral and essentially passive observer who decides the case on the basis of the conflicting arguments presented by the parties and their lawyers. The role of the lawyer is that of resolute advocacy and to present the client's case in the strongest possible light.

The adversary system is based on the proposition that the best way to arrive at the truth and justice of a case is to allow the parties to define the dispute, investigate the case, and present starkly conflicting evidence and arguments before a neutral judge. But how sound is that theory and when and how do we need to modify its operation to ensure a fair and efficient system of justice? The adversary theory assumes a rough "equality of arms." Does our system of justice do enough to compensate for the fact that many litigants lack the resources to mount an effective case against a rich and powerful opponent?

The adversary system also shapes our view of legal ethics. It requires lawyers to dedicate themselves to resolute advocacy on behalf of their clients. Many people, and certainly many first-year law students, find it difficult to accept the partisan role of the lawyer.[8] The duty of resolute advocacy gives rise to what has been described as "[t]he central question for legal ethics"; namely, how can a lawyer "justify doing an act that, if performed outside the context of a professional role, would call for moral condemnation."[9] I thought that it was vital for law students to grapple with this question and that civil procedure was the place for them to do so.

My experience in practice, my reading, and my teaching persuaded me that partisan advocacy by lawyers is not only morally justified but also essential for the maintenance of the rule of law. Without legal advice, the law is inaccessible to ordinary citizens. The law is complex, and non-lawyers lack the training and knowledge required to plead a case in court. Ordinary citizens need lawyers to open the doors of our justice system and to secure their legal rights. The lawyer's job is not to judge the client. The client is legally entitled to have the judging done by an impartial court, and that fundamental promise of our system of law can only be secured by ensuring that all clients, however good or bad they may seem to be, have the benefit of resolute advocacy.

But, as lawyers are always asked, "How can you defend someone you know to be guilty?" Although the question involves criminal law, it represents the paradigmatic challenge to legal ethics in the adversary system, and I grappled with it in my civil procedure course. The answer is simply this: everyone has the constitutional right not to be convicted and imprisoned for a crime unless the prosecution is able to prove their guilt beyond a reasonable doubt. The only way we can secure that right is if lawyers offer their clients resolute advocacy rather than judgment.[10]

As the very long and growing list of wrongful conviction cases demonstrates,[11] it is often the case that an accused who seems to be "obviously" guilty is not, in fact, guilty. There are many reasons. People confess to crimes they did not commit. The police may have "tunnel vision" and, when they have someone who seems to be obviously guilty, they may fail to conduct a thorough investigation. If lawyers were ethically bound to refuse to defend accused persons they thought to be guilty, the right not to be convicted unless proven guilty would be lost. And even if the lawyer knows for certain that the client is guilty, guilt does not strip the client of all legal rights, including the right to a fair trial and the right to have the prosecution prove guilt beyond a reasonable doubt.

I believe that it is wrong for lawyers to be closely identified with the cases they argue. I derive this from the English "cab rank" rule, described by the UK Bar Council as the "bedrock obligation for the independent referral bar."[12] Barristers must take on any case offered to them provided it is within their competence, and they are available and appropriately remunerated. This principle ensures that unpopular clients and those charged with serious offences get proper legal advice. The idea does not appeal to idealistic law students who see themselves as crusaders for just causes but when it comes to arguing cases in court, especially criminal cases, it is an important principle to maintain.

However, it is also important for law students, lawyers, and the public to understand that implicit in this role-differentiated moral justification for a lawyer's duty of resolute advocacy are certain limiting principles that even the most partisan lawyer must respect. Since the lawyer's duty of resolute advocacy is to secure the *legal* autonomy of the client, it follows that an advocate can discharge this duty *only within the confines of the law*. There is no moral justification for securing for the client benefits or advantages not sanctioned by the law. The duty of resolute advocacy is also qualified and limited by the lawyer's duty to the court and society to act in a responsible and professional manner. This is disputed by some American commentators who argue that resolute advocacy may even justify the lawyer lying on behalf of a client.[13] That view is clearly not shared by the Anglo-Canadian vision of legal ethics, which posits that the advocate must never mislead the court or knowingly present evidence that is untrue. The duty of resolute advocacy must be reconciled with the fundamental principle of professional conduct – namely, that advocates ought to act "honourably within the limits of the law, while treating the tribunal with candour, fairness, courtesy and respect."[14]

Criminal Law

Probably the most enjoyable course to teach in my early years was my "small group" in criminal law. Most first-year courses at U of T and other law schools are taught in large sections of about seventy-five students. But, since 1972, every first-year student at U of T has taken one course in a seminar setting with fifteen to eighteen students. This provides a setting that facilitates discussion and debate in which every student is expected to participate. The students get to know their small group classmates well, and participation is less threatening than in a large class. Friendships and even romances are formed – several marriages have resulted from a first meeting in a small group. The faculty also used the small group to offer students instruction on legal research and writing. All other courses involved 100 per cent evaluation based on a final examination, while in the small groups, a significant part of the grade was based on written work submitted during the term. Another function of the small group is to ensure that every student gets to know and work closely with at least one faculty member.

I found criminal law to be an ideal small group subject. The students came to the course with opinions they were eager to express. I was interested in the subject, and few topics failed to provide ample fodder for debate. For most classes, we would discuss the assigned readings in a seminar format. For some classes, I set up moots and debates, often asking the vociferous pro-prosecution students to take the role of defence counsel to face off against the "bleeding heart" pro-defence students to whom I assigned the role of Crown counsel. This was not mischievousness on my part. I was trying to find a way to have the students step away from their preconceived ideas and understand the analytical legal problems that had to be confronted. Having to argue on the "wrong" side of a case, the side with which one does not initially sympathize, forces one to confront the issues from a more intellectual perspective. My intention was certainly not to beat my students into submission, surrendering the morality and humanity they brought to the law, but rather to develop in them the necessary analytic skills required to see all sides of an issue as well as the forensic skills needed to present a difficult case.

I got to know my small group students very well. Small group teaching gave one a good feel for the ever-changing habits and mores of incoming classes, and some of my small group students became good friends. Many of my small group students have gone on to distinguished careers as practitioners, judges, and academics, although I have to admit that few of them decided to devote themselves to criminal law.

I first met Ron Daniels as a student in my small group in criminal law. Ron later joined the faculty, became Dean, and has gone on to serve with distinction as President of Johns Hopkins University. I learned an important lesson about teaching from Ron when he was my student. He told me that his friend, Joanne Rosen, a psychology student, was thinking about applying for admission to law school, and he asked if she could sit in on one of our classes. I agreed and, as it happened, we were about to discuss the insanity defence. That seemed to be an ideal class for a psychology student to attend. Joanne came to the class. I thought that it had gone brilliantly. I asked several questions, and the students responded with more questions. It seemed to me that they were grappling with the most interesting and difficult issues in this area of the criminal law. When I saw Ron the next day, I told him that I was so glad that Joanne had attended, since I thought it was our best class of the year. Ron paused and then said, "Professor Sharpe, I don't know how to say this, but that was the most confusing and unhelpful class so far." I was stunned. Our conversation made me realize how important it is to understand that the instructor's perspective can be very different from that of the students. I still think that the discussion that day was first rate. I can only hope that, in the end, the students realized that the confusion was not theirs but the law's and that, by grappling with these questions, they had gained a better understanding of a difficult area of the criminal law. Fortunately, Joanne was not dissuaded by the experience from studying law and went on to a successful legal career, as well as marrying Ron.

Remedies

My third course was an upper-year optional offering in remedies. The course had not previously been offered at the law school, so I had to design it from scratch. The importance of the subject seemed obvious to me: what is the point of a right if it is not protected or vindicated by a court order giving the right concrete, practical effect? In an often-quoted passage from an eighteenth-century English case, "indeed it is a vain thing to imagine a right without a remedy."[15] The common law tradition had long emphasized the importance of remedies, but the rules and principles were not well developed. It was simply assumed that the court would somehow always find a practical way to assure that a wronged party was given an adequate remedy. There were texts and articles on specific aspects of remedies law and course outlines from other law schools, but I could find no generally accepted scholarly definition of the subject. I found that there was (and there continues to be) a lively debate about exactly what the subject of remedies does or should include, but in the parlance of today, the subject was certainly "under-theorised."[16] Despite its importance, the law of remedies had received relatively little attention from academics. Nor, in my view, had it produced sustained and refined or systematic judicial thought. It seemed to me that a great deal of judicial soul searching often went into the concluding paragraphs of judgments, which told successful plaintiffs the order they would actually receive.

The lack of a definition was certainly also a blessing for a new scholar with a background in litigation and an interest in procedure, looking for an interesting and relatively undeveloped area to study. By taking on remedies, I was building on my work on *habeas corpus*, which is one of the common law's remedial gems. My thesis and book involved taking a systematic look at an important area of law that had always been dealt with piecemeal. I had done my best to give *habeas corpus* a structure and to identify and articulate coherent organizing principles that would assist in decision making and explain the subject for scholarly purposes. I was keen to do the same for remedies. The major difference was that *habeas corpus* was a public law remedy, while my course would focus on private law remedies.

I set to work preparing a case book for the course. In the age before the internet and electronic versions of cases and other materials, this involved going to the library and finding and photocopying cases and articles that illustrated significant aspects of the subject. To avoid overloading the students with too much to read and to ensure that the casebook covered the subject, the next step was to attack with scissors and scotch tape the mound of paper I had collected. I had to assemble a collection that would have about thirty pages of condensed reading for each of the fifteen or so two-hour classes. Some of this work could be delegated to a research assistant, but, as I recall, for my first case book, I did it myself with some assistance from a secretary. At the time, the law school had its own printing equipment to produce the required number of bound copies of the materials. Although both the course and the instructor were new, I attracted a reasonable enrolment of about thirty-five interested second- and third-year students.

I was intrigued by the strong historical theme that ran through the subject of remedies. To understand civil remedies, it was necessary to grasp the role played by the courts of equity, a separate stream of jurisdiction until the late nineteenth century. Equity had tamed the rigours of the common law by granting a variety of remedies – declarations, injunctions, and specific performance – not available from the common law courts. Those innovative remedies still bore the marks of their history, and one of the questions I posed was whether the constraints imposed by history upon remedial choice remained valid today.

In most cases, courts award money damages to compensate injured parties. Although damages are the most frequently granted remedy, I decided not to be swallowed up with that subject. It was an enormous field to cover, and for this upper-year course I had to be selective. Damages were already canvassed in first-year torts and contracts, and I decided that from both a teaching and a scholarly perspective, it would be better to focus my course on specific remedies, especially injunctions and specific performance. These remedies protect and vindicate rights by requiring defendants to do or refrain from doing actions that violate plaintiffs' rights. Specific performance requires defendants to actually perform what they promised to do, giving plaintiffs exactly what the contract entitles them to. Injunctions protect plaintiffs from harm by forbidding rights-violating conduct or even requiring defendants to act precisely as the plaintiffs' rights require. I had argued injunction and specific performance cases in practice. I was intrigued by the historical development of these remedies and the possibilities they offered by their perfect correspondence with the substantive right. I was also intrigued by the fact that, despite this perfect correspondence, specific remedies were the exception rather than the rule.

I had always regarded teaching remedies as part of my larger project to write a book. Once my book *Injunctions and Specific Performance* was published in 1983, I decided to look for a new teaching challenge.

Constitutional Law

After the *Canadian Charter of Rights and Freedoms* was enacted in 1982, I replaced remedies with a seminar on civil liberties in 1983–84. I prepared a casebook dealing with legal rights in the criminal process, freedom of speech, freedom of religion, and equality. The *Charter* had just come into force, and how it would be interpreted by the courts was hotly debated. I had little to go on, and at least half the materials in my casebook were American, a stark contrast to what would be expected today given the Supreme Court's insistence on a distinctively Canadian approach to *Charter* interpretation.

In 1984–85, I co-taught the Law Review seminar with Marty Friedland. The students were tasked with writing papers on the new *Charter* suitable for publication in the *University of Toronto Faculty of Law Review*, a unique journal that only publishes student work. We had a very strong group of students who, under our supervision, produced an excellent collection of nine published papers on *Charter* issues ranging from mobility rights to minority language education rights, free press and fair trial, Aboriginal self-government, obscenity and censorship, interrogation, and cruel and unusual punishment.[17] One of the papers, "No Room at the Top: Interest Group Intervenors and *Charter* Litigation in the Supreme Court of Canada," written by Jillian Welch, has been frequently cited by court decisions and the subsequent literature.

Encouraged by this initial foray into the *Charter*, I decided to try my hand at teaching constitutional law. Until the *Charter*, constitutional law had been an upper-year course. Because of the *Charter*'s pervasive significance for the legal system as a whole, the law school decided to move it into the first-year curriculum, making it an eligible small group subject. This afforded aspiring constitutionalists like me a terrific opportunity. I could switch from teaching my small group in criminal law to a small group in constitutional law without having to compete for the assignment with other faculty members who had a more established profile in constitutional law.

The students were keenly interested in the *Charter* but considerably less enthused by the first part of the course, federalism. I found it fascinating to puzzle through the judicial decisions from the early days of Confederation down to the present, sorting out the conflicts between provincial and federal jurisdiction. I tried to show the students how these seemingly arid and technical debates were deeply rooted in Canada's history and commitment to the ideal of bringing a geographically and culturally diverse assortment of communities together in one country that respected their differences. I am not sure I succeeded, but I did my best. There certainly was an audible sigh of relief when we finally got to the *Charter*.

Teaching the *Charter* in the late 1980s was a delight. We were dealing with a steady stream of decisions from the Supreme Court of Canada written by outstanding jurists such as Brian Dickson and Bertha Wilson confronting the challenge of establishing a proper framework for *Charter* adjudication. The Court's willingness to make something of the *Charter* surprised many, including me, who feared that we might see a repeat of the Court's disappointing performance under the *Canadian*

Bill of Rights. The early *Charter* cases fascinated me. The assurance of a large, liberal, and purposive interpretation of rights and the guarantee of requiring a robust governmental justification wherever rights were limited held great promise for the protection of fundamental rights and freedoms and marked a clean break with the legalistic formalism of the past.

I enjoyed teaching constitutional law and decided to see if I could combine my interest in the subject with my litigation experience. The Law Review seminar experience proved what I already suspected: given the chance, our students were capable of taking on challenging projects and delivering first-class work. That realization led me to my next teaching venture, the subject of Chapter 8, the Constitutional Litigation Program, which allowed me to combine teaching, student initiative, the *Charter*, and my interest in advocacy before the courts.

Scholarly Work

While I enjoyed teaching, I would not have stayed in the academic world if I had seen lecturing as my only occupation. The Oxford experience of writing my DPhil thesis and book on *habeas corpus* had given me a lifelong taste for (or, as Geraldine would put it, addiction to) research and writing. I could see that the effort one had to put into teaching could be doubly rewarding if linked to a scholarly project.

I enjoyed teaching criminal law, but with one exception, I did not write on the subject. Early in my time on the faculty, at the urging of Jacob Ziegel, I wrote a case comment for his *Canadian Business Law Journal* on an important Supreme Court of Canada decision on strict liability in criminal law,[18] a topic of great interest to commercial enterprises when dealing with regulatory offences. For some reason, Jacob insisted on calling me "John." I corrected him several times, but he persisted, and I eventually gave up. However, I had to put my foot down when I received the galley proofs for my article showing the name of the author as "John Sharpe." As I will explain in Chapter 9, my case comment may have been an important factor when I was selected as Chief Justice Dickson's Executive Legal Officer ten years later.

I managed to link teaching civil procedure with some of my scholarly work as well as my outside work. I became very interested in the issue of privilege. There are two forms of privilege. The first is solicitor-client privilege, under which everyone is entitled to seek legal advice from a lawyer with the assurance that any confidence shared with the lawyer will not be revealed. The second is litigation privilege, under which parties are permitted to shield from disclosure documents prepared for the purpose of advancing or defending a claim. It seemed to me that very often these two distinct forms of privilege were confused. I wrote a paper[19] trying to clarify the difference and was pleased to find that it was frequently cited, including by the Supreme Court of Canada.[20] I was also interested in the jurisdictional limits of the Federal Court of Canada, a topic I had confronted in practice, and I co-authored a paper with my then colleague, now Justice of the Federal Court of Appeal, John B. Laskin.[21] I also worked with Gary Watson, Alan Hutchinson, and Bill Bogart on a revised edition of the casebook we all used to teach civil procedure.[22]

When I moved into teaching constitutional law, I wrote articles on Bora Laskin's views on the *Canadian Bill of Rights*,[23] commercial expression and the *Charter*,[24] and the role of the judiciary under the new regime of the *Charter*.[25]

Cross-Border Litigation

In 1978, I was asked by a law school friend, Jonathan Guss, with whom Roger Timms and I had worked to establish a legal aid clinic during our time as students, to undertake a project examining some of the complex procedural and jurisdictional rules that governed claims by claimants injured by defective products. Jon was working in the federal Department of Consumer and Corporate Affairs on a large project to study the law of product liability in Canada.

My mandate was to focus on claims that implicated parties in more than one province. This involved careful consideration of what lawyers call conflict of laws or private international law, the legal rules that apply when a claim in one jurisdiction has a cross-border dimension. I was asked to address three questions. When was it permissible to invoke the jurisdiction of a court in one province against a defendant who was outside the borders of that province? When would the courts of one province give full enforcement to a judgment rendered by the courts of another province? Where manufacture, purchase, use, or damage occurs in different provinces, which principles and legal rules determine the appropriate law to govern the lawsuit?

Surprising though it may seem, the existing law treated each of Canada's provinces as if they were truly foreign entities. The rules governing a claim by a Nova Scotian resident against an Ontario manufacturer were the same as if the claim was brought against a German manufacturer. Indeed, I found that, in some respects, the Nova Scotian claimant would be treated more favourably if suing a truly foreign defendant. The existing legal regime applied rules developed in the English courts in the nineteenth century, when England was the dominant economic power. Not surprisingly, those rules were highly protective of English merchants and manufacturers and strongly favoured English law and English jurisdiction. It was obvious that those rules needed to be modified to deal adequately with product liability claims in a modern federal state and that this was an area ripe for legal change.

My study, later published by Consumer and Corporate Affairs in both English and French[26] and as a monograph by Butterworths,[27] surveyed the existing law on jurisdiction, choice of law, and enforcement and recommended significant change. I concluded that the unmistakable trend towards stricter liability rules for defective products had not been matched by changes to procedural rules. The pro-defendant conflict of laws regime failed to provide a fair or efficient means of implementing the substantive law shift in favour of claimants. Claimants were often not allowed to bring their claims in their home province or to base their claims on the laws of their home province but were forced to sue in the defendant's province even where the defendant knew of or encouraged the sale of its products in the claimant's province. Even if claimants could sue in their home province, they were often unable to enforce a judgment in the defendant's home province.

I argued that the jurisdictional rules should be liberalized, and that claimants should have the benefit of the law most favourable to their claims. I argued that the rules for enforcement should be altered to reflect the needs of a modern federation. Where there was a reasonable basis for a province to assert jurisdiction, the courts of a sister province should enforce the judgment.

When Supreme Court of Canada Justice Gerard La Forest wrote the first of several judgments that revolutionized Canadian conflict of laws in 1990,[28] I was delighted to see that he cited my book in support of reforming the archaic rules for enforcement of interprovincial judgments. My future colleague on the Court of Appeal, David Paciocco, wrote a favourable review in the *Canadian Bar Review*, agreeing that my study was "a worthwhile and timely contribution to the continuing product liability reform debate."[29] Years later, as a judge, I was able to build on the work I started with the product liability study when deciding several cases involving extra-provincial jurisdiction.[30]

Injunctions and Specific Performance

My scholarly focus gradually shifted from civil procedure to remedies. When designing and teaching the course on remedies, it struck me that the area had strong potential for the kind of scholarly work that interested me. I wrote several papers on remedies, most notably one co-authored with Stephen Waddams published in the *Oxford Journal of Legal Studies*.[31] We attempted to reconcile the proposition that common law damages were measured by the loss suffered by the plaintiff, not any gain made by the defendant, with the fact that sometimes courts did award gain-based damages. These cases involved a variety of situations in which the defendant had ignored or appropriated the plaintiff's right or entitlement. Our explanation was that what appeared to be gain-based damages could be explained as being the loss the plaintiff had suffered by being deprived of the opportunity to bargain for the right the defendant had denied. Our argument was influenced by the economic analysis school of thought that had become a strong feature of the faculty's interdisciplinary project. Stephen and I both focused on legal doctrine and were sceptical (Stephen even more than me) of the capacity of overarching theories to explain the law. Neither of us adhered to the law and economics approach, but we were both prepared to borrow insights it revealed. The paper attracted considerable attention and controversy. While many scholars have disputed our theory, I believe that it remains a useful and plausible way of looking at the issue.[32]

I also wrote a few articles and book chapters on remedies and a paper on remedies for the Ontario Law Reform Commission Law of Contracts Amendment project. This work, combined with teaching the remedies course, led to me embarking on what became my second book, *Injunctions and Specific Performance*, a book that has gone through several editions. This project is still very much with me, because it is now published with annual loose-leaf updates. It has been widely cited by courts across Canada, including the Supreme Court of Canada.

I worked closely on this book with Stephen Waddams who was at the same time embarking on one of his influential texts, *Law of Damages*. We thought about writing one large book covering all remedies but decided that it would be more manageable to write two separately authored, but closely linked, books. We continued to collaborate on the preparation of our annual updates and new editions of these books until Stephen passed away in 2023. It was a privilege to work with Stephen Waddams, a remarkable and generous scholar. His knowledge of private law was vast. He had a wonderful ability to see how enduring legal principles applied to new situations and to see when the law had to change to meet the demands of justice. We certainly did not agree on everything, but any disagreements were readily accommodated as we were writing different books. Stephen loved to talk about legal problems with his students and with his colleagues in the faculty common room. His interests ranged well beyond contract law and remedies, and he was always ready to subject to his discerning legal eye the latest pronouncement from the Supreme Courts of Canada or UK on virtually any legal subject.

Injunctions and specific performance are court orders made in civil proceedings that require a party to do something or to refrain from some course of conduct. For example, if a property owner's actions unreasonably interfere with a neighbour's enjoyment of property, a court can, at the suit of the neighbour, order the wrongdoer to stop such conduct. If a party refuses to complete a contract to sell land, a court can, at the suit of the purchaser, require the seller to complete the transaction. These remedies are exceptional in the common law tradition, which strongly favours the award of monetary damages to remedy civil wrongs. They are derived from the tradition established by the courts of equity, a parallel system of courts that developed in England and existed until equity was fused with law in the late nineteenth century.[33]

Courts still used the language of the pre-*Judicature Act* era, when law and equity operated as parallel streams, to explain when these remedies could be awarded. I argued that it was time to formulate principles governing the award of these remedies in modern terms. I saw my task as working with the historical precedents and explaining them in terms of the advantages and disadvantages they presented. The result was not radical change, but instead an explanation focusing on the advantages of one remedy or another, rather than blindly following criteria that had evolved in a different court system more than 100 years earlier. I tried to put historical factors, which seemed to dominate analysis, in a proper modern theoretical perspective.

Sabbatical and Return to Oxford

Writing *Injunctions and Specific Performance* was a major task, one that was greatly facilitated by the one-year sabbatical enjoyed in 1981–82. Sabbaticals are one of the great privileges of academic life. Stephen Waddams and I arranged to be on sabbatical for the academic year 1981–82 in Oxford to work on our remedies project. I was keen to return to Oxford. I loved the atmosphere, I knew the library, and I was confident that I would be able to settle in quickly and make good progress on the project. Geraldine and I had enjoyed our two years in Oxford a decade earlier, and we were looking forward to living in England for another year. Our children, ages nine, seven, and two, were still young enough that moving them for a year would not unduly disrupt their lives or their education.

We managed to arrange a house exchange with John Eeekelaar, an Oxford family law scholar who was spending a year at the University of Toronto. The Eeekelaars had a pleasant house in Boar's Hill, a quiet and pastoral village within a ten-minute drive of Oxford city centre. Our two older children, Anne and Claire, enjoyed their year at a Church of England school. They could walk to school through "Matthew Arnold's Field," which was adjacent to the house. Very quickly we noticed that they were picking up English modes of speech, saying things like "have a go," "this wretched jacket," and "getting muddled." Geraldine managed to find a day care for Stephen run by Balliol College near the law library, where she was able to continue her work as a freelance translator. We enrolled the girls in riding lessons, which were very popular.

I was received at Magdalen as an Honorary Member of the Senior Common Room, which meant I could have lunch and the occasional dinner at my old college. I enjoyed renewing my connection with the law Fellows and being welcomed back as a scholar in my own right. I gave a couple of classes on criminal law, and attended the Atkin Moot when Lord Denning, a Magdalen graduate and a reform-minded judge who was a hero to law students around the common law world, delivered an amusing and crystal-clear oral judgment at the end of the moot.

My DPhil supervisor, Ian Brownlie, by then back at Oxford as the holder of the Chichele Chair in Public International Law, invited me to traditional dinner at All Souls College. This was perhaps a strange place for a left-winger like Brownlie, but with some irreverence, he seemed to be enjoying the place.

We made regular visits to London, travelled a few times to France to visit Geraldine's sister and her family, spent a few days in Wales showing the children castles, went on a package tour to Tunisia in December, and spent a week in Florence at Easter. The children were thrilled to see the spectacle of the Oxford-Cambridge "old boys" polo match and to stand a few yards away from Prince Charles as he mounted one of the three horses he brought along for the occasion. Part way through our time, Argentina invaded the Falkland Islands, and we were glued to the television news to watch what seemed to me to be an unlikely British victory in the ensuing war.

I interrupted my work on remedies to review the proofs for my book on *Interprovincial Product Liability Litigation* and to make a trip to Belgium to visit Mons, Ypres, and Vimy Ridge to help me along with my book on the Currie libel trial, discussed in Chapter 7. Richard Hart, the founder of Hart Publishing, then legal editor at *Oxford University Press*, met me to arrange the publication of the second edition of *The Law of Habeas Corpus*. Despite these distractions, I was able to devote most of my time to *Injunctions and Specific Performance* and, by the end of the year, had essentially completed the manuscript.

The remedies books Stephen Waddams and I wrote were well received. We were awarded the Foundation for Legal Research's Walter Owen Book Prize, which "recognizes excellent legal writing and rewards outstanding contributions to Canadian law."[34] I was encouraged when I read several highly favourable reviews of my book,[35] with one notable exception. Feminist Professor Christine Boyle, of Dalhousie Law School, took me to task in the pages of the *Canadian Bar Review*.[36] She praised our books as being "outstanding examples of the genre" of "apolitical exposition of legal doctrine" and said the publication of the books was a "major event in the world of legal scholarship." But most of her review criticized us for writing what she regarded as sexist books. Indeed, she wrote that the books betrayed a "phallocentric world view." Not only had we followed the then common convention of using the pronoun "he," but I had failed to discuss in sufficient detail the use of injunctions to protect *Charter* rights and to pay adequate attention to the types of injunctions women might seek, in particular in family law.

I was quite stung by the review. While I did not agree with much of what Professor Boyle said, I had to admit that she had a point on the use of male pronouns, and I remedied that in the next edition. My treatment of injunctions as a *Charter* and public law remedy expanded in later editions as the law developed, and perhaps I should have offered a better explanation for why I avoided detailed treatment of specific substantive areas such as family law.

Travels

An enjoyable feature of academic life is the travel and interaction with other scholars and lawyers that often flows from one's writing. Over the years, I have given a long list of presentations on remedies, including one in 1985 to the Alberta Court of Queen's Bench where I enjoyed spending time with Alberta's trial judges, an experience that planted in my mind the idea that, one day, I might like to become a judge. My long involvement with the Canadian Institute for Advanced Legal Studies and the world of judges began with a paper I presented at the Institute's conference at Stanford University in 1986 that combined my interest in remedies and constitutional law, "Injunctions and the Charter."[37] My interest in constitutional law took me to England, Japan, Italy, and Israel for lectures and conferences. My work on conflict of laws took me to a comparative law conference in Australia in 1986 where I was invited to give a paper at the University of Sydney on "A Lawyer's Look at the Economic Analysis of Injunctions and Specific Performance." An invitation to apply for a Chair at the faculty followed, an offer that I declined.

Grassy Narrows Project

In 1983, I was retained by the federal Department of Indian and Northern Affairs to prepare what was described as a "prelitigation study" to assess the legal remedies that might be available to the Islington Band, Whitedog Reserve, for the devastating harms they had suffered from mercury pollution caused by an effluent from a pulp and paper mill into the Wabigoon and English River Systems. The mercury was ingested and retained by fish, a staple in the diet of the affected Indigenous communities. Members of those communities suffered severe health consequences. I was asked to consider remedies available to individuals and the bands collectively, whether claims would be available against the companies responsible or against the Province of Ontario.

The case came to me through some work I had done for Justice Patrick Hartt at the Indian Claims Commission on the recommendation of John Olthuis at Citizens for Public Justice, the lawyer behind the Mackenzie Valley Pipeline case described in Chapter 4 and the separate school funding case described in Chapter 8. It was my first exposure to Indigenous legal issues. I had two very capable student research assistants, Robert Scavone and Patricia Bregman, to help with the work, and my U of T colleague Denise Réaume drafted two chapters on issues related to negligence.

The study involved many difficult legal issues relating to the law of public and private nuisance, Indigenous title and treaty rights, riparian rights, negligence, strict liability under the *Rylands v Fletcher* doctrine, statutory liability, limitation periods, governmental liability, damages, class actions, and whether the case would fall within the jurisdiction of the Ontario or federal courts.

These issues were highly contentious, and my report was over 200 pages long. I did my best to point out what I thought to be the strengths and weaknesses of the bands' claims. My overall assessment was that achieving success would break new legal ground on several issues. The bands came close to having a strong claim on several issues and, when looked at cumulatively, "a court with the will to do so could quite properly give relief."

I submitted my final report in July 1984. I heard nothing until April 1985, when I had a call from retired Supreme Court Justice Emmett Hall. He told me he was in Toronto mediating the case, that he had my report, and that he would like to meet me. I went to see him at his hotel. He greeted me warmly, complimented me on my report, and said that he had found it very useful in his efforts to bring the parties together.

My work and that of Justice Hall were only the start of a very long and still unfinished process to find justice for the victims of the Grassy Narrows disaster. The corporate entity responsible for the harm agreed to pay compensation but insisted on a release that would preclude further claims. The bands would not agree, and the impasse was broken when the Ontario government agreed to provide the company with an indemnity against future claims. But that was only the beginning. Complete justice for the bands raised broad issues of policy and would likely require more than the law and the courts could offer. The bands have continued to press, with considerable, but less than total, success at both levels of government for compensation, remediation of the waterway, and proper treatment of the victims of mercury pollution.

Progress Through the Ranks

I was very fortunate to have worked under three strong and supportive deans. I have already mentioned Marty Friedland, my Dean until 1979. He hired me and inspired me with his scholarly ambition. Frank Iacobucci, Dean from 1979 to 1984, was a team-builder, a man of exceptional warmth and charm, who fostered a warm collegial environment. He represented the faculty well to the wider university community and to the legal profession. Rob Prichard, Dean from 1984 to 1990, had the vision to urge the law school to expand its outlook with interdisciplinary work and to aspire to new heights of scholarly excellence. He was a formidable fundraiser, his energy and enthusiasm were infectious, and I appreciated his support for me and my projects.

At the law school, the Dean conducts annual performance reviews examining the contribution made by each faculty member to scholarship, teaching, and administration. My reviews were always positive and encouraging, placing me at or near the top of merit pay awards made by Deans Friedland, Iacobucci and Prichard. In 1979, after three years on the faculty, I was promoted to the rank of Associate Professor with tenure and, in 1983, I was promoted to Full Professor. This was faster than usual, and certainly faster than would happen today, again a reflection of the changes that have occurred in the academy since I first joined it.

A New Approach to Legal Scholarship

Four years before I joined the faculty, Michael Trebilcock came as a lateral hire from McGill. Michael is a New Zealander who began his teaching career in Australia. He came to Canada to join the McGill faculty in 1969, and after his appointment at U of T, he quickly became a foundational figure in the law school's commitment to serious scholarship. Invigorated by leaves spent at the University of Chicago and Yale law faculties, Michael started the Law and Economics Program, a school of thought that by then had gained significant traction in leading American law schools, including Yale Law School, which by then was replacing Harvard as the model to which U of T aspired. Rob Prichard, who joined the faculty the same year as I did, was an active member of the law and economics group, as was Don Dewees, an engineer, turned lawyer, turned economist, cross-appointed from the economics department.

Law and economics, or economic analysis of law, approaches legal problems through the application of microeconomic theory. The operation and effects of legal rules are assessed from the perspective of economic efficiency. Rules that promote efficiency are favoured over those that do not. The theory posits that there has been and will be a natural progression towards efficient rules.

Although I had only taken one course in economics as an undergraduate, I was a regular attender at a lively series of lunchtime workshops at which visiting scholars would present their work for discussion and debate. I found these sessions fascinating. They demonstrated to me the advantage of taking a familiar legal problem and subjecting it to scrutiny from the perspective of a different discipline. While I was never persuaded that justice under law could or should be equated with economic efficiency, I could see that efficiency concerns had a role to play in understanding how legal rules operate and in fashioning better rules.

Of particular interest to me was that economic analysis scholars had turned considerable attention to remedies.[38] While I did not always agree with what they wrote, they certainly provided useful insights into how remedial rules can and should operate. My work on remedies was influenced by the economic analysis of law literature on the operation and effect of injunctions and specific performance. One law and economics insight that had been ignored by lawyers and judges was that a court-awarded legal remedy might be only a point along the way to a final resolution of the problem. A court order gives one party a remedy it can enforce, but that does not preclude post-judgment bargaining, a feature of remedial law rarely discussed in court decisions or in the conventional legal literature. To fully understand the impact of a legal rule or remedy, one has to look beyond the court award to what economic and efficiency considerations are likely to produce on the ground.

Shortly after the establishment of the Law and Economics Program, the law school initiated another workshop series devoted to legal theory, initially under Ernie Weinrib's leadership, and later under that of Brian Langille. Again, despite my lack of sophistication in philosophy or legal theory, I was an eager and regular, although largely silent, participant at these workshops. They covered a broad spectrum of legal issues, and I found them to be intellectually stimulating. They made me think about law differently and greatly enriched my outlook. Some of the speakers I found to be largely impenetrable. I remember going home one day and expressing my exasperation to Geraldine with one presenter who appeared to me to be obsessed with trying to answer the question "how do I know this chair is not a table?" It seemed to me that presenters at these workshops were often arguing ideas that were novel and interesting with no regard to whether they had any hope of practical implementation. Was this just a game where it was better to be controversial and interesting than to be reasonable and practical? But, for the most part, as with the law and economics papers, I gained valuable new insights into how legal problems should be understood and analysed.

The women and the law workshops, started by female law students and subsequently led by Denise Réaume, soon followed. I was also a regular attender at these workshops, which were influenced by the critical legal studies movement. This school of thought is sceptical of the pretence that legal doctrine can be considered to be independent from social and political forces and sees law as a tool used to maintain the existing power structures. Feminist scholars exposed the law's sorry history of misogyny and baked-in discrimination against women.

More workshops came and went, but the idea of approaching the law from the perspective of another discipline became mainstream. Many faculty members have graduate degrees in some discipline other than law, and their scholarship is shaped by their extra-legal training.

During my time as a faculty member, the injection of the scholarly insights from other disciplines was combined with a strong spirit of collegiality. We did not agree on everything, but we realized that we had more to gain by listening and learning from each other than by falling into warring camps. Collegiality was encouraged by the leadership of my three Deans, Friedland, Iacobucci, and Prichard. The range of interests and approaches were expanding, but our sense of common purpose and mutual respect prevailed. We had managed the inevitable tension between academic law and law in practice by widening our horizons while remaining loyal to our mission to educate future lawyers.

The Law and Learning Report

In 1983, the Social Sciences and Humanities Research Council published the *Law and Learning Report*,[39] principally authored by Harry Arthurs, one of Canada's leading legal scholars, former Dean of Osgoode Hall Law School and shortly to become President of York University. The report urged law schools and legal academics to adopt a more scholarly and interdisciplinary approach.

A survey of Canadian law professors revealed that the rather dismal picture I described earlier still prevailed. Forty per cent of respondents said they were planning to leave teaching, forty per cent said they devoted ten per cent or less of their time to research, and only twenty per cent devoted more than one-quarter of their time to research and writing.

The report described four types of scholarly work: (1) conventional texts and articles, expounding legal rules and explaining authoritative legal sources; (2) legal theory, designed to provide a unifying theory or perspective to better understand legal rules; (3) law reform research designed to improve the law; and (4) fundamental research "designed to secure a deeper understanding of law as a social phenomenon, including research on the historical, philosophical, linguistic, economic, social, or political implications of law."[40] The first three categories of research considered the law on its own terms. "Fundamental" research considered the law from an external perspective gained through the insights of other disciplines.

My work included the first three types of research, but until I ventured into legal history, nothing I did would qualify as "fundamental research." The tone of the report was clear. In the view of the authors, fundamental research ranked the highest in the hierarchy. I did not agree with that hierarchy. Legal scholars have much to gain from viewing the law from the perspective of other disciplines, but I saw more conventional forms of legal research that speak to all lawyers – be they academics, practitioners, or judges – as being central to the law school's mission.

The report also suggested that legal education should be divided into two streams – one professional and the other academic, devoted to fundamental research. That suggestion troubled me greatly. There will always be a tension between the academic and professional visions of legal education. The lament that legal education has become too academic is frequently heard, as is the contrary plea for more innovative legal scholarship. But that tension is to be expected in a discipline that strives to accommodate both professional and scholarly objectives. It is that combination of objectives that attracted me to the study of law in the first place and that has always been a central feature of my fascination with the study of law.

I strongly believed in the scholarly mission of law schools, and I thought that the report's two-stream approach would undo most of the positive developments that had happened to legal education in Canada since it had been rescued from the grasp and control of the legal profession in the late 1950s. Aspiring lawyers would be deprived of the broadly based legal education they so badly needed to be able to serve the public, and the purely scholarly stream would be cut off from the stimulation gained from our connection to practice. We were the only social science that had the advantage of a direct connection with the real world, and I could not understand why we should throw that advantage away.

The report generated a lively and healthy debate about law teaching and legal scholarship. But at the time of the report's publication, I was less sure. I was not alone in thinking that it unfairly denigrated the type of work Stephen Waddams and I were doing in the area of remedies.[41]

An amusing review of our books, written by future Supreme Court of Canada Justice Thomas Cromwell, then a professor at Dalhousie, took the form of an arbitral award resolving the grievance of "the union of doctrinal and theoretical scholars" against the "Consultative Group on Research and Education in Law."[42] The imagined grievance complained that the consultative group had "failed to support valuable scholarly enterprises" and "unfairly denigrated doctrinal and theoretical legal research and writing." Tom concluded that a reasonable observer would conclude that the report denigrated our work and that any denigration of work such as ours was wrong, unfair, and unjustified. He wisely added, however, that the denigration was the unintended product of the report's enthusiasm for "promoting the ideal and the unexplored" and that the legal academy should embrace a welcoming approach to all forms of legal scholarship and see them not as independent pockets but as being integrally related.

The legal academy rejected the *Law and Learning Report*'s two-stream approach to legal education but the encouragement of a more welcoming approach to theoretical, interdisciplinary, and empirical research was embraced. That fit nicely with U of T's ambition to be a leading centre for scholarly work in law and to maintain a healthy relationship with both the wider university community and the legal profession.

My work on *habeas corpus*, civil procedure, and remedies was largely doctrinal. I researched the decided cases, read the existing literature, and tried to present an orderly, coherent account of what the law was and how it might be improved. While I was not a theoretician, I strived to write at the level of what I describe as "mid-level theory," probing the existing rules and doctrines to identify the underlying and driving general principles that structure the law.

I believed then, and I still believe today, that doctrinal scholarship is useful and important. Doctrinal scholarship provides a ready and reliable source for lawyers, judges, and other scholars to access foundational principles of law. Doctrinal scholarship also provides a basis for more theoretical or philosophical enquiry. Strong doctrinal scholarship carefully sifts through the case law and existing literature and provides the reader with a coherent and readily available account of the law in a given area. This promotes consistency and efficiency in the legal system. Doctrinal scholarship also assists lawyers, judges, and other legal scholars in settling unsettled areas of the law, identifying emerging trends, and providing an overarching structure into which a decision on an unsettled point must fit.

It is a frequent complaint of practising lawyers and judges that legal scholarship has become too esoteric. I share that concern, but only up to a point. Many modern legal theoretical and interdisciplinary scholars are writing for specialized audiences, making their work inaccessible to those outside the field. But lawyers and judges should not overlook the value of theoretical work that advances our understanding of the essence of law, its philosophic underpinnings, and its coherence. Ideas that survive scholarly scrutiny and debate may seem esoteric today but often become more mainstream and influential in the future.[43] I only say that this type of scholarship should not entirely displace strong doctrinal scholarship.

The *Law and Learning Report* and the trend that I have described towards interdisciplinary research influenced me to broaden my horizon and to undertake writing projects in legal history that I describe in the next chapter. I am not sure that they qualify as "fundamental research," but they have been a welcome turn from the more doctrinal work of my other projects and from my work as a judge.

7
My First Adventures in Legal History

My time as a law professor coincided with the change in the direction of legal scholarship that I described in the previous chapter. The law school I attended as a student emphasized teaching and devoted little attention to research and writing. By the time I joined the faculty as a professor, things were starting to change. We were encouraged to research and write, and gradually the focus of those efforts shifted to embrace interdisciplinary and more theoretical approaches to legal scholarship. I continued to work on more conventional projects, but I was influenced by the shift towards interdisciplinary scholarship, and I gradually shifted my focus towards legal history, a field in which I continued to work even after my appointment as a judge.

I have written four case studies, one, an article and the other three, books, and a judicial biography. In this chapter, I will discuss my first two projects, written while I was still a professor, the Eddie Guerin *habeas corpus* cases, and the Currie libel trial.

Case Studies

All lawyers trained in the common law tradition are familiar with one form of the case-study method. Law students cut their teeth by carefully dissecting the facts of reported cases and debating how the result might be different if this or that fact changed. But the case-study method familiar to lawyers reflects a sterile version of history. When we look back to the past to find precedents, we restrict our reading to what is found in the reported decisions. The decisional facts are often very detailed and provide a thorough account of who did what to whom. However, every decision is not only rooted in decisional facts but is also the product of the prevailing social, economic, and political context. Reading past decisions rarely provides a full picture of the context underlying the case, yet that context will often have exerted a powerful influence on the decision. Legal history reminds us that law is not made and does not exist in a vacuum. It is the product of social, political, and economic forces that are constantly shifting and changing. We can gain a much more complete and richer understanding of the law, its content, its development, its impact, and its possibilities if we pay attention to the context in which disputes arise and cases are decided.[1]

Eddie Guerin – The Man Who Escaped from Devil's Island

My first scholarly project in legal history was an article-length study[2] of a 1907 *habeas corpus* case that I had stumbled upon when writing my thesis at Oxford. The case was not well reported when it was decided.[3] I mentioned it in my book but only in a footnote. However, it was so unusual that I always thought it merited further study, so I turned to it when I decided to undertake a legal history project.

Eddie Guerin, a notorious criminal, had been convicted in France in 1902 at the age of forty-two of having committed a daring robbery of the American Express office in Paris. He was sentenced to penal servitude for life at Devil's Island, a notorious French penal colony in French Guiana, but after three years in 1905, he managed to escape and make his way to England. His escape attracted considerable attention in the popular press, and sensationalised accounts of his exploits made him famous. The French authorities, determined to return him to Devil's Island, made an extradition request. Guerin was arrested. He challenged his detention by way of *habeas corpus*, arguing that he was, in the words of a treaty between England and France, a "native born or naturalised" British subject, and therefore exempt from extradition.

The puzzle was that almost twenty years earlier, in 1888, Guerin, then twenty-eight years old, had made exactly the same argument when he faced an earlier request for extradition to France for another robbery. In 1888, the English courts refused his request for *habeas corpus* on the ground that he had not been able to prove that he was born in England and that he was a British subject.[4] When he faced extradition again in 1907, he made precisely the same claim to English birth and this time he succeeded.

How could precisely the same issue about the same individual that had arisen in 1888 have been decided differently in 1907?[5] Guerin's case was also significant from a legal perspective. It raised a fundamental issue about *habeas corpus*: upon whom does the burden of proof lie? In 1888, the Court ruled that Guerin had the burden of proving that he was a British subject and that, since he had failed to do so, his *habeas corpus* application failed. In 1907, with no mention of the 1888 decision, the court ruled that the French government bore the burden of proving that Guerin was not British and that, since it had failed to do so, Guerin's *habeas corpus* application succeeded.

In a case like Guerin's, where the facts were anything but clear, the burden of proof determined the result. I had argued in my book that, since the liberty of the subject was at stake, the burden of proof should rest with the authorities seeking to justify the detention and that any doubt should be resolved in favour of the prisoner. I agreed with the 1907 decision, but how could I explain the 1888 ruling or the fact that it had no impact on the later decision? Could I unearth the real story and the reason for these conflicting results on what seemed to me to be a neglected yet fundamental issue of constitutional law?

I discovered that there were many sources that might help me unlock the puzzle. First was Eddie Guerin's own account of his life and of his two *habeas corpus* cases. Guerin achieved such notoriety from his escape from Devil's Island that, in 1928, he was able to publish a memoir, possibly ghost written. In England it was published under the title *Autobiography of a Crook*[6] and in the United States, under the title *I Was a Bandit*.[7] I managed to find a copy of this highly romanticized account of Guerin's criminal exploits in America, England, and France and his vivid accounts of life in the penal institutions of all three countries. Guerin had embarked on a life of crime in adolescence. He had a lengthy criminal record for crimes of dishonesty and robbery. He was a self-admitted career criminal, but he did his best to present himself in his book as a likeable and sympathetic rogue who rose from poverty to travel the world with panache and style, financed by clever and daring criminal exploits that he tried to characterize as harmless. He described the hell of Devil's Island in such graphic terms as to make his escape seem justified and perfectly understandable.

Guerin's book was hardly a reliable source. As I will explain, however, it provided a clue as to why, by the time of his 1907 *habeas corpus* case, Guerin was perceived by the public less as a notorious criminal and more as a daring and romantic figure who had managed to extricate himself from the cruel and inhumane French penal colony. This assessment was confirmed by my detailed review of newspaper accounts of Guerin's criminal exploits, his escape from Devil's Island, and the *habeas corpus* proceedings themselves.

Archival sources provided some insight. This was my first encounter with archival research, and I found the process fascinating. A very helpful man in the old Chancery Lane Public Record Office managed to uncover the original court files for the two *habeas corpus* cases. They contained the affidavit evidence about Guerin's place of birth. He claimed to have been born in England, but there were no birth or baptismal records to support that claim. He also claimed the status of a British subject through his father, who was Irish and who had deserted from the British Army during the Crimean War and subsequently immigrated to Chicago. In the 1907 proceeding, there was considerably more evidence. The prosecution went to great lengths, retaining lawyers in Chicago and Ireland to investigate Eddie's place of birth and his claim that his father was an Irishman.

There was also a helpful Foreign Office file in the Kew Public Record Office that provided a picture of the behind-the-scenes political aspects of the case and its importance to British-French relations. The French were keen to get Guerin in 1888 and especially in 1907. Ironically, it had been the French who insisted on the Treaty provision precluding the extradition of nationals, a provision the English did not want. In English criminal law, jurisdiction resides with the territory in which the crime is committed, while in France, criminal jurisdiction is based on the nationality of the accused person. This difference produced a gap in the law that Guerin sought to exploit. If he could avoid being sent to France, he would be in the clear, because he could not be prosecuted in England as the offence had taken place in France. The English authorities regarded Guerin as a dangerous criminal and did not want to protect him even if he was a British subject. This was made clear to the jury empanelled to try the issue of Guerin's nationality in 1888. The trial judge summarized the evidence and instructed the jury (unfairly, I thought) that the issue was whether Guerin should be sent to France to face trial or be allowed to stay in England and "defy the law."[8]

I discovered that some very prominent legal figures had been involved in the Guerin cases. Most notably and most unusually, Lord Alverstone, the Lord Chief Justice who presided over the 1907 proceeding, was Richard Webster, England's Attorney General, in 1888. I was astonished to discover that, as Attorney General, he had argued the 1888 case on behalf of the prosecution against Guerin. I could not imagine that Webster, now Lord Alverstone, the senior judge presiding in the 1907 case, had forgotten about his earlier *habeas corpus* encounter with Eddie Guerin, yet no mention was made of what today would be seen as a glaring conflict of interest. The conflict certainly did not affect his decision, since he ignored his 1888 submissions and ruled in Guerin's favour in 1907.

Digging through newspaper accounts, I found that the 1888 and the 1907 cases each coincided with a significant contemporary event that could well have influenced the outcome. The 1888 case followed closely on the highly charged debate on the Irish Home Rule question. Guerin's claim of British status through an Irish father who had deserted the British Army was hardly one to attract much sympathy in England. The 1907 case coincided with one of the most notorious miscarriages of justice in modern times, namely, the case of Alfred Dreyfus, who had been wrongfully convicted of treason and, like Guerin, had been sentenced to penal servitude in Devil's Island. The French military and legal establishment dug in and refused to admit that they had made a terrible mistake. The Dreyfus case, front page news in England in 1907, painted French justice in the worst possible light. As Guerin put it in his memoir, having "read all about the treatment to which Dreyfus had been subjected," everyone agreed "that whatever I had done was not sufficiently bad to condemn me to a poisonous hole where men rotted away and were never heard of for ever more."[9] Although the Foreign Office was keen to have Guerin extradited, I discovered that when the matter was argued in court, Sir Robert Finlay, the Attorney General, did little to resist Guerin's case. As I wrote in my article, one hardly needs to be a legal cynic to imagine that these contextual factors tipped the balance in an area where the law was uncertain.

Eddie Guerin remained in England, and his name appeared regularly in the police court columns for having committed various crimes of dishonesty. His death at the age of eighty was recorded in the *Times*: "Eddie Guerin, the man who escaped from Devil's Island, has died at Bury, Lancaster."[10]

The Currie Libel Trial[11]

The Guerin project whetted my appetite for legal history and the case-study approach. Reading a biography of Stephen Leacock, the Canadian political scientist and humourist, I came across a short account of the 1928 libel action brought by Sir Arthur Currie, the commander of the Canadian Corps in the 1914–18 War. Ian Kyer, then a student and my research assistant, found that Currie's papers had been deposited with Public of Archives Canada (now Library and Archives Canada), and the finding aid suggested that there was a considerable volume of material on the case. In days before digitised online records, a trip to Ottawa was required. It only took me a day at the archives to see that there was an interesting book to be written. I would have to expand my research beyond the Currie papers, but what I had found was very encouraging. Currie's papers included a complete transcript of the trial, Currie's wartime diary and correspondence, and his correspondence with his lawyers and his military colleagues about the case.

Currie's papers gave me a picture of the man. He was a hard-working, well-organized individual who had become a war-time general almost by accident. He was articulate, formal, correct, and driven to succeed. He had risen to positions of authority beyond his education and training and likely beyond his own expectations. He had no formal military training apart from his involvement as a volunteer in the militia in Victoria, British Columbia, yet he became Canada's most senior general. He had no university degree, yet after the war, he became Principal of McGill University.

Reading his papers, I could see that the 1928 libel trial represented Currie's attempt to remove what he bitterly resented as a blot on his record – the suggestion that he had been personally responsible for the needless deaths of Canadian troops during the last days of the war.

Before the war, Currie worked in the insurance industry and, around the time the war broke out, he had suffered a severe financial setback from real estate speculation. He escaped that situation in part by means of a serious defalcation from militia funds that would later haunt him and by enlisting in the army. He quickly rose to the senior ranks, eventually becoming the commander of the Canadian Corps.

Currie was a careful officer known for his meticulous planning of every operation, but he suffered a fate common to other World War I generals: he was not liked by the men in the ranks. Given the high casualties and appalling conditions in the trenches, this was hardly surprising. But in Currie's case, there was an added sting. Annoyed by Currie's refusal to promote his son and spurred on by the complaints he heard from men in the ranks, Sir Sam Hughes, Minister of the Militia, attacked Currie for what he saw as needless loss of life. Standing in Parliament in 1919, where he was protected from being sued for libel, Hughes stated that Currie should have been court-martialled for needlessly sacrificing lives on the last day of the war to capture the town of Mons in Belgium.

When the Port Hope *Guide*, a small-town Ontario newspaper, repeated and embellished Hughes's attack almost 10 years later, Currie decided to strike. In an editorial written by W.T.R. Preston, a veteran political operative, journalist and author of dubious repute, the *Guide* deplored the erection of a plaque in Mons to commemorate the capture of the town by the Canadian forces on November 11, 1918. The front-page editorial accused Currie of "conceiving the mad idea" to capture Mons and causing "a deliberate and useless loss of life" at "the last day: and the last hour, and almost the last minute" of the war. Despite being advised by Stephen Leacock and other senior colleagues at McGill and by his legal counsel that legal action was ill-advised and dangerous, Currie was determined to fight. His decision to sue for libel led to one of the most sensational trials in Canadian history.

The more I dug into Currie's papers, the trial transcript, contemporary newspaper accounts of the trial and the literature on the 1914–18 war, the more I became convinced that I had struck gold in my search for a case study. The Currie libel trial concerned one of the great events in world history. The idea of trying to understand and unravel a complex military operation in the courtroom fascinated me. Could the legal process fairly examine and judge the complex events of the last days of the war? One naturally had sympathy for Currie if, as he insisted, he was not guilty of the charge that he had needlessly sacrificed lives. But was protecting Currie's reputation more important than allowing for open debate on an important historical event? Should Currie, an important public figure, be able to silence criticism of his actions during the war? These were legal issues I would later explore in my academic and judicial work.

I thought I could write the book, but would anyone be interested in publishing what I wrote? A vitally important factor in my decision to tackle the Currie project was the support I received from the Osgoode Society for Canadian Legal History. The Osgoode Society was established in 1979 on the initiative of Roy McMurtry, then Ontario's Attorney General. Roy was concerned that Canada's distinctive legal history was not being written. He convinced members of the three branches of the legal profession – practising lawyers, legal academics, and the judiciary – to join in a society that would publish at least one "members' book" per year. Since its founding, the Osgoode Society has published more than 120 books and created a significant archive of oral histories from all branches of the profession – a remarkable achievement, fulfilling Roy McMurtry's vision of preserving Canada's legal history.

I told Peter Oliver, the Editor-in-Chief of the Osgoode Society, about my project, and he assured me that if the manuscript survived academic peer review, the Osgoode Society would publish it. This assurance and Peter's support and guidance as I proceeded with the research and writing gave me the confidence that I needed to take on a major project.

The Osgoode Society has been a vitally important part of my scholarly work ever since. In subsequent chapters I will describe the help and encouragement I received from Peter Oliver and his successor as Editor-in-Chief, Jim Phillips, for my other Canadian legal history projects. Not long after the publication of the Currie book, I became a Director of the Osgoode Society, and then I succeeded Roy McMurtry as President when he retired from that role in 2015. I am proud to have been a part of the Osgoode Society's achievement in bringing scholars, lawyers, and judges together in a common cause.

I greatly enjoyed the archival research. To see and read the original documents was riveting. To unravel the story the papers told was intellectually challenging and exciting. Reading Currie's wartime correspondence gave me the feeling that I was with him as he worked through the problems he faced. Reading the transcript and newspaper accounts of the trial gave me the feeling that I was with the lawyers, strategizing about how best to present the case; with the judge as he did his best to manage a difficult trial and ensure its fairness; and with the twelve men on the jury as they struggled to come to a fair verdict.

I returned home from my trips to the archives filled with enthusiasm about what I had found. My wife seemed to understand, but my joy was incomprehensible to my three children. They still tease me that my idea of a really great day is a trip to those boring and dusty archives.

My research also took me to northern France and Belgium. I visited Vimy Ridge, where, in early 1917, four Canadian Divisions fought for the first time as the Canadian Corps under Currie's leadership. The Corps mounted a carefully planned and highly successful attack that became a huge source of Canadian pride. I felt that I had already been there, since my mother often told me about attending the commemoration of the Memorial with her grandmother in 1936 on a tour organized for veterans and the relatives of veterans. The Vimy Memorial is a sombre and inspiring sight that every Canadian should see. I also visited Ypres, where, to this day, every evening at 8 p.m., buglers sound the "Last Post" at the Menin Gate Memorial. I visited several war cemeteries. It is one thing to read about the massive casualties of the war and quite another to stand in a cemetery with countless rows of simple but elegant white military headstones, many of them marked simply "A Soldier of the Great War."

At Mons, I saw the plaque installed in 1928 on the wall of the Hotel de Ville commemorating the capture of Mons by the Canadian Forces on 11 November 1918, which had led directly to the Currie libel trial. The report of its installation had prompted the Port Hope *Guide* to publish the editorial condemning Currie for needless slaughter. I visited the City's war museum, which contains considerable information and memorabilia about the capture of the city. I went to the grave of George Lawrence Price, a Canadian private who was shot minutes before the armistice and who is buried near Mons in a beautiful small cemetery also containing the graves of British and German soldiers who fell in 1914 when the town was captured by the Germans.

Currie was represented by one of Canada's great lawyers, William Norman Tilley, KC. Tilley argued cases in the trial courts, the courts of appeal, the Supreme Court of Canada, and the Judicial Committee of the Privy Council. He advised Currie not to sue, but when Currie insisted, he took on the case with professional vigour and enthusiasm.

Currie and a long list of his fellow senior officers strongly denied that they had taken Mons to glorify themselves for having captured the town the Germans had taken from the British in their first engagement in 1914. Currie insisted that he was simply following the Allied strategy in the final days of the war: to maintain contact with the Germans and keep pushing them back in order to prevent them from regrouping for a final stand.

The Port Hope *Guide* was represented by Frank Regan, a scrappy lawyer who was more at home in the criminal courts. Regan's witnesses were embittered men from the ranks. They had played no part in planning the strategy: they simply followed the orders that kept them in harm's way right up to the end.

The trial was very much a David and Goliath battle. The smooth, sophisticated Tilley, Currie, and the senior officers on one side, and the feisty Regan and the men from the ranks on the other. Tilley insisted on confining the case to what happened on the last day of the war, while Regan tried to expand the issue to what happened in the final several days of the war. Regan, representing a client with limited resources, often tried to introduce questionable second-hand or hearsay evidence. He tried to rely on published reports, war diaries, and other similar sources that were not admissible in law. Tilley resisted, but as the case wore on, perhaps worn down by Regan's ingenuity in letting the jury know what was in the reports, he wisely decided to cut Regan some slack to avoid giving the jury the impression that Currie had something to hide.

W.T.R. Preston, the author of the editorial that so offended Currie, insisted on representing himself, and he did a credible job. He made an argument that fell upon deaf ears at the time but that deserved more attention than it received. Why, Preston pleaded, were Currie's actions during the war not a fair subject for public debate? Holding him and the Port Hope *Guide* to the strict proof of the truth of every word of the editorial according to the strict rules of evidence could only stifle debate on a subject of great public importance. Years later, I confronted this issue as a judge when I wrote a decision accepting the defence of responsible journalism: where a media defendant can show that it acted in accordance with the standards of responsible journalism in publishing a story that the public is entitled to hear, it has a defence even if some of the facts are incorrect.[12] I am not sure that Preston would have been able to show that he had acted in accordance with the standards of responsible journalism, but the case would have been a closer call than it was under the law prevailing in 1928.

I enjoyed trying to understand and explain the tactical interplay between Tilley and Regan, as well as the efforts of the austere trial judge, Justice Hugh Rose, to keep the case on the rails. I was also fascinated by the details of the horrors of war that emerged from the evidence.

The jury returned a verdict in Currie's favour, but his victory was qualified. He asked for $50,000 in damages and received only $500, and one juror, an ex-serviceman, dissented.[13] Currie was awarded his legal costs, but the defendants lacked the means to pay. He was left with a significant debt for legal fees, from which he was rescued by the generosity of some wealthy McGill supporters. Even a prominent man like Currie faced access to justice issues. The press treated the verdict as a victory, but fighting the case took a huge toll on Arthur Currie. Shortly after the trial, Currie collapsed and suffered a serious breakdown in his health.

Currie was a straightforward man who expected straightforward solutions. But, as he was told by those who advised him not to sue, the legal process can be draining and unpredictable. I found a letter he wrote admitting that he had suffered "a complete nervous breakdown caused largely by the harrowing thought that ten years after the war one was forced to fight another battle to retain hold of any good name one had."[14] He took a lengthy leave of absence from McGill but never fully regained his health and died at the age of almost fifty-nine in 1933.

My book was well received, and a second edition in paperback was published in 2009. I knew that the Currie case would not be my last legal history project. As soon as it was finished, I began to think about what I should turn to next.

8
Constitutional Litigation

I was committed to an academic career, but I retained my interest in advocacy before the courts. The law school gave me the flexibility to combine those interests by allowing me to create the Constitutional Litigation Program. I found myself arguing some fascinating cases and at the same time giving my students an opportunity to be involved in advancing fundamental rights and freedoms in the early years of the *Charter.* This corresponded with my vision of the law as an engaging intellectual discipline that offered immediate practical outcomes.

The Constitutional Litigation Program

My most adventurous and challenging teaching initiative was the Constitutional Litigation Program launched in the mid-1980s. I was riding the wave of *Charter* cases that were starting to make their way into the courts. My idea was to have an upper-year seminar of about twenty students that would have several objectives. First, we would explore in a seminar setting current issues in constitutional litigation, such as standing, intervention, forms of evidence, and constitutional law remedies. The second and most significant component was to give the students an opportunity to become directly involved in constitutional litigation. Each student would be assigned to me or to a practitioner to assist with preparing a *Charter* case for hearing. I was able to assemble an impressive list of practising lawyers who were willing to involve our students in their work. The students were expected to make a presentation in the seminar discussing the issues with which they were dealing. The other objectives were to sponsor research and experience through workshops and seminars dealing with issues arising in constitutional litigation and to provide a service to individuals and groups that lacked the resources to litigate worthwhile cases.

My idea coincided with an emerging trend in legal education, namely the recognition that law schools should provide clinical programs where research and theory are related to practice in an immediate but academically rigorous fashion. The program recognized the exceptional quality of our students and would provide them with an opportunity to pursue an interest in constitutional law in a concentrated and intensive manner.

The *Charter* provided an ideal setting, linking theory and academically rigorous research, including the kind of interdisciplinary work that was the pride of the faculty, to practical implementation. And we would be providing a service to public interest groups and individuals who lacked the resources to litigate worthy cases. The project also reflected my view, instilled by my time with MacKinnon McTaggart, that law should be seen as a form of public service. Lawyers are certainly entitled to gain a livelihood, but they should also be willing to offer their services pro bono for deserving causes.

Dean Rob Prichard was very supportive when I proposed starting the Constitutional Litigation Program. As a launch, I put together a one-day conference on current issues in constitutional litigation. Former Prime Minister Pierre Elliot Trudeau, who had retired less than a year earlier, politely declined my invitation to deliver the keynote address, stating that he was on "sabbatical in order to enjoy a time of rest and reflection" and that he did not "know exactly when [he would] call a halt to this period of non-activity." He added that he congratulated me "on a very worthwhile initiative." Fortunately, we drew a large and enthusiastic audience without him, since people were hungry for discussion of *Charter* issues. Among those attending were 10 future judges, a future provincial premier, and a long list of distinguished lawyers and academics. The papers were written by leading constitutional scholars and practitioners and covered a wide range of topics, including standing, intervention, the use of American and European sources as authorities, the use of legislative history and social science evidence, mootness, and remedies. They were later published as a collection in a book that I edited with the assistance of a very able student, Jennifer Aitken.[1] Several chapters have been cited by the courts, including the Supreme Court of Canada.

The "Man-in-the-House" Case

I trace the origins of the Constitutional Litigation Program back to 1978, when Dick Gathercole, the Director of the law school's legal aid clinic, asked me if I would take on one of the clinic's cases that was headed to the Court of Appeal. Mary Eberts, then a colleague on the faculty and a friend from my days at Western, was also interested. We agreed to argue the case together. The case involved an interesting public law issue; namely, the "man-in-the-house" rule, which disentitled a woman from receiving family welfare benefits if she was not living as a "single person" and, more specifically, if she was living "with another person as [his] wife."[2]

Our client had two children and had been deserted by her husband. Before the split, they had been friends with another couple who also had two children and then separated. Our client eventually lived in the same house with that man and undertook childcare and housekeeping duties in exchange for her share of the rent. It was established that there was no sexual relationship between them and that they led separate and independent lives apart from the arrangements for childcare and housekeeping. The Divisional Court had upheld the decision of the Social Assistance Review Board, which had affirmed the decision of the Director of Family Benefits of the Ministry of Community and Social Services to deny benefits to our client. The Board and the Divisional Court applied what I would call a mechanical interpretation of the regulation that simply asked if the woman claiming benefits was living under the same roof as a man. If she was, her benefits were terminated. That interpretation was certainly administratively convenient for the welfare authorities. It relieved them from having to inquire into the precise nature of the living arrangements. But it was also very unjust when applied to our client, who was struggling to meet her family's living expenses and had a purely business-like arrangement with the man for whom she worked as a housekeeper.

I was worried that the Court of Appeal might not find the case worthy of its attention, but leave to appeal was granted, and the Court patiently listened to Mary and me when we argued the case. The Court accepted our argument and rejected the government's submission that living "with another person as [his] wife" could be interpreted by reference only to economic considerations. Justice Gordon Blair wrote: "I can find nothing in the context which would compel departure from the usual rule that the ordinary interpretation is to be placed upon such commonplace expressions as 'living with another person as husband or wife.'" There was no conjugal relationship, our client was a housekeeper, not a spouse, and it followed that her welfare benefits had been wrongly terminated.

Arguing this case was a rewarding experience. I enjoyed the challenge of taking on a difficult case and reversing what I saw as an unjust result for a very needy client. It was Mary Eberts's first venture as an advocate, and I was happy to be part of the story that launched her successful career as an effective counsel for equality-seeking groups. The case convinced me that I would enjoy doing more pro bono litigation. I had the security of my faculty position, so I did not have to worry about being paid for my advocacy, and I could see that there were interesting cases to argue on behalf of deserving clients.

Canadian Civil Liberties Association

In early December 1982, I joined the Canadian Civil Liberties Association (CCLA) and, in my letter, enclosing my thirty-five-dollar cheque for membership, I asked to be added to the list of volunteers to act as advocates to argue cases. I heard nothing until the spring of 1984, just as I was thinking about starting the Constitutional Litigation Program. Alan Borovoy, General Counsel at the CCLA, contacted me to ask if I would be willing to take on a case involving restrictions on the freedom of expression rights of lawyers. I am not sure if my earlier letter triggered Alan's request, or how he knew about me, but his request was the first step in what became a very interesting and rewarding personal and professional relationship.

Freedom of Expression Cases: Law Society Rules

The case Alan asked me to take on involved two lawyers who had run afoul of the Law Society's rules prohibiting advertising. The first, David Klein, was a careful lawyer but one willing to push the boundaries. He provided brochures in his office to clients outlining the nature of certain routine legal services and the flat rate he would charge for those services. The Law Society Rules forbade lawyers from advertising the price of legal services, even in this modest way, because it feared that there was a risk that the brochures would find their way into the hands of non-client members of the public. Mr. Klein retained one of Canada's best advocates, Ian Scott, QC, to sue for a declaration that the Law Society's rule violated the right of freedom of expression guaranteed by the *Charter*. The Law Society was represented by a senior and respected lawyer, Brenden O'Brien, QC.

The second lawyer who had run afoul of the Law Society's rules, Robert Dvorak, was considerably more brazen, as was his legal counsel. Dvorak had started his own practice and, to attract clients, resorted to advertising his services in the *Toronto Star*. I am not sure that the ads brought him any clients, but they certainly caught the attention of the Law Society. Dvorak was charged with professional misconduct.

Incensed by those charges, Dvorak went to the media to complain. That led the Law Society to charge him under another rule providing that "a lawyer should not initiate contact with the news media on behalf of himself in respect of any cause or matter in which he is involved in his professional capacity."

Dvorak retained Harry Kopyto to take on his case. Harry was one of my law school classmates with whom I shared a locker, and he was later disbarred for allegedly over billing the legal aid plan. He held strongly leftwing views and was always willing to take on any case that would provide him with the chance to give the establishment a poke in the eye. Dvorak's case fell into that category.

Alan Borovoy was less interested in lawyer advertising than in the rule forbidding lawyers from initiating contact with the news media. A staunch defender of freedom of expression, Alan thought that justice was more likely to prevail on important issues if lawyers were allowed to explain their cases to the public.

I eagerly accepted Alan's invitation and got to work on putting together an application to intervene in the case that was set to proceed before the Divisional Court, a court comprising three Supreme Court of Ontario trial judges that dealt with public law issues. I worked closely with Alan to prepare written and oral argument setting out the CCLA's position.

Alan was a University of Toronto law graduate, but he never engaged in private practice. He spent his first decade as a lawyer as a labour activist and, as a founder of the CCLA, became its General Counsel in 1968. His passions were the eradication of racial discrimination and the protection of freedom of expression. He delighted in devising tactics and schemes that would promote those values in public discourse.[3] As I would soon learn, Alan was a *Charter* sceptic. He strongly believed in the rights guaranteed by the *Charter*, especially freedom of expression, but he worried about conferring too much power on unelected judges. He feared the *Charter* would divert debate on civil liberties from the robustness of the public forum to the sterile atmosphere of the courts. But Alan was also a realist and when it became clear that Canada would have a *Charter*, he lobbied hard for strengthened legal rights and remedies and for a robust section 1 "reasonable limits" clause requiring governments to show that limits imposed on rights were demonstrably justified. On the other hand, his distrust of the judiciary made him a supporter of the notwithstanding clause giving legislatures the right to override judicial decisions under the *Charter*.[4]

The *Klein and Dvorak* case was the only time I recall Alan coming to court to watch me argue a case. I was sitting at the counsel table when he stormed into the courtroom and promptly made an obscene gesture towards the bench. Fortunately, the judges had not yet entered the courtroom, but I could tell that Alan was sending me a message. First, nobody, and certainly not judges, was to be spared from his mischievously irreverent sense of humour. Second, Alan did not trust authority, and that certainly included the authority of the bench. Third, while he was prepared to let me argue his cases, I must never forget that he called the shots – and, so far as he was concerned, the only truly effective and meaningful shots would be fired by Alan Borovoy to the public at large, and not by some lawyer arguing the case in court. Needless to say, in the many cases that followed, I was always relieved when Alan did not show up.

It was never even clear to me whether he wanted me to win or lose. When I won, he would have to admit that the courts were not that bad after all. When I lost, I gave him another target for his invective. After one win, he wrote to thank me for my "stellar advocacy" but added: "Please ensure, however, that you follow your instructions next time. You are not supposed to win. You are supposed to lose – with splendor." He often called his lawyers "beautiful losers." There is no doubt that, for Alan, it was a lot more fun to fight no-holds-barred in the streets, in the newspaper columns, and in the media than in the courts. His amazing ability to capture a difficult argument in a simple phrase and his wicked sense of humour would often shine. Alan firmly believed that civil liberties cannot be forced on people by judicial fiat. He thought that while the CCLA might win the odd battle in the courts, the war for civil liberties could only be truly won if he could capture the hearts and minds of ordinary Canadians.

The *Klein and Dvorak* cases were heard by three senior judges, Justices Henry, Eberle, and Callaghan. Our first hurdle was to obtain standing as a friend of the court. We argued that the CCLA had a distinctly different perspective to offer. Klein and Dvorak sought to advance their professional interests, while the CCLA sought to represent the public's interest in receiving information regarding cases pending before the courts and the availability of legal services. Our intervention application was welcomed by the two lawyers and not strongly resisted by the Law Society. We were granted leave to intervene, by no means a foregone conclusion in the early days of the *Charter*, since the judges were generally unfamiliar with the practice.

Brenden O'Brien, counsel for the Law Society, relied heavily on the argument that the *Charter* did not apply to the Law Society, because its powers were inherent and rooted in the history of the common law. This seemed to me to ignore the obvious fact that the Law Society had a statutory mandate and exercised statutory powers. For reasons I did not understand, the judges seemed attracted to O'Brien's pitch, and I spent much of my limited time for oral argument refuting it.

The interplay between Ian Scott and Harry Kopyto was amusing to watch. Scott knew how to present and usually win cases. While Kopyto was passionate about any case he took on, his strategic sense of how to win the case was nothing like Scott's, and he seemed to be more intent on needling the judges with his provocative behaviour. Although the three of us were on the same side, at times it was difficult to say whether Kopyto's impassioned advocacy was going to hurt us more than help us win the day.

Ironically, despite the marked discrepancy in forensic skills, Kopyto was partly successful, while Scott was not.[5] The Court rejected Scott's argument that commercial speech was protected by the *Charter*, but the majority accepted Kopyto's submission, supported by the CCLA, that the Law Society's injunction against lawyers going to the media ran afoul of the *Charter*'s guarantee of freedom of expression. I was delighted when I read the majority's decision on this point, since it adopted verbatim substantial portions of the CCLA factum. This was done without attribution. Alan Borovoy thought that we should have been given some credit. I think I persuaded him to be happy with the fact that we had made some law and that he should regard judicial copying of our factum as the one and only acceptable form of plagiarism.

Given the mixed result, Klein, Dvorak, and the Law Society all sought leave to appeal to the Court of Appeal. Leave was granted, and I was looking forward to arguing the case in that Court. However, the Law Society decided to change the rules on advertising and lawyers speaking to the media to make them *Charter* compliant, rendering the appeals moot, and they were abandoned.

The experience of arguing and winning this early *Charter* case on behalf of the CCLA bolstered my confidence that I had the advocacy skills to handle cutting-edge *Charter* litigation and that there were deserving clients who would welcome my assistance.

Freedom of Expression Cases: Keegstra, Zundel, and Film Censorship

I worked with Alan Borovoy on an intervention application to the Alberta Court of Appeal in the case of the infamous holocaust denier James Keegstra. Alan was fully aware that fighting the hate propaganda law would cost him support, particularly in the Jewish community, but he was very firm in his belief that the difficulty of defining what constitutes hate speech posed an unacceptable risk to freedom of expression.[6] As we put it the Keegstra factum: "The real issue ... is to ask whether the criminal law can define with sufficient precision and clarity that which is unworthy and leave unthreatened legitimate forms of expression and public debate." Vigorous advocacy, we argued, will often be disturbing to some, and the attempt to punish "destructive hatred ... poses a constitutionally unacceptable risk" of "impeding or discouraging" speech, which "creates constructive tension." To this we added: "There are in our society too many members and descendants of too many nations, races and groups with too many historical grievances to imagine that [the hate speech provision of the *Criminal Code*] could always be applied to curtail only the outrageous and malevolent excesses of those tempted to re-write history." Alan argued that the "chilling effect" of the hate law would deter legitimate speech and that prosecuting odious hatred was counterproductive, giving hate mongers a platform and access to an audience they could not expect to reach if left undisturbed. He wanted the CCLA to intervene to avoid having the freedom of expression argument advanced and tainted by Keegtra's lawyer, Doug Christie, who, he thought, shared Keegstra's obnoxious views.[7]

I also worked with Alan on another case involving another notorious holocaust denier, Ernst Zundel, who had been convicted under the *Criminal Code* offence of spreading "false news." I prepared a factum arguing that the provision "creates a dangerously sweeping restriction upon freedom of expression" and that, "if used to criminalise attempts to recount historical or political events," it posed "a potentially serious threat to freedom of expression." I was disappointed when our leave to intervene application was dismissed by the Court of Appeal, but in the early days of the *Charter*, courts were still reluctant to grant intervenor status, particularly in criminal cases. The false news provision was loosely framed and more vulnerable to *Charter* attack than the hate speech offence, an assessment borne out by the fact that when the two cases reached the Supreme Court of Canada, the hate speech provision survived in *Keegstra*,[8] while the false news provision was struck down in *Zundel*.[9]

The next freedom of expression case I argued for the CCLA concerned the power of the Ontario Film Review Board to censor films.[10] We joined the applicant Ontario Film Appreciation Society's challenge to the Board's order that explicit sexual scenes be cut from a film. The Divisional Court set the Board's decision aside on the narrow ground that the Board had failed to properly consider the statutory test giving it the power to require the cuts and that it was not necessary to consider the constitutional arguments. This familiar technique of dodging *Charter* issues was attractive to judges but considerably less so to the parties hoping to secure a broader ruling. Although I did not watch it, the film, *Amerika*, was described as a political diatribe of two and a half hours and had a few brief scenes of explicit sexual activity. The Court's reasons suggested that we succeeded essentially because the film was so boring that no one would watch it for the sex scenes. Justice Edward Sanders wrote: "I do not consider that the viewing of the film could have any possibility of affecting local standards of sexual morality or increasing the likelihood of crime. No one would view this film because of an interest in the depiction of explicit sexual activity."

Almost all the cases I took on involved arguing as an intervenor. Gradually, we overcame the judicial wariness to intervenors by establishing that we could be helpful by making concise and well-crafted arguments. Appearing as an intervenor allowed me to become involved in some fascinating cases without having the burden of putting the entire case together and marshalling the required evidence, and without the client facing the possible consequence of an adverse costs order if we lost.

Freedom of Religion Cases

The CCLA was also concerned about freedom of religion, particularly freedom from religious compulsion. I appeared for the CCLA as intervenor in a case challenging mandatory prayer in public schools.[11] A regulation enacted under the *Education Act* required that "a public school shall be opened or closed each school day with religious exercises consisting of the reading of the Scriptures or other suitable readings and repeating of the Lord's Prayer or other suitable prayers."[12] The Sudbury Board of Education mandated that the requirement be satisfied by the recitation of the Lord's Prayer. We joined the applicants and the other intervenors, including the Canadian Jewish Congress, represented by my future judicial colleague John I. Laskin. We argued that by mandating the Lord's Prayer, the regulation and the Board's practice were a form of coerced religious observance, contrary to the *Charter*'s guarantee of freedom of religion, as well as the promise of equality. The regulation was defended on the basis that it allowed parents and students to ask to be absent during religious exercises. We argued that the exemption provision did not save the regulation, since children of different faiths would naturally feel coerced to comply lest they be singled out by their peers. These arguments persuaded Justice Robert Reid, but he was in dissent, and the other two judges, Justices Dennis O'Leary and William Anderson, each wrote reasons rejecting the *Charter* challenge.

I recall Justice O'Leary asking if there was anything "offensive" about the Lord's Prayer. As a Christian, he was very familiar with its recitation, and he could not see how anyone, whatever their religious beliefs, could object to anything that it contained. He relied on the preamble to the *Constitution Act, 1982,* stating that "Canada is founded upon principles that recognize the supremacy of God and the rule of law." The majority were dismissive of the compulsion argument. Justice O'Leary held that if children came from a different background, which would be obvious to their classmates, they would take no particular notice of their absence from prayers and religious exercises. Justice Anderson found that it "offends logic and common sense" to say that the regulation that gave parents and students the right of exemption amounted to coercion. The majority reasons, written by two experienced and respected judges, reflected the wary attitude many judges took in the early years of the *Charter,* uncomfortable with the new mandate it conferred and unwilling to view matters from other than a majoritarian perspective.

Justice Reid, dissenting, viewed the matter quite differently. Like Chief Justice Dickson in the *Big M Drug Mart* decision,[13] he was prepared to view the matter from the perspective of those who held religious views different from those of the majority. In a passage that might have rankled his two colleagues, he wrote that "[i]t may be difficult for members of a majoritarian religious group, as I am, to appreciate the feelings of members of what, in our society, are minority religions … [or] the feelings of agnostics and atheists."

Fortunately, Justice Reid's dissent was not in vain. At the Court of Appeal, a five-judge panel reversed the Divisional Court's decision by a 4–1 majority.[14] By the time the case was heard, I had moved on to work at the Supreme Court of Canada as Executive Legal Officer, and the CCLA brief was argued by my former law school colleague, John B. Laskin. The majority, Justices Brooke, Blair, Goodman, and Robins, had no difficulty in finding that the regulation and the Board's practice constituted a form of coerced religious observance that contravened both freedom of religion and constituted discrimination on grounds of religion contrary to section 15 of the *Charter*. The presence of two Jewish judges – Goodman and Robins – likely made it easier to persuade the Court of the minority perspective. Like Justice Reid in the Divisional Court and Chief Justice Dickson in *Big M,* they were prepared to view the matter from the minority perspective, and they had little hesitation in striking down the regulation.

I put together another case from scratch involving freedom of religion. It was also on behalf of the CCLA, which had taken on the cause of a Baha'i family living in Elgin County in southwestern Ontario. Religious instruction was mandated by a regulation that required two periods of religious instruction every week. Matters of a controversial or sectarian nature were to be avoided. However, the local Board of Education had given a local Bible study group control of its mandatory religious instruction program, and the instruction the group offered was from a decidedly fundamentalist Christian perspective. As with school prayer, the regulation allowed parents to claim an exemption for religion classes.

The case was heard by the Divisional Court before the Court of Appeal's decision in the school prayer case.[15] Two of the three judges, Justices David Watt and Mac Austin, would become my colleagues on the Superior Court and Court of Appeal years later. Another future Superior Court colleague, Blenus Wright, defended the regulation on behalf of the Attorney General of Ontario. John Sopinka, future Justice of the Supreme Court of Canada, was joined by another future judicial colleague, David Brown, to defend the practice of the Board of Education.

Once again, I only succeeded in persuading one of the three judges, Justice Austin, that by permitting compelled religious indoctrination of school children, the regulation infringed freedom of religion. Justice Austin also accepted our submission, supported by the expert evidence of a U of T psychology professor, that given the pressure children would be under to conform with their classmates, the exemption did not adequately address the religious coercion or denial of equality. However, Justice Watt wrote a lengthy judgment upholding the regulation and the Board's program of instruction, with which the third judge agreed.

The case proceeded to the Court of Appeal after John Sopinka was appointed to the Supreme Court and after I was working there as Executive Legal Officer. John B. Laskin argued the appeal successfully, and a five-judge panel unanimously allowed the appeal.[16] This was a major victory for the CCLA, for the Baha'i family, and for religious freedom and equality, of which I was proud to have taken part, even if I did not manage to carry the day at first instance. When I discussed the outcome with Justice Sopinka, with his characteristic good humour and bravado, he insisted that had it been the two of us arguing the case before the Court of Appeal, the result would have been different.

Equality Cases

I took on several equality cases, including an application for leave to appeal to the Supreme Court of Canada on behalf of Irene Bregman, the widow of a veteran who had served in the Soviet Army during World War II. Legislation provided that allied veterans were entitled to a pension provided they had resided in Canada for at least ten years.[17] Our client's husband had become a Canadian citizen, but he had not resided in Canada for ten years at the time of his death. The case was challenging to argue, because it arose before the Supreme Court of Canada had pronounced on section 15, the equality guarantee, and because the cases that had been decided provided limited guidance. Bregman's claim had been denied by a unanimous Court of Appeal, with my former mentor, Associate Chief Justice Bert MacKinnon, presiding.[18] Working with a very capable student, Veronica Bedard, we developed an argument that citizenship was a precisely defined legal category that established a more meaningful link to Canada than mere residence. We argued that it was arbitrary and irrational to deny the benefit to a Canadian citizen who fought for an allied force. We also suggested that leave to appeal should be granted to afford the Court an opportunity to tackle the difficult issue of how best to remedy underinclusive statutes, in particular whether to strike them down and deny the benefit to all, or to extend the benefit to those who had been excluded. The case was presented in the era when the Court heard oral argument on leave to appeal arguments, so I travelled to Ottawa and appeared before a panel that included Justice Bertha Wilson. Justice Wilson, herself a naturalized citizen, seemed interested in the case, but leave to appeal was refused.[19] I was disappointed by the result but pleased to have been before the Supreme Court, if only on a leave application. When the Supreme Court did pronounce on section 15 in the *Andrews* case[20] in early 1989, it seemed unlikely that Ms. Bregman's case would have succeeded had leave been granted.

I was pleased when the Women's Legal Education and Action Fund (LEAF) came to the program for assistance on several matters. One of the LEAF cases renewed my acquaintance with the "man-in-the-house" issue. My previous win on behalf of the Student Legal Aid clinic had not ended the pattern of women being arbitrarily denied welfare benefits. On behalf of LEAF, we undertook the representation of two single mothers who had their benefits denied in circumstances where the "man" was neither living "in the house" nor making any financial contribution. We launched appeals to the Divisional Court from the Social Assistance Review Board, challenging the validity of the regulation as a *Charter* denial of equality. Before the appeals were argued, the Ontario government agreed to settle the cases and to alter the way it dealt with entitlement to these benefits. The students in the seminar had been fully engaged in preparing the case and, while they were delighted by the result, they were disappointed not to see it argued in court. At our year-end dinner, they presented me with an engraved wall plaque, which I now proudly display in my law school office, which says:

OFFICIAL SARB INDICATOR
MAN IN THE HOUSE!
CON. LIT. 85/86

Another LEAF case had a similar outcome. A law student and his spouse wanted to give their child the spouse's last name. The *Vital Statistics Act* denied a married woman that right. We brought a *Charter* challenge, arguing that the provision amounted to a denial of the equality right guaranteed by section 15. Once again, the province conceded the point, and the declaration we sought was granted on consent. I was pleased with the result but disappointed that I did not have the chance to argue the case and that, since the decision was on consent, no reasons were given, and no precedent was established. Another LEAF case challenging mandatory retirement at age sixty-five settled when the employer agreed to make a satisfactory arrangement with the employee.

The reason these cases were resolved was that the *Charter*'s section 15 equality guarantee had caused governments to conduct comprehensive reviews of the statute book and to change those statutes that seemed to be inconsistent with section 15. There was a three-year phase-in period from 1982 to 1985 after the *Charter* was adopted before section 15 came into force. The three-year grace period had passed, but the government remained willing to concede section 15 challenges that were likely to succeed rather than face defeat in the courts.

Student Projects

Several students prepared research papers for various public interest groups. For the CCLA, we undertook studies on the constitutionality of the hate literature provision in the *Criminal Code* and the constitutionality of the compulsory detention of persons suffering from mental illness. The faculty's future Dean, Ron Daniels, prepared a detailed memorandum on the possible uses of social science evidence in *Charter* litigation, and another student completed a study of the use of the "Brandeis Brief" in American constitutional litigation to introduce the court to such evidence. Other projects included a brief for an organization now called the Canadian Association for Community Living for the Boyer Parliamentary Commission's study on equality, and a brief on the Supreme Court of Canada's intervention rules on behalf of LEAF.

Several students worked with the practitioners who had agreed to involve students in their cases. These cases concerned mandatory retirement, pension benefits for widows of veterans, opposite sex prison searches, age discrimination in housing, minority language education rights, and whether the *Charter* protects the right to engage in collective bargaining, and a variety of criminal cases dealing with search and seizure law, whether the duress defence was unduly limited, and a prosecution of *The Joy of Gay Sex* for obscenity. Several of these cases went all the way to the Supreme Court of Canada and are still cited as leading authorities, including the *Lavigne* case[21] challenging the right of trade unions to spend money on political activities and a Supreme Court of Canada decision on Sunday closing.[22]

My future colleague and co-author Kent Roach prepared an excellent memorandum for the argument of *R v Swain*[23] and the challenge to the discretionary detention of individuals found not guilty by reason of insanity. In the memo, Kent foreshadowed his work that was to come years later on constitutional remedies, advocating a "two-track approach" that moves from individual remedies to more general reform when he argued that "to ask for a personal remedy simply for [Swain] ... will ignore much of the reform potential of this *Charter* challenge."[24]

Perhaps the most notable involvement with a practitioner involved the case of Shalom Schachter, argued by Brian Morgan of Osler, Hoskin and Harcourt, challenging the parental leave benefits offered by the *Unemployment Insurance Act* on the ground that adoptive parents were given benefits not available to the parents of natural born children. The case posed a very difficult question. If the law did deny equality, what is the appropriate remedy? Should the court "throw the baby out with the bath water" and strike down the benefit afforded to adoptive parents, or should the court "read in" to the statute and give the same benefit to natural parents? The case eventually ended up at the Supreme Court of Canada[25] and established an important precedent on *Charter* remedies. As might be expected, the Court's answer was "it depends."

Separate School Funding Reference

My most ambitious undertaking was the representation of the Ontario Association of Alternate and Independent Schools in a section 2(a) freedom of religion and section 15 equality *Charter* challenge to the Ontario government's extension of full funding to Roman Catholic separate secondary schools.

The arrangements in place at the time of Confederation for denominational schools were constitutionally guaranteed.[26] However, the effect of that guarantee was limited by the 1928 *Tiny Township* decision of the Judicial Committee of the Privy Council holding that, at Confederation, funding was provided only to the equivalent of Grade 10.[27] That meant, as a practical matter, that publicly funded separate school education ended at Grade 8 and most Catholics attended the publicly funded non-denominational high schools. The Catholic Church long regarded the limitation of funding as an injustice and, in the mid-1980s, persuaded Ontario Premier Bill Davis to extend full funding to the end of secondary school.

It became apparent that the extension of full funding would be challenged from two very different perspectives. The non-denominational public schools, their teachers, and their supporters were strongly opposed, because they feared the measure would lead to the erosion of the public school system. They wanted to strike the measure down. Non-Catholic religious and private schools contended that the province could not fund the schools of one religion without giving the same benefit to other schools. They welcomed the extension of full funding to Catholic schools but argued that could be justified only if they were given the same benefit. Although these two camps sought diametrically opposed results, they joined in a common cause to attack the extension of full funding to Catholic schools as a denial of equality. Knowing that a challenge was coming, the government wisely directed a reference to the Court of Appeal to determine the constitutionality of Bill 30 before the full apparatus of fully funded separate schools was established.

I was contacted by John Olthuis to see if I would take on the case on behalf of the Ontario Association of Alternative and Independent Schools, a broadly based association of religious and independent schools. I knew John from my days in practice, when I worked with Ian Binnie to represent an organization he worked with in the Marshall Crowe bias case, discussed in Chapter 4. The Association was prepared to pay a very modest fee. I eagerly accepted the brief, because it would present the students with a chance to be engaged in a major piece of *Charter* litigation. I knew taking on the case would be a significant undertaking, and I was delighted when John B. Laskin, my former academic colleague who had gone on to practise civil litigation with Torys, agreed to come on board.

Our client was given standing by the Court of Appeal and, with the help of the students in the seminar, we crafted what we hoped would be a winning argument. The case presented a fascinating challenge. A guarantee in the original 1867 Constitution had to be reconciled with the promise of equality in the new 1982 Constitution. Did the *Charter*'s section 15 equality guarantee limit the capacity of the province to expand what had been promised to separate school supporters in 1867? A central issue was whether the Court should adhere to the admittedly questionable 1928 ruling that separate school funding was only guaranteed to Grade 10.

The case posed an interesting issue for me. I have always supported a strong non-denominational system of education, and that put me at odds with the objectives of my client, which sought full funding for all religious and independent schools. I took the brief because I thought it represented an excellent opportunity for me and for the Constitutional Litigation Program and because I firmly believe that lawyers should not be identified with their clients' cases. At a meeting with representatives of the client, I was asked for my personal views. I thought my answer might mean the end of the case for the Constitutional Litigation Program, but I had to be honest. I told them I was a strong public school supporter but suggested that my views on funding independent schools could make me a better advocate for the client, since I would be aware of the opposing view and better able to craft a sound legal argument. I added that while I was not keen on seeing more public funding for denominational and independent schools, I could see no legal or moral justification for selecting one religion for special treatment. I am not sure whether it was my honesty or the persuasiveness of my response, but it satisfied the questioner, and the retainer was not lost.

The case was argued over thirteen days before a five-judge panel in the Court of Appeal. There was a long list of intervenors, and the courtroom was packed with counsel, including Ontario's Attorney General Ian Scott, the legendary John Robinette, future Supreme Court of Canada Justice John Sopinka, and several other future judges of the Superior Court and Court of Appeal, including my future colleagues Mac Austin, John I. Laskin, Paul Rouleau, and David Brown.

The case was steeped in history. It required a detailed look at the system of education in pre-Confederation Ontario and the complex bargain struck in 1867 with respect to the rights accorded to religious minorities in both Ontario and Quebec. Ian Scott made one of the most brilliant arguments I had ever heard, weaving law together with history, to make the case that the fundamental promise of separate school rights that made Confederation possible had been broken when funding only extended to Grade 10 and that it was time to repair that wrong.

The solemnity of the legal arguments was broken when an in-person litigant, Reverend (and beekeeper) Bill Morris from Bloomfield Ontario, handed the bench jars of honey he had gathered from his hives, graciously accepted by a bemused Chief Justice.

When I stood up to argue our case towards the end of the thirteen days, I admitted that the Court might well be sceptical that I would have anything new to add to the arguments that had already been made. However, I asked for their patience and assured the Court that our perspective was different. The parties opposing the extension of full funding to Roman Catholic separate schools were using the *Charter* to defeat historic rights. We urged using the *Charter* to provide equal rights. The other parties had presented the case as requiring a stark choice between preferring the old 1867 Constitution's guarantee of separate school funding or the 1982 Constitution's guarantee of equality. Our client would show how to resolve that conundrum and respect both guarantees: extend the funding to Roman Catholic separate schools, as required by the 1867 Constitution, but give independent and denominational schools equal rights, as promised by the 1982 Constitution. Indeed, we argued, our client was asking the Court to follow the very principle upon which funding for separate schools had been promised in 1867 – namely, to recognize the importance to certain minorities of the infusion of moral and religious values on education. That was precisely what Roman Catholics sought in 1867 and what our client sought in 1986: to have their children educated in a manner consistent with their conscientious or religious views. In 1867, Roman Catholics were the predominant religious minority. By 1985, things had changed. Roman Catholics had become Ontario's largest single religious group, and we now had a much more religiously diverse population. Special privileges should not be extended to one group simply because they were here first. By all means, allow the province to fulfil the 1867 promise and extend separate school funding, but on the condition that the province respects the 1982 promise of equality.

By a 3–2 majority, the Court of Appeal upheld the validity of Bill 30.[28] Chief Justice Howland and Justice Robins, dissenting, concluded that "Bill 30 is inconsistent with s.15(1) of the *Charter* which gives to every individual the right to equal benefit of the law without discrimination based on religion. If this right is to mean anything, it must mean at least that the followers of one religion are not to be the beneficiaries of greater benefits provided by law than the followers of other religions." The majority, Justices Zuber, Cory, and Tarnopolsky, found, in a much shorter judgment, that the promise in section 93 of the *Constitution Act, 1867* of funding for Roman Catholic separate schools in Ontario had to be read as part of a package of rights that included the province's legislative authority to define the extent of denominational school rights. That authority, they held, was protected from *Charter* scrutiny by section 29, which provides:

> Nothing in this *Charter* abrogates or derogates from any rights or privileges guaranteed by or under the Constitution of Canada in respect of denominational, separate or dissentient schools.

I did not find the majority judgment persuasive. I could see why section 29 protected from *Charter* scrutiny the rights that were granted by the Constitution in 1867, but by choosing to extend those rights in 1985 beyond what the courts had previously held to be their scope, it seemed to me that the province was exercising a legislative authority that had to comply with the *Charter*.

Not surprisingly, the case was appealed to the Supreme Court of Canada. It was argued over six days, undoubtedly longer than the Court would allow today, and once again a long list of distinguished counsel appeared. The case was heard by a panel of seven judges because of the illness of Justice Julien Chouinard, who died shortly after the case was argued.

The Court remained oddly silent and asked very few questions during oral argument. Once again, there were three perspectives. The first was that of the public school supporters. This group comprised school boards, teachers' unions, and my sometime client, the CCLA. Led by John Robinette, showing his years but still compelling and convincing, this group argued that section 15 precluded any additional funding for separate schools. The second group included separate school boards, teachers' unions, and the province. Ian Scott was again brilliant, forcefully arguing that the time for fulfilling the promise made at Confederation to separate school supporters and to the Catholic minority in Ontario – a promise that had been fulfilled for the Protestant minority in Quebec – was long overdue. He even brought his family into the mix: one of his forebears was responsible for the 1859 "Scott Act," which gave certain funding rights to separate schools. We formed the third group, those who supported full funding for separate schools but insisted that section 15 required that the same rights be extended to other religious and conscience-based schools. John B. Laskin and I worked closely with Donald Brown and Guy Pratte, a former student and close friend, who represented a group of independent Christian schools. We also worked closely with John I. Laskin, who acted for the Canadian Jewish Congress.

My turn at the podium came first thing on Monday morning, 2 February 1987. I certainly felt the pressure as the court clerk announced to the room packed with distinguished counsel "The Court, La Cour" and swung open the large doors through which the judges pass to enter the courtroom. I managed to get hold of my nerves and, at just the right moment, I felt an unexpected surge of energy and confidence that carried me along. Again, I argued that both the old and the new Constitution had to be respected and that an interpretation that reconciled the guarantees of both should be preferred over an interpretation that prefers the old over the new.

Because the judges remained silent, it was very difficult to predict the outcome. We knew that we faced a difficult battle, even though our legal argument seemed strong. Ian Scott's historically based argument was very attractive. The separate school system was here to stay, and it made little sense in the late twentieth century to have it end at primary school. The consequences of accepting our submission would be significant for the public school system and for the provincial purse. When we reported to our client, we pointed out that, even if we were successful, there would be a political battle ahead, since the province might decide not to extend full funding to separate schools, thereby depriving the client of the lever it needed to secure funding for its schools.

The judgment dismissing the appeal was released six months later at the end of June 1987.[29] In three separate judgments, the Court unanimously rejected the section 15 challenge. Ian Scott's argument that denominational school rights were a fundamental aspect of the 1867 constitutional bargain that made Confederation possible won the day.

Hill v Scientology

My last appearance as counsel came a few years later in 1995 while I was Dean and shortly before my appointment as a judge. Alan Borovoy enlisted Kent Roach and me to seek intervener status in *Hill v Scientology*,[30] a defamation case in which a Crown attorney, by the time of trial a judge, had recovered a very large damage award for defamation. Morris Manning, the lawyer representing the Church of Scientology, held a press conference on the steps of Osgoode Hall. Wearing his barrister's gown, Manning read from and commented on court documents alleging that Casey Hill, the Crown attorney dealing with protracted proceedings against Scientology, should be found guilty of contempt of court for misleading a judge and breaching court orders sealing documents belonging to Scientology. The allegations were found to be without foundation and the jury awarded Hill $1.6 million in damages.

The CCLA position was that the traditional law of defamation unduly restricted freedom of expression. If a statement harmed reputation, subject to a few specific defences, defendants could only escape liability by proving the truth of what they had said or written. This created a "chilling" effect on freedom of expression, discouraging media scrutiny and criticism of public figures borne of the fear of being sued. The CCLA took what I would describe as a middle-of-the-road position. We did not advocate the American approach, formulated in *New York Times v Sullivan*,[31] that a public figure could recover damages only upon proof of malice. On that standard, plaintiffs can succeed only by proving that the media defendant knew that what it published was false or was reckless as to the truth of the statement. Our position was that the media should have a defence if they could show that they had a reasonable belief in the truth of what they had written. The CCLA also argued for limits on defamation damages.

Alan was furious when counsel for Hill decided to cross-examine him on his affidavit filed in support of the intervention application. Kent and I managed to calm him down sufficiently to get him through the ordeal. We were given intervenor status.

The Court gave us more time than we expected, but most of that time was taken up by the judges' questions. It was clear that they were not with us. The facts of the case were far from ideal from the CCLA's perspective. The judges were sympathetic to Hill and offended by a gowned lawyer holding a press conference at the courthouse door and making false statements about the conduct of an officer of the Crown. The defendant was not a media outlet but a quasi-religious organization that had played fast and loose with the truth. The plaintiff, ably represented by my friend and future judicial colleague Bob Armstrong had been badly maligned and he was someone with whom the judges could readily identify. The decision of the court did say that the *Charter* value of freedom of the press and expression could be used to modify the common law of defamation, but the judgment fell well short of what the CCLA was asking for. However, fourteen years later, the Supreme Court did accept the defamation defence of responsible journalism that largely corresponds to the CCLA position in the *Hill v Scientology*.[32]

The case marked Kent's first appearance as counsel before the Supreme Court. When I left the Dean's office to become a judge, I gave Kent my court gown as he was keen to take on more advocacy. I was delighted to be part of his initiation as counsel, an experience that was followed by a long list of other appearances, several of them considerably more successful than his first, on behalf of the CCLA and other public interest groups.

Benefits of the Constitutional Litigation Program

I thoroughly enjoyed the work of the Constitutional Litigation Program. It gave the students a valuable learning experience, and I was personally thrilled to find myself in court arguing some fascinating cases. The combination of teaching constitutional law and arguing these cases in the early days of the *Charter* was both challenging and rewarding. The experience coincided perfectly with my interest in the law as an intellectual discipline that had immediate practical application. Although I certainly did not plan the trajectory, it also seemed to lead quite naturally to my next legal adventure as Executive Legal Officer at the Supreme Court of Canada.

9
Executive Legal Officer at the Supreme Court of Canada

After I had been teaching for eleven years, my legal career took an unexpected turn when I accepted a position at the Supreme Court of Canada. I spent three fascinating years working with Chief Justice Brian Dickson, one of Canada's greatest judges. He involved me in the historic endeavour he shared with his colleagues to meet the new challenge of giving life to the promise of the *Charter of Rights and Freedoms*. I learned an enormous amount about the nature of law and how it evolves, and about the work of judges and the courts. Most importantly, I enjoyed the privilege of working closely with a great Canadian and a wise and compassionate judge.

An Invitation to Ottawa

In the late spring of 1987, Jim MacPherson, then serving as Chief Justice Brian Dickson's Executive Legal Officer, called me to ask if I would be willing to come to Ottawa in the next day or so to be interviewed by the Chief Justice. I did not know Jim at the time – we have since become close friends and colleagues – but I did know that he had been named as the new Dean of Osgoode Hall Law School. Jim's term as Dean did not begin until January 1988, but the Chief Justice was anxious to have a new Executive Legal Officer named as soon as possible.

Jim was the first person to fill the position of Executive Legal Officer. The post had been created by Chief Justice Dickson. No doubt influenced by his military and corporate law experience of working in a team, Dickson decided that he would benefit from the assistance of a mid-career lawyer or professor to assist him with the many duties he has as Chief Justice of Canada.

I had not applied for the job, nor had I given the position any thought or known that my name was being considered. I was not even sure that

I wanted the job. I was enjoying academic life and arguing my pro bono *Charter* cases. But I knew that opportunities like this do not come along every day. Jim told me that I was on the short list. It was clear that I had little time to reflect, since the decision would be made quickly.

I decided to follow my instinct and not let the opportunity pass me by. I had nothing to lose by travelling to Ottawa to see the Chief Justice. I had long been a Dickson admirer. I knew him as a judge who wrote in a clear and accessible style and who was prepared to stake out new jurisprudential ground when appropriate. He firmly rejected the excessive formalism that prevailed when he joined the Court. Along with Chief Justice Bora Laskin, Dickson worked to free our law from excessive reliance on English authority and to create a distinctively Canadian jurisprudence, attuned to the needs of Canadian society. It would be interesting to meet him and to explore this unexpected opportunity.

Within a day or so, I met Jim at the entrance to the Supreme Court Building, situated west of the Parliament Buildings on Wellington Street. It sits high above the Ottawa River to the north and is set back from the street to the south by a wide lawn. The building was designed by a Montreal architect, Ernest Cormier, and has a dignified but austere feel, softened somewhat by its art deco features. At the entrance, one passes impressively solemn statues of Justicia and Veritas. The large and rather daunting marble entrance hall leads to the Federal Court's courtrooms at either side and the Supreme Court's courtroom up some stairs at the back.

Jim escorted me to the second floor. We walked along the red carpeted hall, lined with portraits of previous chief justices, passing by the chambers of Justices William McIntyre, Gerard La Forest, and Willard Estey to reach the northeast corner and the chambers of the Chief Justice of Canada.

I had visited the chambers of the Chief Justice once before, when I appeared as Ian Binnie's junior counsel in the Marshall Crowe case in 1978. As mentioned in Chapter 4, on that occasion, along with a long list of other lawyers, I was escorted into the Chief Justice of Canada's chambers to discuss how Justice Ritchie would be participating in the hearing. I do not recall how Chief Justice Laskin had the office organized or decorated, but in Dickson's time, the office was meticulously neat, with no files or papers in sight except a single sheet on Dickson's desk, apparently his notes for my interview. The wood-panelled walls were decorated with paintings, a sign of Chief Justice Dickson's interest in art and art collecting.

Chief Justice Dickson was at his desk. He rose to greet me warmly and invited me to sit down. He was clearly prepared for the meeting.

He asked me some questions about my work. He seemed to be very interested in my writing, some of which he had read. He was particularly interested in the case comment I had written about his decision in *R v Sault Ste Marie*,[1] a leading case that still governs the fault element for regulatory offences. He came across as being very business-like, rather formal in his demeanour, but at the same time very warm and welcoming.

He described the job of Executive Legal Officer in some detail. It was clear from what he said, and from what Jim had told me, that if I received the position, I would be working closely with him on almost all aspects of his work as Chief Justice. He invited me to join him for lunch at the Rideau Club. I am not particularly good at small talk, nor, I sensed, was he. I wondered how the lunch would go, but largely thanks to his gracious manner, we had a very pleasant time talking about Ottawa, my family, and his son, Brian, who had been my law school classmate. As we sat at our table, several people – lawyers and political figures – came over to say hello to the Chief Justice. I could see that even when the Chief Justice of Canada just shows up for lunch, it is an event.

Within a week or two, Jim MacPherson called to say that the Chief Justice wanted to offer me the job. I knew that this might happen but still had not made a firm decision about whether to accept. I would be asking Geraldine to move away from her friends and activities, and we worried about disrupting the lives of the children, then ages fourteen, twelve, and eight. If Geraldine had said no, I would have understood and turned down the offer. But, to her credit, she saw this as a wonderful opportunity for me. She had moved a great deal when she was a child, and she thought that it would be an interesting adventure for us all.

When he interviewed me for the job, Brian Dickson was seventy-one years old. He had been a member of Court for fourteen years and Chief Justice of Canada for three years. He had four more years to serve before he reached the mandatory retirement age of seventy-five.

I had to receive a leave of absence from the law school. Dean Rob Pritchard was very helpful in that regard. He even provided me with a travel allowance so that I could maintain contact with the faculty during my time in Ottawa. I used it several times, including once to add some bench strength to the professors' hockey team to answer a challenge from the women's team.

Jim MacPherson was not leaving the job until January 1988, and Chief Justice Dickson wanted me to commit for two years from that date. That was awkward, since it would involve breaking up the children's schooling twice mid-school year. Fortunately, I was going on sabbatical from 1 July, and I had not made any plans to be away. We agreed that I would take the position for twenty, rather than twenty-four, months but that I would come to Ottawa in September. I could fulfil my academic responsibilities by finishing the book on the Currie libel trial and working on the second edition of *Habeas Corpus* and, at the same time, becoming familiar with the job which I would take up full-time in January 1988. In a very short period, I managed to find a house to rent in the Sandy Hill area of Ottawa, and we rented our house in Toronto for two years. We still managed to make a previously planned trip to France for the month of August. The salary for the Executive Legal Officer position was in line with my U of T salary, and all our moving expenses to and from Ottawa were covered.

Members of the Court

I got to know the members of the Court reasonably well. The one exception was Justice Jean Beetz. I had great respect for Justice Beetz, largely because, when teaching constitutional law, I found his decisions beautifully crafted, especially his dissent in the *Anti-Inflation Reference*.[2] He was a quiet and private man who kept very much to himself. He formed close bonds with his law clerks, in particular, during my time at the Court, with future Supreme Court Justice Nicholas Kasirer. Dickson appreciated Beetz's intellectual strength but was frustrated by his consistent failure to write his decisions in a timely manner. When I saw Justice Beetz, he was invariably pleasant and correct, always calling me "Mr. Sharpe." To the rest of the Court, I was "Bob."

After Justice Beetz's retirement for health reasons in November 1988, Justice Antonio Lamer became the Senior Puisne Judge. He and Dickson were close, both personally and jurisprudentially. Once he became the Senior Puisne Judge, Dickson counted on him as the "second-in-command." Lamer shared Dickson's concerns about excessive delay in rendering decisions. He also shared Dickson's relentless work habits, and the two men formed a bond. Because my responsibilities included assisting Dickson in court administration, I had a great deal of interaction with Lamer, and we got along well together. I am an admirer of his judicial contribution,[3] which, sadly, was not enhanced by his decline towards the end of his time as Chief Justice. As I will explain in Chapter 11, Lamer was instrumental in my appointment as a judge.

At the time, there was no formal process in place for the appointment of Supreme Court judges. The Minister of Justice consulted the senior representatives of the bench and bar, but the process was opaque. The final decision was that of the Prime Minister. Dickson made a point of maintaining a relationship with the Minister of Justice and the Prime

Minister, and I believe that he was regularly consulted on appointments to the Court.

Justice Beetz was one of the three Quebec judges on the Court, and that meant that he had to be replaced by a lawyer or a judge from Quebec. The *Supreme Court Act* provides for three Quebec judges to ensure that Quebec's distinctive civilian tradition is reflected by the membership of the Court. Justice Beetz was replaced by Justice Charles Gonthier, a quiet and scholarly judge who had been very active in judicial education. I first met him when he came to the opening of the Canadian Judicial Centre in 1988. He had served for fourteen years as a Quebec trial judge and less than a year on the Quebec Court of Appeal before his appointment to the Supreme Court in 1989. Justice Gonthier was a highly gracious man. He took to the work of a Supreme Court judge with ease. He seemed to work quietly and steadily and certainly did not suffer from the indecision of his esteemed predecessor. I did not have a great deal to do with him, but he was invariably cordial and interested when we had anything to discuss.

Justice Willard Estey occupied the office adjacent to that of the Chief Justice. He was a brilliant but at times difficult man. He could be very entertaining, especially at after-dinner legal events, which made him popular in the profession. I found him to be less distant than Justice Beetz, but more distant than the other judges, perhaps because he distrusted my background in academe rather than in practice. Many people who are entertaining and humorous in public are sad in private, and perhaps Estey was an example. He displayed outspoken disdain for Ottawa, for the work of Court, and for the Meech Lake Accord when he left the Court in 1988 to pursue a career in business. When he resigned, there were twenty-five cases on reserve, and under the *Supreme Court Act*, he had six months to complete his work on those cases. His injudicious and embarrassing outburst provoked a complaint to the Canadian Judicial Council, which led Estey to recuse himself from further participation in the work of the Court and depart before he had completed his work, putting added pressure on the judges who remained.

Estey was from Ontario and, although there is no guarantee of three Ontario judges on the Court, there is a strong convention to that effect. The arrival of Justice John Sopinka, a senior Ontario counsel, as Estey's replacement was like a breath of fresh air. Sopinka was a brilliant advocate who had no difficulty in adapting to his new judicial role. I knew him slightly before he arrived in Ottawa, because I had argued cases against him in my Constitutional Litigation Program work, and I had served on a Law Society committee that he chaired. One day, not long after he arrived, he strode into my office and told me I was working too hard. I needed to get out and have some fun. He invited me to a game of tennis at his club. I had limited experience on the tennis court, and I did not have proper equipment, but he insisted. I was uneasy about the invitation, because Sopinka was an accomplished athlete who had played professional football with the Toronto Argonauts of the Canadian Football League. He was intensely competitive. He beat me, of course, but not nearly as badly as he could have, and I enjoyed the game. I took his message about getting interested in a sport to heart and became a regular, although average, tennis player as a result.

Justice William McIntyre, from British Columbia, like Dickson, was a World War II veteran. He had a rather gruff demeanour, but it did not take long to realize that, behind that façade, he was a warm and generous person. He was a very hard-working judge. I always had the impression that he wanted to return to British Columbia as soon as he could. Before I came to the Court, I thought that Justice McIntyre was unduly conservative in his judicial outlook, despite his courageous *Canadian Bill of Rights* dissent stating that capital punishment offended the guarantee against cruel and unusual punishment.[4] When I worked at the Court, even though I often disagreed with his decisions, I could see the importance of having a voice of caution and restraint. Dickson had deep respect for Justice McIntyre despite their frequent judicial disagreements, and no doubt that respect rubbed off on me.

Justice McIntyre, one of the two judges from western Canada, was replaced in 1989 by Justice Beverley McLachlin, then serving as Chief Justice of the Supreme Court of British Columbia. She had a brilliant run as a Supreme Court Justice for eleven years and as Chief Justice of Canada for seventeen years. I was amazed by Justice McLachlin's ability to turn out her judgments quickly and efficiently. She was exactly what the Court needed as it struggled to keep up with the workload, which she seemed to relish rather than dread. We had both taught courses on remedies and, while I had never met her, she had written a favourable review of my book *Injunctions and Specific Performance*.[5] I am a strong admirer of her judicial work, and I greatly enjoyed getting to know her when she joined the Court.

Justice Gerald Le Dain, another World War II veteran, greeted me enthusiastically when I arrived at the Court. I always enjoyed talking to him. He was bristling with ideas. Like Justice Beetz, he was a brilliant constitutional scholar, but also like Beetz, he suffered from indecision, and his judgments were often long delayed. This quality did not endear him to Dickson, who was very concerned about the fact that the Court regularly missed its six-month target for the release of judgments. I was occasionally dispatched to their offices to ask when we might expect to see a draft judgment on a particular case, a task I did not relish but one I had to perform. Justice Le Dain's resignation from the Court for reasons of ill health was a tragedy for him, his family, and his law clerks.

Le Dain was an Ontario appointment, although most of his time in academe and practice had been spent in Quebec. Justice Peter Cory, a member of the Ontario Court of Appeal, replaced Justice Le Dain, and, like Justice Sopinka, he was a breath of fresh air. Like Dickson, Cory was a wartime veteran, and, like Dickson, he had worked his way up the judicial hierarchy from trial judge to appellate judge and finally to the Supreme Court. Justice Cory's generous and polite demeanour in and out of court was legendary in the profession. He never said a bad word about anyone. At the Court, he regularly circulated the hall on the second floor in the afternoon with a tin of cookies, offering them to anyone he encountered. He dropped by one day with his tin of cookies when I was meeting with a journalist. My visitor was convinced we had staged the whole thing. I got to know Justice Cory very well, and he became a mentor when I embarked on my career as a judge.

Justice Bertha Wilson, the first woman to be appointed to the Supreme Court, never lost her Scottish accent or her down-to-earth Scottish outlook on life. I did not have a great deal to do with her at the Court until a reciprocal visit with the Soviet Constitutional Court in 1988–89, which I discuss below. My other contact with her was my involvement in the New Year's Eve parties organized by Jim MacPherson. Bertha and her husband, John, were regular attendees, along with Gordon and Nancy Fairweather, Ottawa Dean Donald McRae and his wife, Sally, and Osgoode Professor John Evans and his wife, Pat. These parties continued, with various other invitees, after our time in Ottawa and after Bertha had retired from the Court, so my contact with her continued. I greatly admired Justice Wilson's courage and work ethic. In the difficult period when Justice Estey resigned and Justices Beetz and Le Dain were suffering ill health, she became very close to the Chief and was an anchor of strength on the Court.

I got along well with Justice Gerard La Forest. I think because of our shared academic backgrounds, he treated me more as a colleague rather than as an underling. More than most of the other judges, he discussed the cases he was working on with me. I suspect that this may have been to lay some groundwork for convincing the Chief of his point of view. I have written about La Forest's willingness to change the law when he thought change was called for.[6] Dickson usually agreed with those decisions, but it did not seem to me that the two enjoyed a particularly strong relationship. That came more from Dickson than from La Forest, and I was never sure of the reason why. Justice La Forest and his wife invited me to their home when they were entertaining his law clerks, and he supported my nomination to the Royal Society of Canada. It was not because of his friendship that I defended his approach to the *Charter* when one of my U of T colleagues labelled him as having "an incontestable claim to be the doyen of the conservatives on the bench."[7]

Justice Claire L'Heureux-Dubé had been appointed as the second female member of the Court shortly before my arrival. She frequently came to my office to chat. It was apparent that she felt that her natural warmth and gallic effervescence were stifled in the austere atmosphere of the Court. At times, I thought she might be telling me more than I had to know, but I did enjoy her visits, and I sympathized with her difficult transition from the work she loved at the Quebec Court of Appeal. She was a prodigious worker, a quality that endeared her to the Chief, who had not been thrilled by the news of her appointment.

Working for the Chief Justice

Chief Justice Dickson set out my duties as Executive Legal Officer in the following language:

> a) To monitor the jurisprudence of the Court, particularly in respect of *Charter* cases to ensure concordance. I am concerned that whatever is said in one case is not contradicted or varied in another, *per incuriam*;
> b) supervise the research of my law clerks and generally be in charge of the law clerk program within the Court;
> c) assist in the preparation of judgments which I have undertaken to write, particularly those related to the *Charter*;
> d) assist in the preparation of speeches;
> e) address groups of students and others who may be visiting the Court;
> f) media liaison;
> g) to assist in protocol matters within the Court;
> h) supervise relations of the Supreme Court of Canada and with other supreme courts in other countries;
> i) assist me in the work of the Canadian Judicial Council, the Conference of Chief Justices and the Order of Canada.
>
> This list is not intended to be exhaustive as something new comes up every day.

This list proved to be more or less an accurate description of my actual duties at the Court. I certainly helped Chief Justice Dickson to monitor the jurisprudence of the Court. There were, however, eight other independent judges who had their own views, did their own monitoring, and did not hesitate to disagree with Chief Justice Dickson on contentious points. I would occasionally have discussions with the other judges on jurisprudential or other issues, but my work was to assist Chief Justice Dickson in carrying out his duties both as a member of the Court and as Chief Justice.

Dickson had the most disciplined work habits that I have ever seen. Everything was done with military precision. He was very good at delegating tasks, but he maintained a firm grip on the critical issues. He had to-do lists to keep track of the tasks he had assigned to me, to Guy Goulard, the Court's registrar, and to his law clerks. At least once a week he would get out his list and ask me what I had done on each item. There was no escape. My objective was to remove each item from that list before it was overtaken by a newly added item.

In the office, his approach was no-nonsense and formal. He was always polite and courteous, but there was no time for small talk. If he thought things were going on too long on something, he would interrupt with "what's next, Bob?" When he called me at home on the weekend, as he usually did, he did not enquire as to what I or the family were up to but almost always started with "Hello, Bob, three things" and then proceeded to tell me three things he wanted me to do. Most of these matters did not have to be done over the weekend, but by calling me, he was able to take three items off his list and add them to mine.

Despite his formality and almost complete focus on work, the Chief came across to me as a warm and generous person. While he was a rigorous legal thinker, he saw his work as a judge in very human terms and was always deeply concerned about the people behind the technical legal arguments. His wartime service left an indelible mark. He knew what it was like to risk one's life for a great cause, to fight alongside others from all walks of life, and to suffer a devastating injury, in his case, the loss of a leg. He suffered from his war injury every day for the rest of his life. It was impossible not to be moved by his wisdom, integrity, and determination to work very hard always to do the right thing.

Dickson's style was to assemble a team to tackle the task he faced. I think this came both from his military experience and from his work as a corporate lawyer. He wanted to have many minds brought together to gather as many ideas as possible to ensure that the problem was thoroughly thought through and that all options were considered. Despite his age and his experience, he remained remarkably open to new ideas and new approaches.

He managed to combine the military-style discipline he imposed on himself and those who worked for him with a very human touch. When he asked me, a law clerk, or a staff member to come to his chambers, he would say "Could you please drop by?" or "Have you got a moment to see me?" as if any of us might have something more important to attend to. He made me and the law clerks feel that we were an important part of his team. One could not help but respect the man for what he had already done and what he continued to do. He was engaged in a lawyer's highest calling, and by involving us and giving us the impression that we were important contributors to his work, he made it our calling as well.

Law Clerks and Judgment Writing

I worked closely with the Dickson law clerks and very much enjoyed my involvement with them and the other law clerks. They were a brilliant and engaging group of recent law school graduates who came to the Court bristling with energy and ideas. More than half of Dickson's twenty-seven clerks have gone on to distinguished academic careers. Several who clerked at the Court while I served as Executive Legal Officer later became my colleagues at the University of Toronto: Patrick Macklem and Martha Shaffer (Dickson clerks) and Jim Phillips, Kent Roach, and Audrey Macklin (Bertha Wilson clerks). Carl Stychin became Dean of Law at the City University in London and Director of the Institute of Advanced Legal Studies. Shauna Van Praagh, a member of the McGill Faculty of Law, is President of the Law Commission of Canada. Nicholas Kasirer, who clerked for Justice Jean Beetz, became Professor and Dean of Law at McGill and is now a member of the Supreme Court. David Lametti, one of Justice Peter Cory's law clerks and law professor at McGill, served for several years as Canada's Attorney General and Minister of Justice. William Lahey, a Justice La Forest clerk, is now President of the University of King's College, Halifax. Marie Josée Hogue, a Lamer clerk, is a judge on the Quebec Court of Appeal and chaired an important public inquiry into foreign interference in Canadian elections.

Chief Justice Dickson enjoyed working with his law clerks. He constantly amazed me with his openness to their new ideas, even if occasionally they seemed to me to be somewhat off the wall.

When I started at the Court, each judge, including the Chief Justice, had two law clerks. During my time there, the number increased to three. There can be no doubt that law clerks play an important and influential role. The judges are confronted with a massive amount of reading and understandably rely on the clerks to distil and analyse the arguments the parties and intervenors present. In their judgments, Supreme Court justices regularly make law-making pronouncements. Judgments must be composed and edited with painstaking care and, as I learned when I was appointed to the bench, judges rely heavily on their law clerks for assistance.

Dickson asked his law clerks to prepare a "bench memo" for every case he heard. He left it to the clerks to divide the work as they saw fit. He wanted these memos to contain more than a summary of the arguments made by the parties and asked his clerks to state their own views and not to hesitate to go beyond the cases and authorities cited by the parties. The bench memos during my time ranged between twenty and fifty pages, and Dickson studied them closely. He regularly met with the clerk and me before oral argument to ask questions and discuss difficult issues.

My favourite moments were when he returned to his office after the day's hearings. He assembled me, the three clerks, and his loyal secretary, Deborah Melanson, to dictate what he called the conference memo. Working from notes he had taken during the conference, he would explain each judge's thinking on the case, how it was likely to be decided, and who had been assigned to write first reasons. He would always ask the clerks what they thought. In one case where he was writing, the result at conference was 9–0 from the judges and an equally decisive 3–0 the other way from his law clerks. They later informed me that if all the law clerks had been polled, the vote would have been 27–0. I remained silent and, as a result, was handed the law clerk's task to marshal the case through to completion.

Dickson often asked me to supplement the work of the law clerks on pending cases, and I was very involved in assisting him with his judgments. This was the most interesting part of my job, even though my contribution and responsibility were clearly limited by the fact that he was the judge and I was there to help him carry out that responsibility. I did my best to assist him to decide cases in a manner consistent with what seemed to me to be his general approach and based on what he had written in other cases. There were certainly times, although very few, when I disagreed with his decision, but I did my best not to allow my own personal views to intrude. That was in part because I knew the limits of my authority and in part because I had such high regard for his judgment that, when I disagreed, I always had second thoughts about my own judgment.

Dickson was a meticulous writer. He inevitably went through many drafts. In the age before word processors, this meant pen and paper, scissors, and scotch tape, and sketching his own thoughts along with appropriate extracts from the clerk's memo, the written arguments of the parties and the briefs of cases and statutes. The law clerks and I were closely involved when Dickson was writing a decision. He welcomed any help he could get to make his judgments clearer and better, but he maintained firm control on the process and on the result.

When the next-to-final draft had been produced by Deborah Melanson, he would assemble the team and we would go through it meticulously, line by line, to ensure that it read well, that there were no gaps or ambiguities, and that nothing had been left out or forgotten. This often occurred at his farm at Dunrobin, about 35 kilometres from the Court, where he liked to work when he was not sitting. I lost count of the trips I made to the farm, almost always driven by Dickson's chauffeur, Gilles Boisvert, often in the company of one or more law clerks.

Dickson made no secret of the importance he attached to the work of his law clerks and the work of legal academics. In a speech he gave at the University of Manitoba in 1977, Dickson said that law clerks "serve many useful purposes, not the least of which … is to bring to the Court an awareness of current teachings and attitudes in Canadian law schools."[8] Dickson did not share what was then a common judicial scepticism regarding the work of academics. In a 1979 lecture at the University of Toronto, he said that "the quality of the law achieved by the courts bears a direct relationship to the quality of the analysis offered by the academic community."[9] His pro-academic attitude probably explains why, when he was looking for a new Executive Legal Officer, my name was on his short list.

Dickson was always interested to know about any academic comment on his work and the work of the Court. He regularly asked me to prepare a memo summarizing what the author said and what I thought of the author's comment or criticism. The Court used a clipping service to monitor press coverage, and Dickson kept a close watch on media coverage. He would often mark up a story and send it to one or all judges to ensure that they too knew what the press was saying.

Media Relations

Dickson made it clear to me that I was to give priority to establishing and maintaining good relations with the media.[10] Increasingly in the *Charter* era, Supreme Court decisions were front-page news. Dickson was determined to see the quality of the media reporting on the Court's work improved. He knew that news reports of the Court's judgments were all that most people – including most lawyers – would read. He thought that the judiciary's traditional reluctance to engage with the media was a mistake and that, by taking a few proactive steps, the Court might be able to improve the quality of the media's coverage.

Before I arrived at the Court, Dickson and Jim MacPherson had established the basic approach. The Court would not attempt to curry favour with the media but would take several steps to make the reporters' jobs easier. Dickson recognized that reporters assigned to cover the work of the Court had a difficult task. Few of them had formal legal training and given the short news cycle, they had little time to digest often complex rulings and explain them in an accessible manner.

Dickson convinced a few of his media-shy colleagues on the Court to form a media relations committee to meet on a regular but informal basis with members of the Parliamentary Press Gallery. Media representatives could raise their difficulties, and the judges could explain media problems from the judge's perspective. He established a pressroom at the Court with telephones, a photocopier, and a place to work. Copies of factums and summaries of the cases being argued were available. An audio feed of oral argument allowed reporters to follow the proceedings from the pressroom, and reporters were permitted to record oral argument to be used for verification when they wrote their stories. The practice of issuing press releases one week in advance of the release of judgments gave reporters a chance to review the case, line up interviews, and generally enhance their capacity to provide a full and balanced report. On the day of release, copies of the judgments were available in the pressroom with headnotes summarizing the case.

As Executive Legal Officer, I was the Court's designated contact person for press inquiries. Dickson instructed me to give priority to responding promptly to media inquiries. My mission was to establish a friendly professional relationship with reporters. That would assist them in accomplishing their task in reporting on the Court's work and, we hoped, it would benefit the Court by encouraging fair and accurate reporting. I established a firm understanding with each reporter that, while they could freely call me for help, my comments were off the record and not for attribution, an undertaking all reporters respected. It allowed me to talk freely to them, providing them with the background information they needed, without violating the fundamental norm that the Court speaks only through its judgments. On days when judgments were released, I went down to the pressroom to assist the reporters, who almost always had to meet a tight deadline to file their stories.

I thoroughly enjoyed my work as media relations officer. I became friends with several reporters, including David Vienneau for the *Toronto Star*, Stephen Bindman for *Southam News*, Kirk Makin for *The Globe and*

Mail, and Viki Russell for the CBC. I admired their ability to quickly absorb and digest the Court's often complex rulings, and I loved their sharp and often sarcastic wit and sense of humour.

Probably the most challenging day I had as media relations officer occurred in late 1988, when the Court handed down its decision in *Ford v AG Quebec*.[11] The case dealt with Quebec's Bill 101, which required publicly displayed signs to be in the French language and invoked the *Charter*'s notwithstanding clause. The Court ruled that the signs law violated the *Charter* guarantee of freedom of expression but made it clear that a more restrained law that did not ban signs in other languages but required a marked predominance of French would survive under the *Charter*'s section 1 reasonable limits clause. Quebec's omnibus invocation of the notwithstanding clause shortly after the *Charter* was adopted in 1982 had protected the signs law, but by 1988 it had reached the five-year expiry date. Despite the expiry, the Court decided to deal with the issue and essentially gave legislatures a green light, stating that the courts would not engage in substantive review of override declarations.

The day the decision was handed down, the pressroom was crowded with reporters, French and English, and the judgment was complex and nuanced. I prepared carefully and did my best to answer a steady barrage of questions. I anxiously awaited the media's treatment of the decision that evening and the next day and was pleased with what I saw and heard. Not everyone liked the judgment. Quebec opinion strongly favoured Bill 101's French language protections, and there was considerable disappointment in the rest of Canada over the Court's refusal to take on Quebec's use of the notwithstanding clause. I had been surprised by the carte blanche the court gave on the use of the override, but I was there to explain the decision, not to deliver my personal views. I felt I had done my job. The reporters understood the judgment and, while I did not agree with everything I read, by and large I considered the reports of the judgment to be fair and balanced.

I was aware of the decision's legal importance, but I had not predicted its profound political impact. It came down during the Meech Lake debate, and the issues it dealt with could not have been more legally and politically sensitive. The Meech Lake Accord, agreed to by Prime Minister Mulroney and all provincial premiers, represented an attempt to heal the constitutional wound felt in Quebec flowing from the adoption of the *Constitution Act, 1982* and the *Charter* without Quebec's agreement. Particularly contentious in the Meech Lake Accord was the clause declaring Quebec to be a "distinct society." I thought that the

Ford decision went a long way to accommodate Quebec's position by upholding the use of the override and ruling that while Quebec could not ban public signs in English, it could require a marked predominance of French. That reflected a constitutional recognition of Quebec's distinctiveness. But that was not enough for Quebec's Bourassa government, which insisted on re-enacting the override clause to shelter the French-only policy. That in turn eroded support in English Canada for the concessions Meech Lake made to Quebec, and in the end the Meech Lake Accord was never adopted.

Groundbreaking Decisions

The *Ford* case was one of several foundational *Charter* cases decided by the Court during my time as Executive Legal Officer. The *Morgentaler* case,[12] attacking the *Criminal Code* abortion prohibition, was argued shortly after I arrived in Ottawa. I was surprised when Jim MacPherson told me that it seemed likely that the Court would strike down the abortion law. I had been a strong proponent of the *Charter*, but I was far from certain that the courts would be prepared to make controversial decisions on issues of social policy. The abortion issue attracted strong opposing views, and it had been a lightning rod for criticism of judicial activism in the United States. I thought that Canadian judges would shy away and leave the issue to Parliament. *Morgentaler* proved me wrong and demonstrated the Supreme Court's determination to make something of the *Charter*. The decision was applauded by many but, as I would soon learn, it also provoked a very angry, hostile, and sometimes hateful stream of letters and telephone calls to the Chief Justice's office from religious pro-life supporters.

Another pro-life challenge was dismissed during the summer of 1989 in *Tremblay v Daigle*,[13] where the Court refused to enjoin a woman from having an abortion at the suit of her estranged partner, the father of the foetus. That case provoked the most dramatic moment I witnessed in the courtroom. The Chief had summoned the members of the Court back from their summer vacations to hear the case on an urgent basis. After the lunch break, the ashen-faced counsel for Ms. Daigle informed the Court that he had just learned that his client had not waited for the Court's decision and that she had recently had an abortion in the United States. Dickson was furious with what he regarded as Daigle's contemptuous behaviour and seemed determined to dismiss her case. Beverley McLachlin urged him to see the situation from the perspective of a desperate young woman who did not want to have the child of the man who had abused her. Dickson came around, and the Court rendered its decision finding that the father had no right to obtain the injunction.[14]

The Court decided a steady stream of *Charter* and constitutional cases that made life as Executive Legal Officer very interesting. To mention a few: *Andrews*[15] laid the foundation for the interpretation of equality; *Edmonton Journal*,[16] together with *Ford*[17] and *Irwin Toy*,[18] laid the foundation for freedom of expression; and *Crown Zellerbach*[19] refreshed the meaning of "peace, order and good government" and the scope of the federal residual power.

Dickson wrote a significant decision holding that sexual harassment was a form of sex discrimination,[20] and there were several important criminal cases that I found fascinating as a teacher of criminal law. *Bernard*[21] dealt with the extent to which drunkenness could be used as a defence to sexual assault. *Corbett*[22] dealt with the issue of cross-examining accused persons on their criminal records; the Court held that they could be cross-examined but that there was a discretion to refuse to allow this where permitting it would operate unfairly. *Mack*[23] recognized the defence of entrapment.

The Court also made important pronouncements in private law. *Just*[24] and *Tock*[25] dealt with governmental liability in tort. *Hunter v Syncrude*[26] dealt with the difficult issue of fundamental breach in contract law. And *Lac Minerals*[27] redefined the scope of fiduciary duties.

To be on the scene and involved in the evolution of Canadian law during this challenging period was one of the highest privileges I have enjoyed in my professional life.

Other Duties

Dickson often asked me to meet with visiting judges, lawyers, law students, and other groups to introduce them to the Court. When the Court was not sitting, I did that in the courtroom. I usually started with the four crucial dates in the Court's history to show how it had evolved from a position of relative obscurity to one of national prominence: (1) its founding in 1875 – not 1867 – to show how it was contemplated at the time of Confederation but not seen as essential; (2) the abolition of appeals to the Judicial Committee of the Privy Council in 1949, making the Court truly Supreme; (3) the introduction of the leave to appeal requirement in 1975, giving the Court control over its docket and allowing it to focus on questions of national importance; and (4) the 1982 introduction of the *Charter*, catapulting the Court into public attention.

Another aspect of my work concerned the Canadian Judicial Council, a statutory body comprising the Chief and Associate Chief Justices of the provincial and territorial superior courts and courts of appeal and the Chief and Associate Chief Justices of the Tax Court, the Federal Court, and the Federal Court of Appeal, and now the Court Martial Court of Appeal. The mandate of the Canadian Judicial Council is broad: "to promote efficiency and uniformity, and to improve the quality of judicial service, in superior courts."[28] The Council's responsibilities include establishing judicial education programs and dealing with complaints against federally appointed judges. The Chief Justice of Canada chairs the Canadian Judicial Council. I invariably attended the Council's meeting with Dickson. I worked closely with Jeannie Thomas, then the Council's Executive Director, in planning agenda items and coordinating follow-up on Council decisions.

I enjoyed meeting and getting to know the leaders of all the courts across Canada. As one might expect, they were a varied lot. Some were distinguished jurists, and others had been appointed for political reasons, but all were committed to maintaining a high standard for the Canadian judiciary. It seemed to me at times that the members from the smaller and less busy courts had a disproportionate influence on deliberations, because their colleagues from the busier courts had less time to devote to the affairs of the Council.

Another of my tasks as Executive Legal Officer was speech writing. Chief Justice Dickson spoke frequently. He was a regular recipient of honorary degrees, and he often spoke at professional conferences and to public audiences. The biggest challenge was that he insisted that every speech or lecture include at least one joke. I do not approve of speakers telling jokes that are not connected to the subject matter of their address, and it was a struggle to find the funny side of most of the topics he spoke on. I put together a collection of books on humour from which I could draw inspiration, but I found many of these sources dated and was surprised to see how much racism and sexism used to be perceived as being funny.

Judicial Education

Before I started my work as Executive Legal Officer, the Council had embarked upon the establishment of the Canadian Judicial Centre, now the National Judicial Institute (NJI). Before the NJI, judicial education was spotty at best. Most courts had some internal education programs, and the Canadian Institute for the Administration of Justice (CIAJ) provided education on a national level. There was, however, no coordinated planning of judicial education for Canadian judges. Many judges were sceptical of the need for education. They felt that their appointment proved that they had all the education they needed. What could be learned from a course that would improve upon the learning gained from the daily experience of deciding cases? These views had a certain anti-intellectual flavour. Traditionalists resisted any appearance of "training" or "instructing" judges as an unwarranted threat to judicial independence.

The advent of the *Charter* changed these judicial attitudes. The *Charter* presented the judiciary with challenges well beyond the experience and education of most judges. Judges faced with the daunting task of making significant decisions in an unfamiliar area under a spotlight that would quickly expose outmoded ways of thinking realized that they needed all the help they could get.

Both the CIAJ and the Canadian Judicial Council looked for a way to improve on the patchwork of existing programs. A 1982 report by Ontario Chief Justice William Howland recommended the creation of a National Judicial Centre. A scholarly judge, Justice William Stevenson of the Alberta Court of Appeal and later the Supreme Court of Canada, was given a leave of absence to come up with a concrete plan. The chance for success of the venture was improved when Frank Iacobucci, a former law professor and future Supreme Court judge, was appointed Deputy Minister of Justice. Stevenson recommended the creation of the Canadian Judicial Centre, with a mandate to plan and coordinate education for all Canadian judges, whether federally or provincially appointed. Chief Justice Dickson fully supported the proposal, as did Justice Minister Ray Hnatyshyn. The Centre was to be an independent entity, located in a Canadian law school, jointly funded by the federal and provincial governments, and headed by a judge.

One of my first tasks as Executive Legal Officer in 1988 was to organize the Centre's first board meeting and to assist the board in the selection of the Centre's first Executive Director, Justice David Marshall from the Northwest Territories. There certainly were growing pains and issues over funding, and I spent considerable time while I was Executive Legal Officer working on these issues with Justice Marshall and the Canadian Judicial Council.

From its very modest beginnings, the NJI has grown to be one of the world's leading centres for judicial education. Years ago, it moved from its first home at the University of Ottawa. Largely through the efforts of several Executive Directors, including George Thompson, Brian Lennox, and Adele Kent, the NJI now has a secure financial position and a wide range of programs. The NJI has developed a strong focus on social context education, encouraging judges to consider factors and forces external to the formal legal rules, but critical for their fair application:

issues such as race, gender, social class, poverty, and sexual identity. My connection with the NJI lasted long after my time as Executive Legal Officer. I served on the Board for several years, and I have been, and continue to be, a regular presenter at NJI programs.

Travel

Dickson liked to have me along when he travelled, and his wife, Barbara, regularly accompanied him on his travels. I had a very positive relationship with Mrs. Dickson. She was an acute observer of the world and a huge support to her husband in his career. She always knew what he was working on, and she did not hold back on expressing her views. She was a very positive person, and, despite her correct and ladylike demeanour, she had a delightfully ironic sense of humour that I thoroughly enjoyed.

Our travels took us to most provinces in Canada. The most memorable trips were to USSR in 1988 and Austria in 1989 on reciprocal visits with the Constitutional Courts of those countries. I was very involved in planning the arrangements for both the Canadian and the foreign legs of those visits. Justice Bertha Wilson and her husband, John, accompanied Dickson on the Soviet visit. Travelling with them, combined with Jim MacPherson's New Year's Eve parties, gave me the opportunity to get to know them both. John Wilson, like Barbara Dickson, was a hugely supportive spouse. John was a retired clergyman. He and Bertha Wilson immigrated to Canada in 1949 to take up a post as a pastor at a Presbyterian church in Renfrew, Ontario. John became a naval chaplain in the Korean war, and the couple moved to Halifax in 1954. Bertha began her unlikely climb to the top of Canada's legal profession when she decided to study law at Dalhousie, and John gradually shifted from pastoral work to public advocacy as Director of the Consumers Association of Canada. Like Bertha, John was a very well-read person with a down-to-earth attitude. He had genuine sparkle and a terrific sense of humour. Getting to know John and Bertha Wilson was one of my most cherished privileges as Executive Legal Officer at the Supreme Court of Canada.

It was an unreal experience to be driven into the Kremlin in a motorcade to meet with the Soviet judges. I was struck by the fact that anyone of any importance in the USSR seemed to insist on having an office in a pre-revolutionary building. In Leningrad, we were taken to Tsar Peter the Great's refurbished Summer Palace, reconstructed not long after the 1939–45 war and before the rest of the city had been restored. Pride in Russian history trumped communist fervour.

We had little time for shopping, and there seemed to be little to buy, but I found an amazing variety of pins featuring images of Lenin for sale at very low prices in hotels and restaurants. Every time I saw a different one, I bought it. When I showed the Chief my collection, I could see that he did not approve. He did not say anything, but he was probably worried about the possible scandal that would erupt if it became known that his Executive Legal Officer collected communist propaganda.

The Austrian visit was less formal and less awkward. We went to the Vienna State Opera and saw a performance of *Der Rosenkavalier*. As the Canadian Ambassador said during the intermission as we sipped champagne, "If only the world really were like this." I was struck by the fact that, at a social event shortly after the opera, one of the judge's wives asked me who had sung the lead role, much in the way that, in Canada, one might be asked who was in goal after a Toronto Maple Leafs game. After the visit, Dickson acquired a new horse that he named Der Rosenkavalier, Rose for short.

I found the Austrian judges much easier to relate to than the Soviet judges, perhaps for obvious reasons. Judge Vladimir Terebilov, Chairman of the Soviet Supreme Court, was a tough old bird who had been a member of the Central Committee of the Communist Party before his appointment as a judge. On the Canadian leg of the visit, we took him to a trial advocacy class at Osgoode Hall Law School and saw a demonstration of cross-examination. Terebilov assured the class that he could show them a thing or two about how to conduct an effective interrogation. I have no doubt that he could have, but I am not sure the lesson would have been useful for an aspiring Canadian lawyer.

Dickson was prepared to overlook the obvious differences between the Soviet and Canadian judiciaries and endeavoured to emphasize what they had in common. He frequently spoke of the judges of the world coming together "with no political ends to serve, no differences to compose, no policies to advance, except the highest of all – the policy of understanding and good-will."[29]

I was deeply moved by two incidents on these trips, one in Vienna and the other in Leningrad. Both reflected the devastating injury Dickson suffered when he lost a leg in the Normandy invasion in 1944. In Vienna, our hosts made a point of introducing him to an Austrian judge who had also lost a leg in the war. The two veterans from opposite sides greeted each other with a warm handshake and a display of mutual respect that only two men with their shared experience could muster. In Leningrad, we visited the Piskryovskoe Memorial Cemetery, which holds the graves of 420,000 civilian victims of the siege of Leningrad and the 70,000 soldiers who died in the defence of the city. Dickson stood like a soldier and saluted, solemnly reflecting on what millions of victims had suffered in the war in which he had served his country and suffered his near-death experience.

Dickson's Retirement

I was scheduled to leave the Court and return to the law school in the summer of 1989. Dickson would not reach the mandatory retirement age of seventy-five until 25 May 1991. Ordinarily, he would have hired a new Executive Legal Officer to replace me and serve for two years until his retirement. However, he decided to retire at the end of the Court year in June 1990 and asked me if I would stay on for another year. I wanted to get back to the university, but I was enjoying the job, the family was enjoying life in Ottawa, and it would have been awkward for Dickson to find a new Executive Legal Officer to serve for a short period. I agreed but said I would have to obtain permission to extend my leave at the law school. Likely expecting that it would be difficult for Dean Rob Prichard to say no to the Chief Justice of Canada, Dickson called Rob, who generously agreed.

Working for Brian Dickson at the Supreme Court of Canada was one of the greatest privileges of my life. I came and left with a deep respect for his wisdom, his humanity, and his contribution as one of Canada's greatest judges. I learned a great deal from watching this wonderful judge and his colleagues do their work. I never realized my dream of being appointed to the Supreme Court as a judge, but I was there as an active participant in the work of the Court during three happy and formative years as Executive Legal Officer.

10
Law School Dean

From 1990 to 1995, I served as the Dean of the Faculty of Law at the University of Toronto. It was a great honour to fill that position, which exposed me to new duties and challenges. I was responsible for leading and administering an institution of over five hundred students and forty faculty members. I represented the faculty to the rest of the university, and I worked at building and maintaining a strong and positive relationship with our alumni. I very much enjoyed the challenge but, in the end, found that my love for the law exceeded my appetite for more administrative duties. After almost five years as Dean, when the opportunity arose, I opted for a judicial career.

Appointment as Dean

I was first considered for the deanship of the U of T Faculty of Law in 1984, after I had been a member of the faculty for eight years. Rob Prichard was selected and he did a superb job as Dean. Six years later, Rob became President of the University of Toronto and, while I was on leave from the faculty working at the Supreme Court of Canada as Executive Legal Officer, I became a candidate for the deanship. My vision of the faculty and the position of Dean had not notably changed in 1990 from what it had been in 1984, but I think that my capacity to meet the challenges of the job had improved. I had spent several more years teaching, writing, arguing constitutional cases, and dealing with the University administration. I had worked closely with the Chief Justice of Canada for three years and watched how he handled administrative matters and the sensitive issues of managing an institution made up of highly intelligent, fiercely independent, and, at times, competitive people.

I could hardly believe that I had become Dean of the law school. It was certainly not something I foresaw as an uncertain first-year student in 1966 or as a lawyer just trying my hand at the academic life in 1976 when I joined the faculty. My appointment surprised others as well. When I told my mother-in-law, of my appointment as Dean, she said: "Well, Bob, that is wonderful. You must be a lot smarter than you seem." Then, not long after my appointment, I faced the intimidating task of welcoming my own classmates back to the law school for our twenty-year reunion. I started by explaining that, when we had been in law school together twenty years earlier, I certainly never thought I would be coming before them as the Dean of the faculty. An anonymous voice at the back of the room yelled, "Neither did we."

Welcoming the First-Year Class

I always found the first day of classes in September to be exciting and energizing, and this was something I shared with our three children. We shared feelings of anxiety and apprehension about facing new teachers and new students. We regularly returned home from our Prince Edward County cottage before Labour Day to escape the weekend traffic and to prepare ourselves for the return to school.

The return to classes in September 1990 was especially challenging. I had been away from the law school for three years, and I was going back with the added responsibility of the deanship. One of my first duties was to give the welcoming address to the first-year class. I worked very hard to strike the right note. I did not want to frighten them the way Dean Wright had frightened me in 1966, but I did want to impress upon them the significance of the path upon which they were about to embark.

When I became Dean, the law school had approximately forty full-time scholars, many of whom were cross-appointed to other U of T faculties. Almost all of our first-year students had an undergraduate degree, and over thirty had graduate degrees. They were selected primarily based on undergraduate grades and Law School Admission Test (LSAT) scores, and especially for students who fell into a special category (mature students who had been out of school for five years and Indigenous students), we also looked at their life experiences revealed by their résumés. While most came from Ontario, two-thirds had degrees from universities other than the University of Toronto. Subjects like political science, history, economics, and philosophy were the most common student choices, although they were not favoured by our admissions process, and we admitted students from a very wide range of disciplines. Each year, we admitted about 175 students from a pool of about 2500 applicants.

The graduate program had expanded to approximately 30 students, about two-thirds of whom were enrolled in the LLM program, which required both course work and a thesis. Most of the graduate students were foreign, and the law school had made a significant effort to make scholarships available.

The first-year LLB class I welcomed in 1990 included two PhDs and one MD. The average age was 25.25 years, and a significant number were over 30, having already pursued other careers. Included in the ranks were a police officer, a nurse, an actor, a United Nations representative, and an IBM executive. I explained that, while it was likely the case that most were headed to the practice of law, they should remain open to the many other opportunities presented to those equipped with a legal education.

I told them to expect a variety of approaches to law and teaching from the faculty. Some professors would lecture, while others would pose endless questions. Some would be gentle, while others would be provocative. They would be exposed to a variety of theoretical approaches to law that would range well beyond the differences in the substantive subjects being taught. I suggested that what the faculty shared was an enthusiasm for our subject and a desire to engage and stimulate thinking and discussion about law. We also shared a genuine community of spirit, a tolerance for different points of view and a commonality of scholarly purpose.

I told the class that they would likely be surprised by the nature of the law. Contrary to popular belief, law is not a set of fixed or rigid rules to be learned and applied in a mechanical fashion. Most of the important questions they would be considering were open textured, unsettled, and open to debate. They would be exposed to a critical approach and an intellectual quest for justice, driven by a commitment to finding better answers to old questions, as well as new solutions to new problems.

They would come to realize that law ranges over so much of human activity that it is next to impossible to define its limits. Law deals with what motivates people, the forces of intellect and the forces of passion. The law is so diverse that some question whether it constitutes a distinct discipline, and they would see how much law relates to and draws upon other disciplines. They would be examining a host of social and political issues from a variety of perspectives, drawing upon philosophy, economics, history, sociology, and theories of literary criticism.

Our task was to take the theoretical insights we could gain from these disciplines and apply them to real problems to find practical solutions.

I explained that, in my view, there had never been a more exciting time to engage in the study of law. Rightly or wrongly, Canadian society was looking to the law and to lawyers for solutions to social problems. Never before had the moral, social, political, and intellectual challenges facing lawyers in practice and in the academy been greater.

I went out of my way to dispel some myths and fears. Law, I told them, is not a monolithic, hard-nosed enterprise with clear answers to every problem. I wanted to dispel two fears common to students embarking on legal study.

The first was that they were not up to the task. I assured them that the very fact that they had been selected by our highly competitive admissions process meant that, if they wanted to succeed, they could. Dean Wright's admonition to my class, "look to the right, look to the left, one of you will not be here next year," no longer applied.

The second fear was that the law will steal their mind and rob them of their moral sensibility. I assured them that that was not the aim of legal education. They certainly would learn new methods of argument and new ways to analyse problems, but that should be seen as developing and challenging their moral sense and not as an attempt to remove it. It was crucial for them to bring their experience and background to bear on the legal problems they were considering. I assured them that a sense of moral rectitude was essential if they were to live up to the highest ideals of our profession.

I urged them to fully engage with legal study. They should be prepared to discuss and debate their views in a spirit of generosity and tolerance and to create an atmosphere in which all could freely express their thinking. I urged them to become involved in the law school community and its many activities – social, athletic, political, and intellectual. They would find they had as much to learn from their classmates as from the teaching faculty.

I also urged them to commit to living a full life both at law school and in their later legal careers. Law study and law practice were demanding. They should aim to become fully engaged without being swallowed. I advised them to experience Toronto's marvellous cultural life of music and theatre. They might even try to become a Toronto Maple Leafs fan. By living a full life, they would be not only a better person but also a better lawyer. They should never forget that there is more to law than cases, statutes, and law review articles. Law is about all of life. More was required than technical competence.

As I looked at the class, I saw that we had achieved over 40 per cent gender parity but that the student body was overwhelmingly white. We had few Indigenous and racialized students, and we recognized that we had to make efforts to improve the diversity of our incoming classes.

The new class would enjoy an LLB curriculum that had greatly expanded since my time as a student. By 1990, we were offering over 140 courses. After the compulsory first year of torts, contracts, property, criminal law, constitutional law, and civil procedure, all upper-year courses were optional. Each year as Dean, I held a session for upper-year students, counselling them to take basic courses like evidence, family law, administrative law, business organizations, trusts, and taxation but also making it clear that the choice was theirs. I encouraged them to consider our many offerings in the areas of legal theory, interdisciplinary offerings with an emphasis on law and economics, and courses involving gender issues and feminist studies.

Administering the Law School

The law school was in excellent shape when I assumed the deanship. My predecessor as Dean, Rob Pritchard, had given the faculty a huge boost of enthusiasm and energy. Rob had done a terrific job fundraising for the new Bora Laskin Law Library and, with the help of the scholarly work of people like Marty Friedland, Michael Trebilcock, Ernest Weinrib, Stephen Waddams, and many others, he worked hard to put U of T on the list of the top law schools in North America.

I knew that my style was not that of a dynamic leader in the Prichard mould, but I believed I could serve the law school well with a steady hand and a commitment to encouraging excellence in scholarship and teaching. I had what was probably then, and certainly is now, a rather old-fashioned view of university administration. I believed that faculty members should assume administrative office on a rotating basis, ensuring that the university and its divisions were governed by dedicated teachers and scholars.

I was influenced by my own experience. When I entered the law school in 1966, Dean Wright and his secretary, Joyce McLennan, ran the place on their own. At Oxford, the colleges were independent. Their affairs were managed by the dons. By the time I became Dean, the administration had grown to include two Associate Deans and other officers. I was able to persuade Carol Rogerson and then Jim Phillips to assume the role of Associate Dean for the LLB program and Denise Réaume to act as Associate Dean for graduate studies. Joan Lax, who became a judge not long after I did, served as Assistant Dean, and another future judge, Bonnie Croll, assumed responsibility for alumni relations. That team, which served me and the law school very well, now looks very small. Today's university is a much more complicated place than it was in 1966 or 1990. Today's law school has a large staff of assistant deans, directors, and administrators.

While I was Dean, I continued to teach constitutional law in the first year, and I did some graduate supervision. Teaching kept me in touch with the students, which I thought to be very important. I did not want to be perceived as remote from either faculty or students. I worked hard to build and maintain a positive collegial environment, one that respected and valued different views. I maintained an open door policy for the faculty. I tried to attend workshops and seminars in addition to the special lectures and events that I was responsible for hosting.

I did my best to face the issues of the day. Feminism was certainly on the rise, part of the push for greater diversity. I tried to understand and accommodate the diversity agenda as best I could. Three of the four professors hired during my time as Dean were women, all excellent scholars. I tried to keep on top of feminist issues and to present a sympathetic image, assisted by the regular advice I got from my colleagues, especially Kathy Swinton, Carol Rogerson, Denise Réaume, and Martha Shaffer. I was very sympathetic to the idea of increasing an Indigenous presence. Somehow, we avoided the rancour and bitterness encountered over diversity issues at some other law faculties.

We faced a financial squeeze, but that, it seems, is to be expected for any academic administrator. With the help of our staff, we introduced efficiencies where possible, and I was able to convince the university to provide us with our fair share of resources. I was not a great fundraiser, and as we had just come out of a successful fundraising effort to build the Bora Laskin Law Library, it was probably not the time to launch another major campaign. I did work hard to project a positive image of the law school to our alumni and the profession in order to build a base for financial support. I did not think we had the option of increasing tuition fees, nor was that something I would have favoured at the time.

Indigenous Issues

I did my best to make our Indigenous students feel welcome and valued. I was taken aback, although I realize that I should not have been surprised, when one of them told me that my idea of law and justice was directly contrary to his belief and experience. To him, Canadian law was a source of oppression and denial. It made me realize how much work we had to do to achieve reconciliation.

We initiated a tutorial program for our incoming Indigenous students to ease their entry into legal studies. When some Indigenous students timidly suggested that we initiate an Indigenous moot, I readily agreed. I thought that the initiative would validate their perspective and allow them to participate in a mainstream law school activity on their own terms. I was deeply touched when the Native Law Students Association presented the law school with a two-row Wampum belt made by Jean Teillet, a Métis student, now a prominent advocate. She explained that it was a traditional representation of peace, friendship, and respect between two sovereign nations and allies, Indigenous people and European settlers.

I tried very hard to appoint an Indigenous faculty member. I did my best to counter that fear of my colleagues who thought we would be compromising our standards of excellence in the name of diversity by recruiting candidates that I thought had strong scholarly potential. In the end, despite making two offers, my efforts came to nothing. I managed to upset the colleagues who thought I was compromising standards without succeeding in making an appointment. But I am glad that I tried and like to think that my unsuccessful effort laid the groundwork for the appointments of Indigenous scholars who came later.

Appointments

I was delighted that my first appointment, Catherine Valcke, was a bilingual civilian and comparative law scholar. She added an important new dimension to the faculty. However, I regretted the fact that I was never able to convince my colleagues that we should expand our offerings in comparative and civil law. Some were so fully focused south of the border that I could not get them to look east to Quebec. Others were dubious about the value of comparative law. I tried to develop interest in collaboration with Laval University but again evoked no interest. I felt that the faculty was failing to take advantage of the prospect of broadening our outlook beyond the common law and to embrace Canada's bi-jural legal culture. I did not think it appropriate for a Canadian law school to adopt the insular attitudes of American law schools.

In each year of my deanship, we made an appointment, and they all proved to be significant scholars and important members of the faculty. Karen Knop, who sadly passed away in 2022, led the faculty in international law. Hamish Stewart is an outstanding scholar of evidence and legal theory. My last appointment was Mayo Moran, a torts scholar, who succeeded my successor, Ron Daniels, as Dean of the faculty and then served as Provost of Trinity College.

Opening the Bora Laskin Law Library

The official opening of the Bora Laskin Law Library on 21 March 1991 proved to be a dramatic and controversial event. Although I could certainly claim no credit for the new library – that belonged to Rob Prichard and the alumni who helped him raise the money – it fell to me as the current Dean to officiate at the day's events. Rob had assembled an outstanding guest list that included former Prime Minister Trudeau, who was to receive an honorary degree. Senior members of the profession and members of the Ontario bench came, as did retired Chief Justice Brian Dickson.

We looked forward to the celebration, but there were clouds on the horizon. The first problem was that the graduating class of 1990 were not an entirely happy and contented lot. They had endured two years of construction and disruption, with classes taught away from the law school, and they felt homeless. We finally got them back to the law school partway through their third year. Some said this made them feel added resentment, since they could now see how much they had missed.

The second problem was that the university's maintenance workers were on strike. They had picket lines at Convocation Hall, where the ceremony to confer Trudeau's honorary degree was to take place. Several faculty members were unwilling to cross a picket line, and I wondered what Trudeau would do given his long history in the labour movement. My reluctant colleagues generously agreed to stay away and not create a fuss and, when the time came, Trudeau did not hesitate to enter Convocation Hall.

The third and most significant source of drama was Trudeau's convocation address. I had no idea what he would say, but I knew that trouble was brewing. When he saw Brian Dickson at the lunch we held in the faculty common room, Trudeau said that he did not know Dickson would be there. He explained that Dickson was not going to like what he had to say. Still in the dark about his address, I simply told him that we were delighted that Dickson and his wife, Barbara, were able to join us. But Trudeau clearly was not about to change anything in his planned remarks just because Dickson was present.

As the Dean, it was my responsibility to present Trudeau for his honorary degree. I had long been an admirer. I presented Trudeau for the degree with these words:

> I am delighted that on this historic day in the life of the Faculty of Law, the University is able to honor two people so critical in Canada's legal

and constitutional development, our faculty's most distinguished graduate and colleague, Bora Laskin, Chief Justice, and our nation's most compelling political leader, Pierre Elliott Trudeau, Prime Minister.

I need not recite the dates of Mr. Trudeau's remarkable life history or the details of his extraordinary accomplishments. These facts are well known to us all. For the past quarter century, his thoughts and actions have been the focal point for debate about the nature of Canada and its future. These have been difficult years. There have been dramatic events and fundamental disagreements. Our honorary graduate has dominated this tumultuous scene through his unique combination of courage, passion and intellect. He has presented us with a vision of Canada which at the same time accommodates and transcends our cultural, linguistic and geographic diversity. Not all Canadians have agreed with his vision, but no Canadian can fail to be touched by his life-long commitment to our nation and a justice for all.

Since our coming together as a federation in 1867, no person can equal Mr. Trudeau's influence as a maker of Canada's Constitution. Under his stewardship, Canada's fundamental law became our own. The *Charter of Rights and Freedoms* will serve as an enduring monument to his profound belief in the ideals of the rule of law and a just society in which basic human rights and freedoms are given priority and are fully protected.

On this day we bring to the University of Toronto a great Canadian, a man who dazzles us with his intelligence, amuses us with his wit, delights us by tweaking the pompous with irreverence, and challenges us with his enduring commitment to our nation and to our most fundamental values.

I take great pleasure, Mr. Chancellor, in presenting to you the Right Honourable Pierre Elliott Trudeau, social activist, scholar and statesman. I now ask that on behalf of the governing council you confer upon him the degree of Doctor of Laws, *Honoris Causa*.

My citation was received with the usual applause. Trudeau proceeded to the podium to give his address.[1] It soon became apparent that he was still seething with resentment over the Supreme Court's decision in the *Patriation Reference* ten years earlier. Until 1982, Canada's Constitution was the *British North America Act, 1867*, an act of the UK Parliament. That meant that it could only be amended by an act of the UK Parliament. When Trudeau could not get provincial agreement to his package of constitutional reforms in the early 1980s that included an amending formula and the *Charter of Rights and Freedoms*, he took the position that the federal government had the unilateral right to ask the British Parliament to amend Canada's Constitution. In the *Patriation Reference*,[2] a decision that Brian Dickson described as "the most important case the Court has ever decided,"[3] a majority of the Supreme Court rejected Trudeau's position. In a complex decision that consisted of four separate opinions, a majority of 7–2 ruled that there was no legal requirement for provincial consent. However, four of the seven judges, including Dickson, held that there was a constitutional convention requiring an undefined but substantial degree of provincial consent for the Constitution to be amended. Constitutional conventions, the decision explained, are essential rules that form part of Canada's Constitution, although they are enforced politically rather than legally. The majority accepted that a court could not enforce a convention, but it could recognize that one existed. The majority held that, while the issue was not one of "pure legality," it concerned "a fundamental issue of constitutionality and legitimacy"[4] and therefore could be answered by the Court. In the result, there were six judges who held that a substantial degree of provincial consent was required, two saw it as a legal requirement, and four, as a matter of constitutional convention.

Chief Justice Laskin was one of the three dissenting judges who doubted the Court's power to rule on the convention and, in any event, found that the historical record fell short of establishing a convention requiring provincial consent. Laskin would have accepted Trudeau's argument that the federal government had the unilateral power to request amendments on strictly legal grounds.

The majority's decision forced Trudeau back to the bargaining table to negotiate further concessions with the provinces and allowed groups such as the CCLA and LEAF to lobby for a stronger *Charter*. Trudeau's anger over the majority's opinion had not abated despite his retirement from politics and the praise he had received as the maker of Canada's modern Constitution. He came to the convocation to commemorate the opening of the Bora Laskin Law Library to praise Laskin's dissent and to condemn those, including Brian Dickson, who had seen things differently.

Like Dickson, Trudeau described the *Patriation Reference* as "arguably the most important decision it ever rendered or ever will render." But their agreement ended there. Laskin's dissent, argued Trudeau, "was not only the better law, but the better common sense, and consequently it was also wiser politically. Had it prevailed over the majority view, I believe that Canada's future would have been more assured."

Trudeau recited the sorry history of failed attempts to define an amending formula that would free Canada's Constitution from the Westminster Parliament. He was determined to free the process from the "insatiable desire" of the provincial premiers "for increased power." He asserted that Canada was more than the sum of its provincial parts and that, as the only body capable of speaking for all Canadians, the Parliament of Canada could unilaterally request the amendment of the Constitution.

The majority judgment had, in Trudeau's view, "fatally tilted the doctrine of Canadian sovereignty away from the people and towards the several governments." At that point, I looked down from the platform to Dickson, sitting in the front row, not far from where Trudeau was standing. Dickson's upset over the tone and the content of Trudeau's speech was visible. As Trudeau continued with his invective against the majority judgment, Dickson turned red in the face and shuffled in his seat, showing obvious disagreement with Trudeau's attack. Barbara Dickson, seated beside her husband, tried to calm him down. The dramatic, one-sided confrontation between two of Canada's constitutional giants transfixed the audience and made me – the Dean of Bora Laskin's law school, who had served Dickson as Executive Legal Officer – very uncomfortable but powerless to act. The temperature rose even higher when Trudeau charged that the majority "chose to turn a deaf ear and a blind eye to the legal arguments which might have led them in another direction." The Court, Trudeau argued, had no business ruling on the alleged convention and then holding, contrary to the evidence, that one existed. The majority, Trudeau asserted, "blatantly decided to *invent* a convention" and wrote a judgment "which tried to lend a fig-leaf of legality to their pre-conceived conclusion." This, he alleged, was "an excessive measure of … judicial law-making."

He blamed the majority judges for the notwithstanding clause that emerged as the deal-breaking compromise in the constitutional negotiations that followed the Court's decision and for weakening Canadian unity by allowing Quebec, "a provincial government whose avowed purpose was nothing less than the destruction of Canada," to cry foul and claim to be a humiliated constitutional victim.

Trudeau's speech deeply wounded Dickson, who was powerless to respond. Trudeau was entitled to disagree with the majority decision, but he was attacking the integrity of the judges who signed it, an extraordinary move by a former Prime Minister. When the two men met after the ceremony, Dickson politely told Trudeau that he rejected everything Trudeau had said. Trudeau tried to soften the blow by responding: "Well, I did appoint you as Chief Justice." Just as Trudeau believed the majority had torpedoed his constitutional project, Dickson believed they had saved it. Proceeding unilaterally with only two provinces on side, Trudeau would have faced a major constitutional crisis and quite possibly a humiliating refusal on the part of the Westminster Parliament to agree to amend the Constitution. Arguably,

Trudeau's constitutional project succeeded because he was forced to negotiate a revised package that secured the support of all provinces except Quebec.

Alumni Relations

One of my roles as Dean was to meet former students at reunions and to attend, and sometimes speak at, professional gatherings. This type of outreach was vital to our fundraising initiatives. We made a concerted effort to connect with our graduates. I travelled to New York, Vancouver, Calgary, Thunder Bay, and elsewhere to meet our alumni and to let them know what had remained and what had changed since their time at the law school. I tried to convey the message that, while we remained true to the ideals of the law school they had attended, things were constantly changing and evolving. I spoke of the moral leadership that I thought had to come from the university, particularly in what I saw as an increasingly cynical environment. Academics certainly had no claim to superiority, but a university-based law school did have an important role to play as the guardian of the intellectual and moral integrity of the law. I suggested that, through our teaching and scholarship, we had a duty to promote the ideal of law as a stabilizing, civilizing force and as an instrument of positive social change.

University Relations

Another of my jobs as Dean was to represent the faculty to the rest of the university. I spent a great deal of time at university-wide meetings and got to know and understand much more than I had before I was Dean how the university functioned as a whole. U of T is a large institution with a complex mix of faculties, colleges, divisions, and centres, ranging over virtually every subject of intellectual enquiry and every profession. I wanted the rest of the university to see the law faculty as an integral part of its mission. Given the strengths of our teaching and research and the impressive credentials of our students, I had an excellent case to present. But there remained a suspicion that the law school was just training lawyers to become rich, so it was important to push the vision of the law school's founders, Deans Kennedy and Wright, that the best professional education was the best academic education, a combination of the abstract and theoretical with the practical and immediate.

Representing the faculty also involved a considerable amount of travel. One initiative was the creation of our Work in Japan program.

Japan's economy was booming, and there was a university-wide initiative to reach out and build relationships with Japanese universities and institutions. With the help of Tak Nakajima, a loyal U of T graduate, we were able to place several students with Japanese law firms that needed help dealing with commercial agreements written in English. I was attracted to this initiative on account of my positive experience in France in the late 1960s. It offered students the chance to live and work in a very different culture and legal world.

Papers, Presentations, and Scholarly Work

My past scholarship was recognized by my election as a Fellow of the Royal Society in 1991. However, the duties of being Dean, combined with my teaching, left me with little time for research and writing. I did manage to write several conference papers, almost all dealing with constitutional law and the *Charter of Rights and Freedoms*.

At the urging of Bill Kaplan, who was starting the publishing company that eventually became Irwin Law, I undertook to write an introductory book on the *Charter of Rights and Freedoms*. I enlisted my colleague Katherine Swinton in the project. We eventually published the book in 1998.[5] Kathy bowed out after the second edition, and my former student and colleague Kent Roach came on board as co-author. The book, now in its seventh edition, has now grown to more than twice the size of the first edition.

I visited the University of Padova in Italy in 1991. The paper I gave was later translated and published in an Italian journal.[6] I sent an offprint to my former colleague Frank Iacobucci, who told me that he was impressed by my Italian. When Joe Di Luca, then an irreverent and amusing student, now a judge of the Superior Court, facetiously complained that our decision not to offer a course in construction law amounted to anti-Italian discrimination, I sent Joe an offprint to dispel any suggestion of anti-Italian bias.

There were also two visits to Israel and the Hebrew University in Jerusalem, organized by Irwin Cotler. At the Hebrew University conference Chartering Human Rights in December 1992, I gave a paper titled "The Constitutionalizing of Rights and the Politicization of the Judiciary." Other papers were given by Justices McLachlin and Gonthier from the Supreme Court of Canada and by Justice Rosie Abella of the Ontario Court of Appeal.

I had never been to Israel, and I found it to be one of the most interesting places I had ever visited. Geraldine and I were fascinated to visit the Church of the Nativity in Bethlehem and, in Jerusalem, the Church of the Holy Sepulchre, the Western Wall and Temple Mount, sacred places of the Christian, Jewish, and Muslim faiths. We floated in the Dead Sea and marvelled at the ruins of King Herod's palace and the fortifications at Masada. The bustle of daily life in Jerusalem's streets and markets, mingled with the tensions and dangers resulting from the ongoing struggle between the Jewish and Palestinian populations, is electric. We saw well-armed young Israeli soldiers roughly handle and search a Palestinian youth, no doubt suspected of some past or planned wrongdoing, while most passersby barely took notice.

On one of my visits to Israel, Justice Aharon Barak of the Supreme Court of Israel and his wife invited the delegates to their apartment for dinner. I had met Justice Barak as he was a frequent visitor to the law school. Their apartment was modest, the food was home-cooked, and the hospitality was very warm. Judges mingled with senior government lawyers and law professors, discussing the issues of the day in a spirited, good humoured, and collegial manner. Part way through the evening, there was a knock on the door. Barak retreated with his callers to a bedroom. He emerged not long after, explaining that he had just heard and decided a *habeas corpus*–type application for the release of a group of Palestinians detained on a bus. There was apparently nothing particularly unusual about being called away from a social function to decide an important matter, and then go back to entertaining guests.

The Israeli Supreme Court, largely under Barak's leadership, was building an impressive jurisprudence of constitutionally protected rights based on the Basic Law, which, unlike our 1982 Constitution, did not contain an entrenched bill of rights. We had much to learn from each other. The Israeli constitutional vision was based on the right of dignity inherent in a modern democratic society, while ours was based on the elaboration of written constitutional guarantees.

In the summer of 1992, I participated in a similar conference in Canberra, Australia, where there was an ongoing debate about whether to adopt a constitutionally entrenched bill of rights. Sir Gerard Brennan, then a Justice of the High Court of Australia and later Chief Justice of Australia, commented on my paper.

I took what I would describe as a cautiously optimistic view of the *Charter* and its impact on Canadian law and politics.[7] I explained why I thought that the *Charter* had brought about a fundamental change to Canadian law and Canadian political debate. Many important public issues formerly within the exclusive preserve of legislative authority were now subject to judicial review. I thought that was a positive development. Governments could no longer avoid scrutiny over measures that threaten basic rights and freedoms. I recognized, however, the issue of the legitimacy of unelected judges striking down laws passed by democratically elected legislators. Constitutional litigation had become an important tool being used by interest groups to advance their political ends. The courts had become embroiled in such intractable issues as abortion, mandatory retirement, and the definition of what may properly constitute a criminal offence. These questions range far beyond what had been seen as appropriate to the judicial function before 1982, when the *Charter* was enacted.

Some critics had decried what they saw as the legalization of politics and argued that the *Charter* represented an inappropriate shift of power away from elected representatives of the people to an unelected judiciary.[8] Others argued that the courts had been too timid and were unduly restrained and deferential to legislative judgment.[9]

I argued that the courts had been conscious of the inherent limits of the judicial function in elaborating *Charter* guarantees. They recognized that, while much could be achieved to enhance the protection of fundamental rights, thought had to be given not only to what could be achieved under the *Charter* but also to inherent limits of judicial function.

I explained that it was perhaps still too early to say whether this important Canadian experiment would succeed but that it seemed to me that, so far, the *Charter* had had a beneficial impact on Canadian law and politics. Fundamental human rights were properly at the forefront of public debate. The claims of those often forgotten in the cut and thrust of day-to-day politics could no longer be ignored. At the same time, the courts had avoided the fears of the left that the *Charter* would be an instrument whereby powerful interests were able to attack progressive social and economic measures.

In his thoughtful paper, Brennan expressed what I would describe as a healthy scepticism about the prospect of an Australian Bill of Rights. He worried that the task of weighing the rights of the individual against the collective interest is "the stuff of politics" and that an entrenched bill of rights "converts political into legal debate, and judicialises questions of politics and morality." He worried that the High Court would have such "a fascinating diet" of constitutional cases that "it would in time have a diminished appetite for the pedestrian issues of law." Brennan feared that, since social and ethical values would be at play, judges could not avoid giving effect to their values "in determining whether an impugned law or executive act is obnoxious to a Bill of Rights and unjustifiable in the collective interest." Brennan also pointed out that governments might gladly shift decision-making authority to the courts to avoid taking responsibility for difficult decisions on issues such as abortion.

Brennan kindly invited me to lunch at the High Court, where we continued our debate. Following the conference, he wrote to thank me for "the stimulus of [my] paper" and reported that, since my departure, he had "been seen by some to be an unqualified supporter of a Bill of Rights." Despite his generous note, I was not convinced that I had been able to persuade him. While several Australian states have adopted bills of rights, the federal level has not done so.

Rereading these papers now, with the added perspective gained from thirty years of *Charter* jurisprudence and twenty-five years on the bench, I would say that they still largely reflect my views on the *Charter*. Much has been achieved, and the risk of an overly enthusiastic judiciary occasionally materializes, but for the most part, the results have been positive and defensible in a modern liberal democracy. Canadian human rights jurisprudence is generally well respected internationally. And even when it seems to me that the judiciary may have overreached and arrived at a conclusion difficult to justify on legal grounds, I almost always agree with the result, even if I question whether it was a proper call for a court to make.

Time to Move On

I was honoured to hold the office of Dean, but I was not long in the job when I decided that my future did not lie in university administration. I received overtures from two top-ranked Canadian universities searching for a new president and reluctantly went for one interview. But I knew that, deep down, I did not want to be a university president. I did not particularly enjoy the tasks of administration, I did not feel that I could muster the enthusiasm required of a successful university president, and, most of all, I remained attracted by and attached to the law. As I will explain in the next chapter, when the opportunity arose, I opted for the bench.

Departure and Return

As I left the office of Dean to become a judge in early 1995, the faculty began preparing for a regular provostial review of the faculty coincident with the selection of the new Dean. The committee – comprising David Johnston, who had recently retired as Principal of McGill, and two distinguished American legal scholars, Martha Minow and George

Priest – reported a year after my departure. I was pleased to learn that the committee's report was positive and encouraging. It found that, although our resources were limited relative to leading American law schools, the faculty was performing at a high level. The faculty was, said the reviewers, "a happy place" where "collegiality and civility had been taken to a high order of operational perfection" and that "lively debate on important legal and organizational differences took place without undue rancour" or division. The committee stated that, to achieve its ambition, the faculty needed more resources. The person appointed to replace me as Dean, Ron Daniels, an energetic and effective fundraiser, was exactly the right person for that job.

The law school to which I have returned as Distinguished Jurist in Residence following my retirement from the bench in 2020 is very different from the law school I left upon my appointment as a judge in 1995. The teaching faculty has grown in numbers and range of interests. The faculty now offers the JD, rather than the LLB, in recognition of the fact that, for our students, law is a postgraduate degree. There are more students entering the law school each year both in the JD stream and in the graduate program, which now emphasizes research and has a significant number of students in the doctoral program. The curriculum has continued to expand the variety of offerings, and theoretical and interdisciplinary approaches to the study of law have become even more dominant.

One of the most encouraging and positive changes is the dramatic improvement in the diversity of the first-year class. Over half the class identify as female, just over forty per cent identify as racialized, and over thirty per cent were born outside Canada. The class now reflects Canada's diversity in a way that it did not during my time as Dean, although there is still work to be done, particularly in Black and Indigenous communities.

11
Trial Judge

I started my twenty-five-year judicial career in 1995 as a trial judge. I found the work to be challenging and rewarding. I was on the front line of the justice system, hearing cases covering a wide variety of subjects. From my time as a law student, I was attracted to law as an intellectual discipline that has immediate practical consequences. It was refreshing to step down from the ivory tower and start working directly with lawyers and litigants to find just solutions to everyday problems, and I spent four and a half happy years as an Ontario trial judge.

Appointment to the Bench

Early in 1994, I received an unexpected call from Chief Justice Antonio Lamer. He told me that he considered it to be part of his job to recommend people he thought to be worthy candidates for the bench. He was meeting with Allan Rock, the Minister of Justice, and he asked me if he could put my name forward. The timing was not ideal. I was only in the fifth year of my seven-year term as Dean. But I knew that opportunities like this did not often arise. I knew Allan Rock, and the happy coincidence of having both the recommendation of the Chief Justice of Canada and a Minister of Justice who knew me might not recur. I thanked the Chief Justice for his confidence in me and called him back the next day to ask him to please put my name forward.

Chief Justice Lamer was very clear on one point. He wanted me to apply to be a trial judge and not to aspire to the Court of Appeal until after I had done some trial work. He had served as a trial judge before being appointed to the Court of Appeal of Quebec. Like Brian Dickson, he loved being a trial judge and, like Dickson, he thought that some trial experience was essential preparation for an appellate role, especially for someone like me, who had an essentially academic background. I knew that some of my academic colleagues would find it difficult to understand why I would accept an appointment as a trial judge, but I accepted Chief Justice Lamer's advice.

I completed the application, much simpler and shorter than what is now required. My work at the Supreme Court stood me in good stead. Brian Dickson and Peter Cory supported my application, as did my former colleague and Dean Frank Iacobucci, by then on the Supreme Court. My application went before the Advisory Committee for Judicial Appointments and, almost a year later, in December 1994, I was told that the committee's assessment had been forwarded to the Minister of Justice.

I was at a law school function when Justice Minister Rock called my home in January 1995 to advise me of my appointment to the Ontario Court of Justice, General Division, now the Ontario Superior Court of Justice. My son, Stephen, then fourteen, answered the phone. No doubt disappointed that the call was not from one of his friends, he said rather abruptly, "No he is not home." Geraldine asked him who had called. He said, "I don't know, but it sounded like Allan Rock. Why would he be calling Dad?" Fortunately, Allan Rock did not give up and called me back later that evening to advise me of my appointment.

I was warmly welcomed to the court by Chief Justice Roy McMurtry (whom I knew from my work as an author and as a Director of the Osgoode Society for Canadian Legal History), Associate Chief Justice Patrick LeSage, and Regional Senior Justice Archie Campbell. I was delighted to find that my office was beside that of Jim MacPherson. Somehow, we managed to have adjacent offices, both on the Superior Court and on the Court of Appeal, for my entire twenty-five years on the bench. Jim, who, like me, had become a judge after an academic career and serving as Brian Dickson's Executive Legal Officer, was a close friend and colleague and great support from the time I joined the trial court.

I was appointed the same day as Fran Kiteley. We did not know each other before but became close friends partly because of our coincident appointments but mostly because Fran has a cottage in Prince Edward County where we often get together.

Brian and Barbara Dickson attended my swearing-in as did Justices Cory and Iacobucci, and many friends and colleagues from U of T and the bar, including Geraldine's uncle, W.R. Poole, QC. My mother was there and, as I said at the time, unlike my wife and children, she probably believed all the nice things that were said about me. I felt it important to strike a note of humility, so I mentioned the law student who told me that he had always held judges in awe but added: "When someone like you is appointed, it kind of demystifies the whole thing." I also related the comment from a U of T colleague that I would be up to the task of judging provided that before I made any important decision, I checked first with Geraldine. I paid tribute to the support of my family and U of T colleagues, what I had learned at MacKinnon McTaggart, and the inspiration I had drawn from my time at the Supreme Court working for Brian Dickson.

Ontario Court of Justice, General Division

The court to which I was appointed had the unfortunate title of Ontario Court of Justice, General Division. Ian Scott, an outstanding advocate and Attorney General from 1985 to 1990, was determined to reform Ontario's court system. He thought that the courts were inefficient and that the judges of the Supreme Court of Ontario had an exaggerated sense of their own importance. The first step in his long-term goal was to merge all Ontario courts in 1989[1] to amalgamate what was then the Supreme Court of Ontario with the County and District Courts. This infuriated the trial judges of the Supreme Court of Ontario, a select group of about sixty judges, who sat at the top of the trial court hierarchy. They sat in Toronto but also travelled around the province on assizes to try the most serious civil and criminal cases. They looked down on their County and District Court judicial colleagues and certainly wanted no part of an amalgamated court. Some of the Supreme Court judges contributed to their own demise by being far too full of themselves and often impatient and nasty in court.

The court was regionalized, and going out on assizes was eliminated. All judges, whether appointed to the Supreme Court or the County Court, were to become judges of the same court. This new court had the pedestrian label of Ontario Court General Division.

By the time of my appointment, many of the former Supreme Court judges had retired, but several remained. Resentment over the change was dissipating. Most of my new colleagues were either former County Court judges or judges who had been appointed to the General Division. But some of the former Supreme Court judges who remained still felt that the Scott reforms were an affront to judicial independence. I did not think that Scott's reforms posed any threat to judicial independence. The purpose of that principle was not to benefit judges but to ensure litigants the benefit of an independent judiciary. We had what we needed to fulfil that: tenure of office, the guarantee of a good salary and pension, and complete independence to decide cases as we saw fit. As a newcomer to the world of judging, I was disturbed by the fact that some judges asserted claims for elevated status or added benefits in terms of judicial independence. I thought that these claims demeaned and threatened the principle of judicial independence. If the public thought that the principle of judicial independence existed for the personal benefit of judges, the public would quickly and properly become highly suspicious of the principle itself.

Gradually, the hard feelings over court merger faded and, shortly before I left the trial court for the Court of Appeal, the court was appropriately renamed as the Superior Court of Justice.

The Toronto region consisted of approximately 100 judges and was organized in "teams" – civil, criminal, family, commercial, or Divisional Court. One served on a team for six months. The "team leaders" worked with the trial coordinators to ensure that a judge was available to hear the cases assigned to the team. My first assignment was to the civil team led by Lee Ferrier, a wise, sound, and practical judge who was very supportive.

Justice Douglas Carrothers, whom I knew from my involvement with the Cambridge Lectures, discussed in Chapter 13, was assigned to be my mentor. This involved me shadowing Doug as he attended his judicial duties for a week or so. Doug had the reputation of being a tough and, at times, impatient judge, but I saw nothing of that during my mentorship. Apart from that week and the helpful casual advice one could receive from other judges, there was no instruction or preparation for the job. There was a course for newly appointed judges, but that took place only once a year, and I had been appointed just after the course had taken place. Like all other judges, I was thrown into the deep end on the assumption that I could swim. But the spirit of the court was highly collegial, and I learned a great deal from lunch time discussions in the judges' dining room, where good humour as well as sage advice prevailed.

Most judges were appointed after a successful career in practice, usually as advocates in the civil and criminal courts. The appointment of Professor Bora Laskin to the Ontario Court of Appeal in 1965 signalled a shift in attitude about the background required for judicial office. By the time of my appointment, it was more common to have academics appointed to the bench, although they were still viewed with mild suspicion by some members of the judiciary and the practicing bar. I did not detect any concern about my background. I was warmly welcomed by my new judicial colleagues and, so far as I could tell, by the bar. Justice Gerard La Forest, a former law professor, wrote to me shortly after my appointment, saying, "Not only is there a place for academics on the Bench; in Canada it is essential if we are not to end up with trees but no forest."

I embarrassed myself on my first day in court. I entered the court room with the registrar's "All rise" and stood behind the dais waiting for everyone to sit down. That, of course, would not happen until I sat down. There was an awkward silence until I finally got the message from the registrar, who looked at me and mouthed the words "sit down!" Shortly after my first day in court, I received a congratulatory note from Louise Arbour, then on the Court of Appeal, advising me to enjoy the work "and don't worry – you will figure out where (and when) to sit, stand and salute."

Transition from Law Professor to Judge

While I was unsure about courtroom formalities, such as when to sit down, I did not feel out of my depth when it came to making decisions. Nor did I find the transition from law professor and law dean to judge to be particularly difficult. My experience teaching civil procedure, criminal law, and remedies, together with cases I had argued for the Constitutional Litigation Program and my admittedly dated experience as a litigator at MacKinnon McTaggart, made me familiar with procedural rules and gave me the confidence that I could handle the work. Judges have to be generalists, ready to deal with cases from across the legal spectrum. I had taught both private and public law subjects, and I had avoided the trend in academe to specialize in a narrow area.

Being a judge certainly involves an element of isolation. When asked about the isolation of the bench, my response was that because I had always led a quiet, boring life, I did not notice any difference. I did notice that my phone did not ring as it had when I was Dean, but the solitude of the bench did not bother me. This was partly because I was working with about 100 other judges in the Toronto region. There are some obvious constraints on outside activities, such as involvement in politics, but modern judges are not as cloistered as judges were in the past and can lead a normal social life.

About two years after my judicial appointment, I gave a lecture in which I discussed the differences between law in the academy and law in the courts.[2] I identified three differences.

First, trial judges find facts, while academics develop doctrine and theory. I found that, as a trial judge, I was preoccupied with the facts. In the real world, facts are both central and troublesome. The best legal theory evaporates in the absence of the facts required to prove the case. The trial judge's focus on the facts makes the trial an engaging human process that requires common sense and compassion.

One of my colleagues on the Court of Appeal, Justice Louise Charron, used to say that when she became an appellate judge, she felt she had moved from being a treating physician dealing with a living body and trying to understand it and make it better, to being a pathologist dealing with a corpse. She saw her job as an appellate judge as trying to figure out what, if anything, had gone wrong. Work in the academy is similarly more pathological than the work of a trial judge.

Second, trial judges provide answers, while academics ask questions. Trial judges face an enormous pressure to decide. Presiding at trial means making many evidentiary and procedural rulings and rendering judgment at the end of the case. Trial judges have no margin for error. Appeals are costly and relatively infrequent, and most cases end at trial. The decisions of trial judges are very important to the litigants, even if the issues involved seem trivial to legal scholars. The judge has a duty to decide promptly and justly. The litigants will have focused enormous amounts of time and energy on their dispute, and they place their fate in the hands of the judge.

Academics can sit back, reflect, and probe the limits of a particular doctrine or theory. There is a considerable margin for error in their speculation. That is not only the luxury of academic work but also an aspect of its important mission – namely, to be constantly questioning and pushing the limits.

Third, trial judges focus on the micro level in resolving discrete, defined disputes, while academics focus on the macro level in trying to see law as an integrated whole. The judge has a discrete, defined dispute to resolve and is asked to find the facts and faithfully apply the law in a way that achieves a practical and sensible result. The academic's view is wider, looking at the law in terms of principle and underlying theory. The academic's concern is for the integrity, consistency, and coherence of the law. The academic is less preoccupied with specific problems and more concerned with the law as a whole and its relation to social needs.

These differences explain why judges need the help of academics. Judges are rightly preoccupied with the need to decide the particular cases that confront them. The reflective approach of strong academic writing can help judges to see the narrow issue they have to decide in its proper context. Strong academic writing offers judges the critical perspective of those who have the expertise and the luxury of study, reflection and even speculation.

Another significant difference from academic life was the lack of reaction to one's work. Academics take part in seminars and debate and have their work scrutinised in the peer review process and by reactions in book reviews and competing articles. Professors must face course evaluations, and the entire academic enterprise is imbued with a sense of intellectual engagement and challenge, rather than deference to authority. By contrast, trial judges receive little feedback. The judgment is released, and the judge moves on to the next case with little idea about how the parties, the profession, or the public reacted to the decision. Most people are deferential and reticent about voicing criticism of a judge's work. Even the occasional reversal by the Court of Appeal, almost always long after the trial, does not match the rather intense scrutiny to which one's work is subjected in the academy.[3]

My experience in the academy led me to believe that there was a need to find ways to provide judges with some form of evaluation of their performance, while respecting the dignity and independence that are the hallmarks of the judiciary. However, I was unable to persuade my judicial colleagues that any kind of evaluation would be helpful.[4] They could see no benefit from an evaluation exercise. They thought that all they would receive would be griping from disappointed lawyers and their clients, and they feared that exposing judges to scrutiny would undermine respect for the judiciary.

Motions Court

I was regularly assigned to sit in "motions court," where a wide variety of matters are heard. Almost all matters are dealt with on the basis of a written record, and live evidence is rarely heard. The lists were often long and, since I would receive the papers only in the afternoon the day before the hearing, there was a great deal of reading and little time to get ready for the hearing. Most matters were procedural, but some were of greater moment – for example, should the plaintiff be awarded an interlocutory injunction or summary judgment?

To survive motions court, the judge must develop a clear strategy. If too many decisions are reserved, the judge will end up with a crippling load. I enjoyed the motions court challenge of dealing fairly and expeditiously with a relatively long list of cases. Reasons are required in every case, but not every case requires lengthy or detained reasons. The judge has to make a quick assessment of the case and decide how to deal with it. I found that most cases could be properly decided with a handwritten "endorsement" on the back of the motion record explaining in concise terms the reasons for the decision. I also found that, by taking a short break to sort out my thoughts, I could often return to court and deliver more extensive oral reasons. I would invariably explain to the parties that my reasons were essentially what I was about to say, but that the reasons would be transcribed and that I reserved the right to edit or amplify them if necessary. I found this to be an effective way to deal with the list while reserving the right to give fuller or more polished reasons if, upon reflection, I thought that more was required. What it did not allow, of course, was for me to change my mind about the result. Inevitably, there were difficult cases that could not be decided on the spot. I enjoyed deciding interesting legal points and did not mind reserving those cases and writing reasons, provided I was able to keep the number of reserves within manageable limits.

I enjoyed sitting in motions court. Most judges did not. Many of them thought that motions were a waste of time and that the parties should be urged to move quickly to trial. I did not disagree with encouraging trials, but the trial lists were crowded, and I thought that some of the better counsel were often doing their best to bring matters to a head through applications for summary judgment, injunctions, or other dispositive relief. Very often, it seemed to me, more serious business was done in a day in motions court than in a day at trial.

I was relatively aggressive on summary judgment motions – cases in which a party asks the court to make a final ruling on the basis of a written record and without having a full-blown trial. I also heard many cases where the defendant argued that, even if the facts as alleged by the plaintiff were true, the plaintiff could identify no legal rule or principle to support the claim being advanced. If I thought the case could fairly be resolved on a written record, I was willing to bite the bullet and decide the case. I felt that early resolution and avoiding a full-blown trial was one way we could improve access to justice. Not all judges shared my view, believing that it was better and fairer to allow the case to proceed to trial. The approach I favoured suffered a setback when a Court of Appeal decision took a narrow view of what cases were appropriate for summary judgment.[5] But after I left the trial court, the more liberal view was accepted by the Supreme Court of Canada in a judgment that urged lawyers and judges to make more use of summary judgment as a way to resolve cases in a cost-effective and timely manner.[6]

Sitting in motions court, I encountered a long and varied list of matters involving planning law; the enforcement of foreign judgments; whether a party was entitled or required to submit a claim to arbitration; the operation of a strip bar contrary to a by-law; appeals from the refusal of building permits; motions to enforce settlements; construction liens; motions to set aside default judgments; the proper classification of a minor hockey team by the MTHL; appeals from the Master (a judicial officer charged with deciding procedural issues); *Mareva* injunctions, or pretrial orders freezing the assets of the defendant; and rulings on solicitor-client privilege. Some of the matters were novel: for example, did the court have jurisdiction to hear a complaint about cable TV charges, or did the case fall within the jurisdiction of the CRTC?[7] The variety was challenging, and I found it stimulating and satisfying to deal with such a range of interesting legal problems.

One of my more notable trial court decisions[8] was made in a motion that extended over eight days. It involved a claim by the United States against a Canadian mining entrepreneur, Robert Friedland, for the cost of remediating environmental harm caused by the operation of an open pit gold mine in Colorado. The United States took the aggressive action of obtaining a *Mareva* injunction, an order that froze $152 million worth of Friedland's assets in Canada to protect the USA's right to collect on the judgment it hoped to obtain in the United States. Friedland moved before me to set aside the freezing order. I was familiar with the issues which I had discussed in my book *Injunctions and Specific Performance*. Freezing orders are made *ex parte* – without notice – on the theory that, if defendants know what is coming, they will take steps to put the assets out of reach. Without notice proceedings carry a serious risk of injustice, because the responding party is not present to meet the arguments of the plaintiff. To counteract that risk, the law requires parties seeking an order without notice to the other side to step out of their usual adversary shoes and make "full and frank disclosure" of both sides of the case. I found that the United States faced serious difficulties in making a claim against Friedland personally for harm allegedly caused by a company. The American lawyers who swore the affidavits to obtain the order knew of these difficulties, yet they had not disclosed them to the judge at the *ex parte* hearing. I ruled that the price of that failure was that the freezing order had to be set aside. The procedural right to a fair hearing trumped the right of the United States to be assured that it would be able to collect on its hoped-for judgment.

Probably my most cited trial decision, *Transamerica v Canada Life*,[9] was made on a summary judgment motion. The plaintiff had a claim against a subsidiary company wholly owned by the defendant and argued that the court should "pierce the corporate veil" and hold the parent company responsible. I dismissed that claim, ruling that the court was not free to disregard a corporate structure simply because it seemed "just and equitable" to do so, and I set out a more stringent test. While the plaintiff's argument might sound attractive, I have always been sceptical about open-ended invitations to do what is "just and equitable" when there are insufficient principles to guide judicial discretion. Without a manageable legal framework to structure judicial decision making, there is a risk of uncertainty, and the result could well be that more injustice than justice would be done. One can hardly oppose "just and equitable" results, but I was not persuaded that requiring the plaintiff, a major corporate entity, to live with a settled rule of corporate law would cause any injustice. And even if justice could be achieved by departing from the rule that corporations have separate legal personalities from their shareholders, that would come at the price of unsettling well-established commercial and business arrangements.

When I heard motions involving procedural issues, my philosophy was to insist that the rules be enforced. This may not sound surprising, but many other judges took a more relaxed view of procedural rules. On the theory that substantive justice should prevail over procedural rules, they thought that everyone should be entitled to a fair trial even in the face of procedural missteps. This seemed wrong to me. I tried not to be rigid and would excuse missteps if they were adequately explained. But if the rules were not given some teeth, I feared that we would fail to achieve fair and efficient justice. I was especially concerned with delay. Litigants are entitled to expect that each step in the litigation will be dealt with within the times prescribed by the rules. There are certainly cases of inadvertent or acceptable delay that should be excused. However, by routinely excusing delay, judges risk gutting the rules of any meaning. To avoid that result, I was prepared to make tough rulings to send the message that delay would not be tolerated.

Class Actions

I was one of the judges assigned to deal with class actions and eventually became the coordinator for class actions in Toronto. Class actions, cases where a representative plaintiff sues on behalf of a larger group of claimants who have suffered the same or similar loss, were relatively new. I was happy to be involved in a new and developing area of law and to be making decisions that broke new ground.[10] I presided over what I believe was the first class action that actually made it to the trial stage in Ontario.[11]

I favoured the development of class actions. Class actions provided access to justice in cases where the individual claims were small, they offered a way to deal with larger claims more efficiently, and they had a disciplining effect on large enterprises. My only reservation was that, often, the real plaintiffs were the lawyers. Many class actions involve individual claims of a few dollars that reach millions of dollars when added together. Individual class members receive little or nothing, while the lawyers, acting on a contingency fee basis, reap huge rewards if the claim succeeds. The benefit society gains from such cases is that forcing defendants to pay huge damage awards disciplines bad behaviour. I was not always convinced that the benefit justified the huge rewards reaped by the lawyers.

Civil Trials

As a civil judge, I presided over many trials. Most were less than two weeks long and often only a few days long. The trial lists were long and often double or triple booked, because many cases settle at the door of the courtroom. The trial coordinators did everything possible to avoid having an empty courtroom or a judge without a case to hear. This was good for efficiency but not for pretrial preparation. It meant that I rarely knew what I was about to hear until the morning of the trial, when I would be given the trial record. And since the trial record only contained the formal pleadings, drafted long before the trial, it often provided only a general picture of what the case was about. To really know what I was dealing with, I had to wait until counsel gave me their opening addresses. Even then, I found, the ground often shifted, both to my surprise and to that of counsel, as the evidence unfolded in unexpected ways. Such is the drama of the trial court.

The civil trials I conducted involved a wide range of subjects. I found the work interesting and invigorating. Most cases did not involve large sums of money, and few of them raised intricate points of law. But what struck me from the start was how important it was to deal with every case fairly and efficiently. The case may not have seemed important to me from a jurisprudential perspective, but I could see how important it was for the litigants. They came looking for justice, and it was my job to ensure that they received it. Inevitably, the loser would be disappointed, but I did my best to ensure that the losers were satisfied that they had been fairly heard, even if they had not been successful.

Running an efficient and effective trial is not easy. Under our adversary system, the judge must let the parties present the case as they think appropriate. But the judge must also remain in control of the proceedings and ensure that the evidentiary and procedural rules are followed and that precious court time is not wasted. Things happen quickly and unexpectedly, and the judge must be ready to make appropriate rulings to keep the case on the legal rails.

I would describe what I attempted to achieve, learned mostly from watching Brian Dickson at work, as being firm but fair. I tried to strike a business-like, no-nonsense tone when presiding. I thought it important to be courteous to counsel and the litigants but to avoid anything suggesting a casual or unduly familiar approach. At the same time, I tried to show compassion to the litigants and their plight and to demonstrate that I was doing my utmost to resolve their dispute in a just manner.

Some judges took a very casual approach to starting on time. I thought that sent a poor message and undercut our effort to show that we were making the best use of the limited resources at our disposal. I insisted on starting court precisely on time and on keeping breaks to their stated times. Because I was a stickler for time, I often went into court before counsel, who were accustomed to the more casual approach of my colleagues. My practice was to simply sit and wait. A surprising number of late-comers did not apologise for being late, but despite their lack of contrition, most learned the lesson and showed up on time for the rest of the trial.

My first civil trial involved a claim for medical malpractice for an allegedly botched nasal surgery. I heard more medical malpractice claims, wrongful dismissal cases, personal injury actions, cases involving fraudulent conveyances, adverse possession cases, actions on guarantees, claims arising from contracts for the carriage of goods, disputed real estate transactions, and condominium disputes. Although most of these were routine, there was sometimes an unlikely twist. I tried an action against Loblaws for personal injuries damages caused when the "L" from the sign on the roof of the store fell and injured an 81-year-old woman. She was a very sympathetic plaintiff, and she persuaded me that Loblaws should be found liable for the harm caused by the falling "L."

I also tried some longer trials that extended over several weeks. One was a case involving a claim by parties defrauded by an errant armoured car money pick-up company that "skimmed" cash on a daily basis, giving it a healthy cash float to play with.[12] An unsolved robbery, strongly suspected to have been staged by the principal of the armoured car company, resulted in a multi-million-dollar loss to the armoured car customers. They sued the insurer, and the insurer sued to void the insurance on the basis that it had been misled by the armoured car company. Another long trial involved the staking of a valuable mining claim.[13] The case was hard fought by some very skilled and aggressive counsel, who insisted on attacking each other. At one point, I became so frustrated with their antics that I simply stood up and walked out. I returned after about 15 minutes, and the situation had calmed down considerably.

Charter Cases

Constitutional cases are a rarity for most trial judges. I heard two notable cases, both in 1997. In the first, I rejected a claim advanced by agricultural workers with respect to collective bargaining.[14] They had been excluded from Ontario's *Labour Relations Act*, but that exclusion was removed by an NDP government. A newly elected Conservative government repealed the NDP law, and the agricultural workers were again excluded. They argued that the law repealing the NDP legislation infringed their *Charter* rights to freedom of association and equality. I ruled that there were two reasons why they had no *Charter* right to strike down the repealing law. First, the law did not prevent them from forming an association and, at the time, the Supreme Court of Canada had rejected the idea that there was a *Charter* right to engage in collective bargaining. Second, the agricultural workers were, in effect, asking the government to legislate in their favour. Freedom of association was seen as a "negative right," one that required the state to refrain from interfering but did not require the state to take positive action. My decision was upheld in a short "rubber stamp" decision by the Court of Appeal,[15] but reversed by the Supreme Court of Canada[16] in a groundbreaking decision, written by Justice Michel Bastarache, that departed from the earlier cases and started to move in favour of protecting collective bargaining rights under the *Charter*. When I was asked a few years later to speak at a dinner to honour Justice Bastarache, I described his decision as a seismic shift in the court's interpretation of freedom of association and the positive application of that freedom in the realm of labour relations.

The second case involved denominational school rights.[17] I agreed with the separate Roman Catholic School argument that denominational school rights included the right to hire Catholic teachers in preference to non-Catholics.

These cases tested my resolve to decide according to the law, rather than according to my own views of what would be best for society. I did not decide with my heart in either case. I was very sympathetic to the agricultural workers, and I have never favoured separate denominational schools. If I had felt it was possible to decide these cases as I liked, my decisions would have been different. In both cases, I felt compelled by the law to decide as I did. Even the reversal by the Supreme Court in the agricultural workers case did not persuade me that I had been wrong to reach the decision I had reached. The Supreme Court changed the law in that decision, as was its prerogative, but I did not think it was for me to take that step as a trial judge bound to follow existing Supreme Court precedents.

Jury Trials

Most of my civil trials were judge alone. However, Ontario is one of the few common law jurisdictions outside the United States that gives litigants the right to elect a civil jury trial. My first civil jury case came as a surprise. When I was handed the trial record, just before going into court, I noted that it was marked as a jury trial. I told the trial coordinator that I had never done a jury trial, and he assured me that I would have an experienced registrar who knew the ropes. When I arrived outside the courtroom, the young registrar was in a mild panic. She informed me that she had never done a jury trial. I quickly got my hands on a model opening, and later a model jury charge, and, so far as I could tell, the trial unfolded in the normal course and without incident despite the combined lack of experience of both the judge and the court registrar.

When I was a trial judge, most civil jury cases were personal injury actions, although I did conduct one jury trial involving a claim against an insurance company for reimbursement for allegedly stolen jewellery. In that case, and in almost all personal injury actions, it was the defendant insurer who elected a jury trial. Contrary to what one might expect from reading about the exorbitant awards of American juries, Ontario juries tend to be very conservative. The combination of public health care and mandatory automobile insurance is likely a factor explaining this difference. Ontario juries know that the injured plaintiff will not have to pay for health care and that large awards will only increase the cost of their motor vehicle insurance. Electing a jury trial also injects an element of uncertainty and, fearful of a low damages award and an adverse costs award, when faced with the prospect of a jury trial, plaintiffs will often settle for less than they had hoped for.

I was surprised by the relative generosity of one jury's award. The plaintiff had injured his back in a car accident. The defendant's surveillance evidence showed him capable of performing ordinary daily tasks and lifting heavy objects. He was exaggerating the extent of his injuries and, had I been trying the case without a jury, I probably would have given him nothing. The jury did not give him what he was asking for, but it did give him what seemed to me to be a significant award.

Upon reflection, I could see the wisdom, compassion, and humanity of the jury's award. The plaintiff was not an altogether unsympathetic character, and he had suffered an injury. The surveillance evidence was persuasive, but the members of the jury may have been put off by its surreptitious and invasive nature, the aggressive approach of defence counsel, and the lengths to which the insurer was prepared to go to defeat the claim. Trials, especially jury trials, are a very human process, and this case reinforced what Brian Dickson taught me, trust the commonsense wisdom of juries.

Criminal Cases

I had only brief assignments to sit on criminal cases. I was disappointed not to have done more criminal work. The problem was that former County Court judges more senior than me did the bulk of the work. Several of them were supernumerary but sat more than they had to. They did an excellent job presiding over criminal trials and had no interest in doing anything else. This left less room for other judges, like me, who aspired to do criminal work.

All of my approximately ten criminal trials involved drug trafficking. All were jury trials. I enjoyed working with juries. Several of them raised *Charter* issues: the section 11(b) right to a trial within a reasonable time, the section 10(b) right to counsel, exclusion of evidence under section 24(2), and issues involving informer privilege, wiretapping, and entrapment.

It is a challenge to explain often complex legal rules to lay persons and, on occasion, I could see that I was probably not succeeding. The fault, I think, was not mine, but with the fact that jury instructions have become very complex because of the need to satisfy the Court of Appeal that all the legal issues have been fully canvassed. Model jury charges were not yet fully established, and I relied on model charges developed by my colleague Justice Michael Dambrot that I thought struck the right balance between legal validity and comprehensibility. Despite the problem of complexity in jury instructions, it seemed to me that juries take their job seriously and that they do their best to render verdicts that were sound both in fact and in law.

In one case, I had the same experience I described with civil juries. The jury convicted an accused I probably would have acquitted because I thought there were gaps in the prosecution's evidence. However, as with my surprise over the civil verdict I mentioned earlier, upon reflection, I could see the soundness of the jury's verdict. I was probably taking too strict a view of the evidence, and I certainly did not think that an innocent person had been convicted.

Pretrial Conferences and Mediation

As a civil judge, I was assigned to conduct pretrial conferences, scheduled after the cases were on the trial list but well before trial. The objective was to settle cases, if possible, or to refine the issues for trial. We were expected to conduct seven pretrials per day, each lasting forty-five minutes, assisted by detailed pretrial memoranda prepared by counsel. Many cases were resolved, but I did not think the process was as effective as it could have been. There should have been some form of triage to identify the more complex cases that warranted more time and more than one conference. To plug that gap, like many other judges, I sometimes scheduled a further conference with the parties, but this had to be done on my own time, since there was no allowance for it in the system.

The push for active judicial involvement in case management and settlement conferences was beginning when I was on the trial court. I was not entirely comfortable with this trend for various reasons, although I was in the minority with my doubts.

Case management works best when one judge follows the case through from commencement. That ensures a consistent approach. For administrative and scheduling reasons, the court did not assign cases in that way. Case management routinely involved a different judge at each stage of the litigation. Different judges have different approaches, and there is a steep learning curve for each new judge who becomes involved in the file. This adds delay and cost. It seemed to me that the hope for efficiency to be gained through case management was lost when cases were passed from one judge to the next.

My other concern was that detailed case management "front-end loads" litigation and, while intended to reduce costs, actually does the opposite. Court management necessarily involves an expenditure of precious judicial time and added costs to the litigants who are billed thousands of dollars by their lawyers for each case conference. I accept that there are times when judicial guidance can help speed the case along efficiently. But I was struck how often at pretrial conferences when I asked parties if there had been any settlement discussions, I was told, "No, we wanted to wait to hear what you had to say about the case first." It seemed to me that, by injecting a judge into a process that should have unfolded cooperatively between counsel, we might be doing more harm than good.

A related issue where I was certainly in a minority was the propriety of judges conducting mediations. Mediation is a process where a neutral person meets with the parties and assists them in coming to an agreement. Mediation is an excellent tool, and I have no objection to its use to resolve contentious cases. My concern was with judges conducting mediations.

I was asked to mediate a highly contentious case arising from the tainted blood scandal in 1997. Actions were brought on behalf of individuals who became HIV positive as a result of blood transfusion. The action named the Red Cross as well as both the federal and provincial governments as defendants. I had never conducted a mediation, either as a lawyer or as a mediator, but for some reason, the parties picked me from a list of judges to conduct it. The process involved three and a half days of hard work. I met with the parties in plenary sessions, but most of the work was done caucusing with each side, moving from room to room to discern what it would take to bring the parties to an agreement and then to prod them to accept those terms. I was delighted when we were able to resolve the case by agreeing on a sum of money to be paid to each party, but I was not sure I wanted to do more mediation.

I have never been opposed to mediation as a technique, and I have done some mediations after I retired from the bench. My concern is with sitting judges acting as mediators. There is a fundamental difference between the role of a mediator and that of a judge. Mediators meet separately with the parties to obtain information and bottom-line positions. They use that confidential information to push for an agreement. This differs from a pretrial settlement conference, at which both parties are present throughout.

The role of the judge is to decide cases according to law in an open and public process. The role of the mediator is to deflect the parties from an insistence on their strict legal rights towards a mutually acceptable accommodation. It seems to me that mingling the roles of judge and mediator poses risks. Should the power and prestige of judicial office be used to push parties towards a non-rights-based resolution of their dispute? The judge remains, in the eyes of the litigants, a judge. The judge's views will be perceived by the parties as reflecting the legal rights and wrongs of the case. Yet that is contrary to the role of the mediator, which is to reach an agreement based on interests, not rights. And mediation often involves some serious arm twisting. I am not sure judges should be twisting arms.

I faced the mediation issue again after my appointment to the Court of Appeal. Some appellate courts – for example, Quebec – pride themselves on disposing of cases by way of pre-hearing mediation. I was wary about judicial mediation at the trial court, and I was even more dubious about mediation at the Court of Appeal. I did not think that the Court of Appeal should be presenting itself as a dispute resolution centre. I believed that our efforts should be focused on our core function of deciding cases according to law and thereby providing guidance to the lower courts, the legal profession, and the public on the governing legal principles. Some colleagues wanted to develop a mediation protocol for family law cases. I had no objection to parties seeking mediation, especially in family cases, to avoid the trauma and uncertainty of judicial proceedings. But I was concerned about judges doing mediations at the Court of Appeal, just as I had been at the trial court. When the pilot project for family cases was proposed, I voiced my concerns. By the time family cases got to the Court of Appeal, they had gone through a trial process that placed heavy emphasis on settlement, and if the parties wanted mediation, there were expert resources available in the private sector. My other concern was that only judges who had a significant interest in family law matters would be involved in court-based mediations, and if mediation failed, a family law expert would be eliminated from hearing the appeal. I thought that we would better serve the public by bringing to bear all the jurisprudential resources we could marshal to our core function of deciding cases. The pilot project was undertaken, but so far as I am aware, it attracted few cases, and the Ontario Court of Appeal never adopted a full-scale mediation initiative.

Self-Represented Litigants

Self-represented litigants present a serious challenge. Most are not familiar with procedural rules or the rules of evidence and, while they feel strongly about their case, they have little idea how to present it effectively. The judge must be tolerant and patient. But at the same time, the judge is required to follow the rules and decide cases according to the law. It is a delicate art to strike the right balance to achieve fair and efficient justice in the courtroom.

One of the most challenging and least sought-after civil assignments that involved in-person litigants was the Landlord and Tenant Court, now replaced by the Landlord and Tenant Board. "L and T court" was our version of the "People's Court," where speedy justice was administered. We were required by law to deal with these cases summarily, although they involved important issues for the parties. The "L and T" judge had their work cut out to get through a list of about forty cases per day. Other judges who had finished their work regularly volunteered to take on part of the load, and I spent many afternoons conducting landlord and tenant trials.

Chief Justice Patrick LeSage asked me to assume responsibility for administrative aspects of the Small Claims Court. This gave me another exposure to "People's Court"–type proceedings. I did not sit in the Small

Claims Court, but I did meet regularly with the dwindling number of judges who had been appointed to that court. I helped them arrange education sessions and advised the Chief Justice on the appointment of lawyers to serve as part-time *ad hoc* judges. I also advised the Chief Justice on complaints brought against judges sitting in the Small Claims Court.

Divisional Court

I sat for several weeks as judge of the Divisional Court, comprised of three Superior Court judges. The Divisional Court, unique to Ontario, hears applications for judicial review of the decisions of administrative tribunals and some appeals from trial judges. This was my introduction to the process of collegial decision making, sitting and working with two colleagues. I found that process engaging, although I was surprised by the rude and dismissive way a few of my fellow judges treated counsel. Having had a brief exposure to the nastiness of old-school judges during my time in practice, I had little patience for this type of behaviour.

It was as a judge of the Divisional Court that I had my first judicial encounter with the law of defamation, the subject of my book on the Currie libel trial of 1928.[18] I wrote a judgment making what seemed to me a commonsense change to the law but one that seemed to cause some consternation to the senior defamation lawyer who argued the case.[19] The issue was whether the defendant newspaper could plead that the article at issue had a lesser meaning than that alleged by the plaintiff and argue that the lesser meaning was true. The plaintiff, a franchise company, claimed that the story published by the newspaper called the plaintiff a "cheater." The defendant newspaper denied that it had called the plaintiff a cheater and pleaded that it had stated that the plaintiff "exploits, takes advantage of, abuses and/or treats unfairly its franchises." Relying on an earlier Ontario decision, the plaintiff disputed the defendant newspaper's right to defend the case by saying that it had not called the plaintiff a cheater, but only that the plaintiff "exploits, takes advantage of, abuses and/or treats its franchises unfairly"; I followed an English decision and held, "It is important, in the interests of freedom of expression and freedom of the press, for the newspaper to be allowed to defend itself fully by presenting its entire case for consideration. From this perspective, it is difficult to see why the newspaper should not be able to defend itself by saying 'this is what we meant and what we meant is true.'"[20]

Scholarly Work

I managed to maintain some scholarly involvement during my time on the trial court. I continued my involvement with the Cambridge Lectures and spoke regularly at NJI programs. I prepared the annual updates for my injunctions book, and I spoke at judicial seminars for other courts, usually on the topic of remedies. I worked rather sporadically on a biography of Chief Justice Dickson that I had started when I was Dean and that I will discuss in Chapter 13. I also wrote a paper on judicial discretion[21] for a CIAJ conference, in which I started to outline some of the ideas that I would develop more fully several years later in *Good Judgment: Making Judicial Decisions*.

My most exotic scholarly adventure was to present two papers at a conference in Kenya: "Fundamental Rights and Freedoms in the Criminal Law: The Canadian Experience" and "The Constitutionalization of Rights and the Role of the Judiciary." The invitation had come while I was still at the law school, but the conference was postponed, and I delivered the papers after my appointment to the bench.[22] My judicial experience had not caused me to change my mind. I defended the judicial protection of fundamental rights in language I am comfortable with today. I argued that "adjudication, constrained by the obligation to justify decisions through reasoned elaboration in terms of principle and precedent, is distinguishable from politics where there are few constraints save the ultimate need in a democracy to attract majority support." There is a risk of politicization of the courts, but that risk can be managed if judicial review is appropriately focused on the values of individual autonomy and respect. Courts should, I argued, steer away from economic rights and focus on the protection of minorities and vulnerable groups and on the values necessary to strengthen democracy: "A true democracy is surely one in which the exercise of power by the many is conditional on respect for the rights of the few."

I also wrote a paper for a conference at the University of New Brunswick Law School to honour the judicial career of Gerard La Forest, who had retired from the Supreme Court of Canada.[23] I considered changes in the vocation of judging from the time La Forest was a law student until his retirement, similar to the changes I had witnessed from my time as a law student in the late 1960s until my appointment to the bench. When La Forest graduated in 1949, the Supreme Court of Canada was slowly emerging from the shadow of the Privy Council. Formalism was the dominant judicial philosophy, and judges were reluctant to openly admit to any law-making role. By the time of his retirement, judicial law-making became a recognized fact of Canadian law and politics, a shift in which La Forest had played a central role. La Forest had studied at Oxford and Yale, practised, taught, contributed scholarly work as an academic, and served in government. I argued that he had combined "Oxford's analytic rigour, Yale's integration of social science, a practitioner's eye for what was needed to achieve justice in individual cases, a scholar's understanding of the broad sweep and direction of the law, a law reformer's zeal for improving the law, and a senior public servant's understanding of the demands and realities of government," a background few judges could match.

Moving to the Court of Appeal

I enjoyed my four and one-half years as trial judge and would have been happy to remain for longer. The work was varied, challenging, and at the heart of the administration of justice. I was proud to be a part of that enterprise.

I did not hesitate to accept an invitation from Chief Justice Roy McMurtry who had moved on to be Chief Justice of Ontario, to sit as an *ad hoc* judge of the Court of Appeal for two different weeks.[24] I enjoyed my two weeks and the further exposure it gave me to collegial decision making and to the very different role of an appellate judge. In one case, I felt compelled to dissent from a judgment given by two senior judges.[25] I feared that my temerity might disqualify me from consideration for an appointment to the Court. My dissent did not persuade my two colleagues, but to their credit, they respected my right to disagree and, about a year and a half later, I was appointed to the Court of Appeal.

12
Court of Appeal

I had the privilege of being a member of the Court of Appeal for Ontario for twenty-one years. The work was intense and demanding, and the responsibility of being the court of last resort for all but a very few Ontario cases was heavy. But the burden was easy to bear because I was part of a group of dedicated, hard-working, collegial, and legally skilled fellow judges. Much as I enjoyed the work of the trial court, as an appellate judge, I found a place where I could make better use of my scholarly background. I could not have found a more congenial professional home.

Appointment to the Court of Appeal

I was appointed to the Ontario Court of Appeal on 25 May 1999, the same day as my friend and colleague, Jim MacPherson. Jim and I shared a great deal: we had both been academics and law deans, and we had both served as Executive Legal Officer at the Supreme Court of Canada under Chief Justice Brian Dickson. The coincidence of being appointed on our mentor's birthday was but one of the unlikely features of our appointments.

Dickson died several months before our appointments, but after we both received the call from the Minister's office, Jim suggested we call Barbara Dickson to share our good news. The three of us had an emotional moment when Mrs. Dickson responded, "Brian would have been so proud." She then said, "Oh my goodness, and today would have been his eighty-third birthday."

Justice Minister Anne McLellan attended our swearing in, and three future colleagues also spoke: Ontario Deputy Minister of Justice and future Supreme Court of Canada Judge Andromache Karatkasanis; Eleanore Cronk on behalf of the Advocates' Society; and Law Society

Treasurer Bob Armstrong. Barbara Dickson and my classmate Brian Dickson Jr. attended, as did Ian Binnie, by then on the Supreme Court of Canada, my family and many friends and colleagues from the bar, U of T, and the trial court. Because Jim was a trial judge before me, his appointment was first. He insisted that he was appointed a minute before me. I say it was a millisecond, but I could not dispute the fact that he was the senior judge so that, when we sat together in the years to follow, he always presided. I sat with Jim on my last day in court in 2020. Jim generously suggested that, for our final day together on the bench, I should take the presiding role, but I demurred and respected his minute – or millisecond – of seniority to the last.

The Court I joined had seventeen members. Roy McMurtry, who had welcomed me to the trial court as Chief Justice, repeated his welcome in his new capacity as Chief Justice of Ontario. I was proud to join a very strong Court that included three future Supreme Court of Canada judges – Justices Abella, Charron, and Moldaver – and several others who were equally capable of filling that role. The atmosphere at the Court was positive and collegial. I could not have felt more welcomed. During my twenty-one years on the Court, I served with over fifty different colleagues. When I retired on 28 February 2020, the Court had expanded to approximately thirty judges, including those who, upon reaching eligibility for retirement, had elected part-time supernumerary status. Only three judges remained from the Court I joined in 1999: Justices David Doherty, Kathryn Feldman, and Jim MacPherson.

I served under three Chief Justices during my time on the Court of Appeal. Roy McMurtry, who served as Chief Justice from 1996 to 2007, can best be described as a legal statesman.[1] He had a successful career as a trial lawyer, politician, diplomat, amateur painter, and finally as a judge. He was one of Ontario's finest Attorneys General when he played a crucial role in brokering the compromise that made possible the adoption of the *Charter of Rights and Freedoms*. I have already mentioned the important contribution he made by founding the Osgoode Society for Canadian Legal History. Roy had the respect of his judicial colleagues who appreciated the strong moral leadership he brought to the office of Chief Justice.

Chief Justice Warren Winkler, in office from 2007 to 2013, had been a successful labour lawyer before becoming a judge. He is a consummate negotiator, mediator, and dealmaker. He had a successful run as a trial judge where he led the development of class actions in Ontario. His appointment directly to the office of Chief Justice of Ontario from the trial bench came as a surprise as it was widely expected that Associate Chief Justice Denis O'Connor would assume the role. Always upbeat and positive with his colleagues, Chief Justice Winkler succeeded in administering the court efficiently and effectively.

Chief Justice George Strathy is an old friend from my days at MacKinnon McTaggart. His legal practice focused on the highly specialized area of admiralty law. This meant that he did not have a high profile in the profession but after his appointment to the trial bench, he quickly earned the respect of the bar as one of Ontario's finest commercial judges. I was delighted when he was appointed to the Court of Appeal in 2013 and as our Chief Justice in 2014. The combination of his superb legal skills and his dignified and professional manner equipped him to be a strong Chief Justice under whom I was proud to serve.

I was also fortunate to serve under three excellent Associate Chief Justices who looked after the day-to-day management of the court. Coulter Osborne, an experienced litigator and trial judge, was in the office from 1999 to 2001. Dennis O'Connor, who had been appointed to Court directly from the bar in 1998, held the office from 2001 to 2012. Alexandra Hoy, who had come to the Court of Appeal from a commercial law background, was the Associate from 2013 to 2020. All three had excellent legal judgment and the respect and admiration of their colleagues, and led with a capable and steady hand.

Preparing for Hearings

As an appellate judge, I no longer faced the uncertainty of the trial court list. We received the files for the appeals on our list about two weeks prior to the hearing. I sat in the days before electronic filing, so when the files arrived, I had a mountain of paper to work my way through. The parties to an appeal are required to provide the essential material from the record of the lower court in the Appeal Book, a written argument or "factum," and copies of the cases and authorities they intend to rely on. In many cases, we would also receive a full trial transcript.

I quickly realized that, given the number of cases we had to decide, and the volume of materials filed, it was not possible to read everything. I had to develop a strategy that would ensure that I was fully prepared for every case, but that allowed me to stay on top of the wave of materials that were delivered to me for each sitting week.

My practice was to first scan the factums to see what the issues were, then read the trial judgment or jury charge, and then carefully read the factums. After that, it depended on the case. Sometimes the case involved the interpretation of a contract or other document, which I would carefully read. Sometimes there were difficult legal issues that required reading a significant volume of case law. And sometimes, especially where factual findings were contested, it was necessary to read the trial transcript.

A strategy I developed, borrowing the example set by Justice Gloria Epstein, was to ask my law clerk to review the files and provide me with an oral briefing before I started my preparation. I found this to be more helpful and more efficient than a written bench memo, which was only one more thing for me to read. It gave me an advance peek at what I faced for the week and a good starting point for my own reading, and provided a way to involve and make good use of my law clerk in the decision-making process.

Oral Argument

Lawyers often ask judges: how important is oral argument? In my view, the importance of oral argument diminishes as one moves up the judicial ladder. Trials can be won or lost by effective oral presentations. By the time the case arrives at the appeal court, the issues have narrowed, and the scope for clever or inventive submissions has diminished. If the case goes to the Supreme Court of Canada, the time for oral argument is severely limited, and its possible impact on the result has further diminished.

The written factum is one of the first things the judge reads and is probably the most important feature of presenting an appeal. One cannot help but form an impression of the case and reach a tentative conclusion about how it should be decided after doing the reading. But in oral argument, points are made or clarified, and after hearing counsel, I often decided the case differently than I thought I would when I did my reading.

Like most judges and lawyers, I found the cut and thrust of oral argument to be one of the most engaging aspects of my work. I agreed with Justice Sydney Robins, who once said that the tone to be struck between judges and counsel should be one of genuine and respectful exchange. Most counsel welcome questions from the bench, since they provide an opportunity to address and, hopefully, answer the judges' concerns. Some of my colleagues were quite aggressive with their questions, and as a young lawyer I saw what I regarded as impatience and rudeness on the part of Court of Appeal judges. The prevailing tone during my time on the Court was more restrained, but we did ask difficult questions, sometimes quite forcefully. Our objective was to let counsel know where we had concerns and to give them a chance to answer.

Law Clerks

I enjoyed working with my law clerks. They came to the Court either immediately after graduation or after spending a year articling with a law firm, full of enthusiasm and fresh ideas. The selection process was and is highly competitive, and our clerks all had very strong academic records. When I started, I shared my law clerk with one other judge, but over the years, we increased the number of clerks, and I sometimes had my own law clerk.

Unlike the process at other courts, I did not have the chance to select my own clerks, something I would have preferred. The task of vetting the applications, interviewing the shortlisted candidates, making the final selection, and assigning clerks to the members of the Court was delegated to a committee. While I would have favoured a more individual approach, the committee's selection and allocation decisions were almost always sound, and I was given excellent clerks to work with.

I relied on my law clerks as a sounding board for my decisions. I encouraged them to be honest and to tell me what they thought. I did not have to agree, but the product was bound to be better if they subjected my drafts to rigorous scrutiny. On occasion, I found it was harder to get the clerk's agreement than that of my colleagues, and that is exactly what I wanted. As I grew older, I realized how important it was to have the benefit of the fresh outlook provided by law clerks. It is too easy to become stuck in one's ways, and I felt that my law clerks provided me with contemporary views I might otherwise have missed – updating my language to ensure properly sensitive usage to social change, and exposing me to the latest views from the academy on legal trends and developments.

Workings of the Court

The work of the Court was divided between civil and criminal cases, roughly equal in volume. However, because many of the criminal cases were sentence appeals that did not take long to argue, more than half of our sitting time was devoted to civil cases. Civil cases included a wide range of subject matter, including contract and commercial disputes, family law cases, personal injury and medical malpractice claims, property disputes, constitutional challenges, and the review of decisions of administrative agencies.

Each week, the composition of the panels changed. We typically sat in court two weeks per month, with the other weeks being reserved for judgment writing and pre-hearing preparation. Since we had seventeen judges, membership on the three-judge panels was quite varied, a feature that I think made us more collegial. We were not facing off against the same colleagues, week after week, as occurs at the Supreme Court and in smaller provincial appellate courts.

Our practice was to go into court with each member of the panel having thoroughly prepared for the oral argument but with little or no pre-hearing discussion. In that regard, we differed from some other provincial appellate courts, where the practice is to discuss the case before the hearing and even to assign the judge who is to write first reasons. I agreed with the rationale for our practice, namely that each judge should come to the hearing fully prepared and with an independent view of the case. Pre-hearing discussions pose the risk that pre-hearing and preliminary views will harden and that a panel member might be reluctant to depart from a view formed and expressed before hearing the oral argument.

We invariably retired to the conference room adjacent to the courtroom to discuss the case at the conclusion of oral argument. The most junior judge was invited to give their view first, followed by the judge second in seniority, and finally the president of the panel. These discussions were respectful, relatively brief, and very frank. It did not take long to determine whether we would agree on the result, as we usually did.

Collegial Decision Making

The most significant change in moving to the Court of Appeal from the trial court was that, apart from when I sat in motions court to deal with procedural issues, every decision I made as an appellate judge was with two or, if the case required a panel of five, four other colleagues.

From the start, I enjoyed the collegial aspect of appellate work. I found that the reassurance of having the support of colleagues when making important decisions easily exceeded the frustration I encountered when there was disagreement.

At one time, each member of a multi-judge court would independently write their reasons with little or no post-hearing discussion. It is now accepted practice for judges to discuss the case after the argument has been heard and to try to come to a collective decision. These deliberations are strictly confidential to encourage an open and frank exchange of views.[2] The process encourages a single or unanimous decision but respects the independence of each judge and accepts that there will sometimes be dissenting or concurring reasons. Collegial decision making combines the independence of each decision maker with the strength of a collective decision.

The collegial process operates as a discipline, discouraging judges from allowing their personal values to unduly influence their decisions. It requires judges to engage with their colleagues when debating the case in the conference room and when preparing reasons for judgment. Being obliged to discuss how and why the case should be decided pushes the members of a collegial court to focus on legal considerations shared by all. Purely personal views are, at worst, diluted, and, at best, eliminated. I also found that the collegial aspect of judging built a feeling of pride in the work of the Court. We had a common interest in maintaining and enhancing the Court's reputation as a stable, reliable institution committed to delivering justice with legal integrity.

During my time on the Court, we enjoyed the essential requirement for collegial decision making: mutual respect for the integrity and independence of each judge. I had colleagues who often saw things differently. I recognized that listening to colleagues with different views could be frustrating and annoying. But in the end, I found that the open discussion of our differences led us to a better result. No court should be a monolith. Judges who lean in one direction will render better decisions if they have to contend with those of a different persuasion.

We felt that we had a duty to strive to reach agreement. But since each judge has a duty to bring an independent mind to bear on the case, each judge has the right to disagree on a point of principle and to dissent or write separate concurring reasons. While we accepted the right to dissent, during my time on the Court, dissents remained very much the exception rather than the rule.

Dissents can be avoided by a willingness to listen to a colleague's different point of view and by accommodating differing views if it is possible to do so without compromising on principle. On a few occasions, I found that writing a draft dissent or concurrence, setting out my views clearly and forcefully, sometimes had an impact on the judge with whom I disagreed. When confronted with what my dissent or concurrence would say, colleagues were sometimes willing to modify their opinion.

The other key to avoiding dissents that was important during my time on the Court was that we usually agreed to settle for minimalist reasons that said no more than necessary to decide the specific case. I decided some cases where it was necessary to make a broad pronouncement to move the law forward, but as a general rule, I am a believer that minimalism is ordinarily the right approach. I had to recognize that each case presented only one set of facts and that it was dangerous to stray from those facts and purport to rule on issues that are not squarely before the Court. What seems right and sensible from one perspective can seem to be wide of the mark when new and unforeseen facts arise.

I rarely dissented. I did not keep a running count, but I believe that I dissented in about ten cases out of approximately two thousand cases I heard over my twenty-one years on the Court. I dissented only when I thought that the majority decision was wrong in principle. I had an equal number of dissents in civil and criminal cases. One of my civil dissents[3] was favourably received by the Supreme Court, which granted leave and reversed the majority opinion for reasons that closely tracked my dissent.[4]

One of the risks faced by a large court that sits in three-judge panels faces is that panels deciding the same issue will reach inconsistent results. Our legal staff lawyers kept a close eye on our docket to try to ensure that cases raising the same issue were argued together or heard by the same panel. If cases slipped through, the law clerks might spot the problem or as sometimes happened, it would be revealed in lunchtime conversation in the judges' dining room.

Decision Writing

When I joined the Court, we faced a backlog of cases. The lists were very heavy. The Court had only recently put time limits on oral argument. We had to place a premium on disposing of cases as efficiently as possible. Because of the backlog, many appeals were launched to buy time. Those cases were straightforward. We could decide them on the spot with brief oral reasons or a handwritten "endorsement" on the back of the appeal book that was read out when we returned to court.

I marvelled at the skill some of the senior members of the Court had developed to craft concise but sufficient language to capture the essence of our decision and to demonstrate to the parties that we had heard and grasped their submissions. Justice Marvin Catzman was an exemplar of that art. Justice George Finlayson often led us back into court after our conference, delivered a rather mumbled oral decision indicating how we would decide the case, and then appeared at my office first thing the next morning with a polished decision that he said he had "dusted up" from his oral reasons.

If the case raised a difficult issue that required further thought and reflection, we reserved our decision and prepared full reasons. One of the members of the panel would agree to prepare the reasons. Once written, the reasons were circulated to the other members of the panel, who would often offer comments and suggestions. The principal author took those comments and suggestions into account, and eventually the final draft signed by all members of the panel was released.

By full reasons, I mean a decision that identifies the issues argued, sets out the relevant facts, provides a full account of the applicable law, and explains how the law applies to the facts of the case. We called this category of reasons "judgments" and applied it if the case we were deciding was likely to serve as a precedent in the future. We also often reserved and wrote fuller reasons when reversing a trial decision out of respect for the judge and the need to demonstrate why the three of us disagreed with the way the trial judge had decided the case.

When I undertook to write first reasons, I worked closely with my law clerk but did not delegate the task of preparing a first draft. I discussed difficult issues with other members of the panel and occasionally with another member of the Court who had not sat on the case. I did not think it proper to discuss our cases with lawyers or academics or to go outside the Court for help or advice. The draft reasons would be edited by my law clerk and circulated to the other members of the panel. Each member of the panel was expected to respond quickly with comments and suggestions. This might involve face-to-face meetings or, more usually, handwritten or "track changes" comments on the draft.

Our practice with respect to reasons evolved and changed during my time on the Court. Once the backlog was cleared, the incentive on litigants to launch appeals to buy time was removed, and the proportion of cases that could be dealt with in brief reasons declined. The principle that a court or judge should deliver a properly reasoned decision had been given added emphasis by the Supreme Court of Canada.[5] We were being asked to reverse trial judges on the ground that they had failed to explain adequately their decisions, and we could not avoid that responsibility in our own work.

These factors made us rethink our practice. We effectively abandoned the "endorsement" approach for the more routine cases and delivered what we called "reasons for decision" of a few paragraphs or pages. Regrettably, I think we may have moved from saying too little to saying too much. The length of our decisions, even for routine cases, increased with the passage of time, and they now read more and more like judgments that provide a full explanation of the background facts and lengthy citation of the legal authorities.

This is but one aspect of what appears to be a general trend in all courts towards more lengthy judgments. I think that development is regrettable. Such judgments often contain excessive factual detail or stray beyond what is required to decide the case before the court. Lengthy judgments are difficult for the profession and the public to digest. The litigants are entitled to a coherent explanation of why they won or lost the case. The profession and the public are entitled to see that there was a principled basis for the decision. Those objectives can be accomplished with concise reasons that go directly to the contentious issues and are missed by lengthy, impenetrable reasons. The bedrock principle that a litigant is entitled to a reasoned explanation of the result can be satisfied in "error correction cases" – cases that do not involve difficult or contentious points of law – with concise reasons of a few paragraphs or pages. I found that, even for cases that decided contentious points of law, my reasons rarely exceeded thirty pages. When I wrote a judgment, I was not writing a textbook explaining everything or displaying my knowledge. Instead, I was deciding a specific case. As my colleague Jean Marc Labrosse used to preach, we are writing judgments, not doctoral theses.

I placed a premium on timely decisions. No doubt to the annoyance of some of our colleagues, Jim MacPherson and I regularly advocated procedures designed to expedite the Court's decisions. This was a view we absorbed from Chief Justice Dickson, who strove to achieve timely decisions at the Supreme Court. I always pictured the anxious litigant who woke up each morning thinking "Will they tell me today whether I won or lost?" I thought that the statutory limit of six months for reserved judgments was more than generous and that there was rarely a good reason for reaching, let alone exceeding, that limit.

When writing a decision, I found it very important to start writing as soon after the oral argument as possible. At that point, the case was fresh in my mind, and I was focused on the precise issues the parties had argued. If I put off writing, my reasons seemed to become longer and less focused. When speaking to other judges about judgment writing, I always said "judgments are not like wine – they do not improve with age."

All judges must write reasons, but it is not the favourite part of the job for all. I found the work intellectually challenging. Judgment writing combined intellectual enquiry with finding practical solutions to real-world problems. This was the feature that had attracted me to the law in the first place. I did my best to come up with legally sound results that provided the parties with a workable solution to their dispute. I was eager to take on the challenging and interesting cases, which meant that I probably had more than my fair share of them. Given the nature of my interest in the law, I could not have found a better place to be than the Court of Appeal for Ontario.

Some of my colleagues told me that I was lucky because I found the task of judgment writing easy. I disagreed. I found it very hard work. The only thing that made it easy was that I liked it. I cannot say how many drafts I went through to get to the final product, since I wrote on my computer, sometimes using a dictation program, and I was constantly changing and reorganizing my judgments. I rarely started at the beginning. I usually began by setting out the issues, which I then used to structure the reasons. I avoided a lengthy recitation of the facts and found that an issues-based structure forced me to limit myself to the important and relevant facts.

My teaching, research, and writing from my days as an academic helped me in judgment writing. I was used to writing and, as an academic, I had tried to write for a broad audience. In my teaching, I tried to make complex legal doctrines accessible to my students by focusing on the basic principles. This was helpful training for a future appellate judge. Judgments should also be accessible and focus on basic principles.

Some of my decisions dealt with issues I had faced as an academic. I wrote several decisions dealing with conflict of laws, the legal rules that apply when a claim in one jurisdiction has a cross-border dimension. While I had never taught the subject as an academic, I was quite interested in it and, as explained in Chapter 6, I had done some writing on the subject. Could an out-of-province litigant injured in a car accident in another province require the other driver to defend the case in the injured party's home province?[6] Did it matter if the accident occurred in the United States or Cuba while the injured party was on vacation or working at a resort?[7] When should a Canadian court recognize an American class action decision?[8]

My decisions on those issues were influential and, as I found when I visited law schools, became staples of the curriculum until the law was settled by a decision of the Supreme Court.[9] The challenge in writing these decisions was that the law had been liberated from its rigid framework, the product of nineteenth-century English cases, by a series of Supreme Court of Canada decisions. Those decisions, however, were cast in terms of broad principles rather that rule-like detail. That meant that my job and that of other judges was to flesh out those principles in workable operational terms that could be used by trial judges. The new principles corresponded closely with what I had written as an academic, and my background in the subject better equipped me to explain how and where I thought the law should go.

I tried to think of three audiences when I was writing a decision. My first and most important audience was the litigants, especially the losing party. I tried to demonstrate that I had understood the evidence, carefully considered their arguments, and not taken extraneous considerations into account. Surprisingly often, not long after releasing a decision, I would encounter the losing lawyer. It was very important for me to be able to look that lawyer in the eye, confident that, however disappointed they might be, they would still think that I had done my honest best to render a properly reasoned decision.

My second audience was the Supreme Court of Canada, even though few Court of Appeal judgments make it all the way to the highest court. Knowing that your decision will be set aside on appeal is a powerful discipline on judicial decision making.

My third audience was the wider legal community and the public at large. I wanted my reasons to demonstrate the legitimacy of my work, that it was based on rationality and sound principle and that the result I reached was just. As I observed in *Good Judgment*, the obligation to provide a reasoned decision cements the judge's adherence to the integrity of the legal regime and the rule of law.[10]

The obligation to provide a reasoned decision operates as an important discipline on judges. It is the legal system's way of enforcing the judge's duty to decide according to law and not according to the judge's personal opinion. The duty to provide reasoned decisions is an aspect of the modern culture of transparency that requires justification from those who exercise public power.

The Judicial Hunch

I know many fine judges who would describe the process of judicial decision making in less cerebral terms.[11] They will say that what really counts are the facts and their impression of what they think would be fair. I think that, to some extent, all judges rely on their "judicial hunch" about the right result. But that does not mean that judges do not decide according to law. Judicial hunches are the product of educated and experienced legal minds. Judges have spent their entire professional lives solving difficult legal problems, and their hunches are not raw gut reactions. And judges cannot decide solely on the basis of their hunches. They have to give reasons. All judges have had the "it won't write" moment: they thought they knew how to decide the case, but when their tentative conclusion was subjected to the discipline of writing, they could not produce a coherent judgment arriving at that result. The result that seemed intuitively obvious could not be supported or explained by proper legal authority. In my case, that happened most often when I did not agree with a trial decision, but I could not justify a reversal because I could not write reasons that would satisfy the standard of review that requires appellate judges to defer to trial decisions absent a clear legal error.[12]

I did not ask my clerks to prepare draft judgments. That practice was very much the exception rather than the rule during my time on the Court, although it is common in American courts[13] and, it is widely believed and, to some extent acknowledged, at the Supreme Court of Canada.[14] In *Good Judgment: Making Judicial Decisions*, I argue that judgment-writing imposes a discipline on decision making. Writing a decision forces the judge to work meticulously through the facts and the law and to provide a fully reasoned justification for the result. I believe that task is central to the judicial role and should not be delegated. Law clerks are bright and enthusiastic, but they lack experience and maturity of judgment. It is one thing to revise and edit a draft judgment prepared by a law clerk and quite another to write the decision from scratch. As I said in *Good Judgment*, "[g]hostwritten reasons create a risk of unacceptably result-oriented decision-making, lacking the rigour derived from carefully working out in one's own mind a proper legal justification for the decision."[15]

Criminal Cases

As I have explained in earlier chapters, I have always been interested in criminal law, but apart from when I was teaching, I struggled to find a way to work in the field. My effort to article at a firm that combined criminal law with other work floundered, and when I was appointed to the trial court, once again my desire to do criminal work was not fulfilled. As a member of the Court of Appeal, I was delighted to regularly sit in Courtroom 10 at Osgoode Hall, where criminal appeals are heard. The Court I joined had several criminal law experts: Justices David Doherty, Michael Moldaver, Marc Rosenberg, and Louise Charron. However, the Court's practice was for the most part to assign panels randomly without regard to each judge's past experience. That meant that I sat as often on criminal cases as did my colleagues who were experts in the field.

A strong case can be made for generalist judges, especially appellate judges. Specialists tend to become fixed in their ways and not to question how things are done. I found it refreshing to sit on civil cases with colleagues who had come to the Court from a primarily criminal law background. They brought a fresh perspective to bear on the issues and often had insights that did not occur to those more familiar with the issue. For example, criminal specialists tend to be sticklers for evidentiary and procedural rules – a healthy corrective to civil law experts, who take a more relaxed approach to such issues.

I felt my non-specialist background made a difference in the areas of delay and the complexity of the criminal process. I found that some criminal law specialists tended to be too tolerant of delay and unphased by the increasing complexity of the criminal process. I decided one case[16] involving informer privilege and the management of the trial process in which that issue arises. Informer privilege protects from disclosure the identity of confidential police informers. Several weeks had been taken at trial to deal with the accused's request for disclosure regarding the informer. That time, I found, was essentially wasted. The blame was to be shared by the defence, the prosecution, and the trial judge. The defence request was excessive, the prosecution's response was less than forthcoming, and the trial judge had failed to maintain a firm grip on the process, leading to an error in the application of the law. I held that, while judicial proceedings were not designed on the basis of a cost-benefit analysis, there had to be a measure of proportionality that informs the way trials are conducted. There had been a significant expenditure of resources with no benefit that I was able to discern. I wrote that "[t]he judicial system, like all other public institutions, has limited resources at its disposal, as do the litigants and legal aid." If every effort were not made to keep trials focused on the essential issues, I wrote, "there is a serious risk that our adversary trial system will simply collapse under its own weight, and we will all be the poorer. It is in the interest of all constituencies – those accused of crimes, the police, Crown counsel, defence counsel, and judges both at trial and on appeal – to make the most of the limited resources at our disposal."[17]

A week in Courtroom 10 routinely involved hearing a mixture of short appeals, usually dealing with sentence, and more complicated cases dealing with all manner of offences. Sexual assault and drug cases are the staple of both the trial and appellate courts. Most cases were heard in half a day or less. On occasion we would devote more than one day to a complex case, usually involving a homicide. *Charter* issues were frequently encountered, often dealing with contested arrests, searches, statements, and the admissibility of evidence.

For the most part, criminal appeals are very well argued in the Ontario Court of Appeal. The prosecution side is argued by members of the Crown Law Office, lawyers who practise criminal law exclusively and who are almost invariably well prepared, knowledgeable, and fair in their submissions. There is a specialized defence appellate bar that regularly appears in the more difficult and complex cases. Most of their work is done on legal aid, but the fact that they are not well paid does not stop them from presenting carefully prepared and effective arguments.

A considerable number of criminal appeals are brought by self-represented litigants. The usual reason for them not having counsel is that they have failed to convince the legal aid authorities that their appeal has sufficient merit. We heard the "inmate appeals" brought by those detained near Toronto at Osgoode Hall, and we regularly travelled to Kingston to hear appeals from inmates detained in the prisons in the Kingston area. When I joined the Court, some inmates were represented by the Queen's University Correctional Law project, but most of them had to struggle along on their own. Justice Marc Rosenberg and defence counsel Marie Henein launched an important and worthwhile initiative to help solve the problem. A select group of defence lawyers, essentially volunteers (they are paid a small daily fee by legal aid), were assembled to assist with inmate appeals. These lawyers receive the appeal materials, meet with the inmate shortly before the appeal is to be argued, and assist the inmate in presenting the argument, surprisingly often with a positive result for the inmate. The skill these mostly young lawyers display in identifying issues and presenting effective arguments is truly impressive, as is their dedication to the ideal that everyone deserves proper representation in court. Their willingness to do this pro bono work and the quality of the service they provide should serve as a model for the rest of the legal profession.

Indigenous Justice

We often dealt with difficult sentencing issues involving Indigenous offenders and the issue of over-representation in the prison population. I decided an extradition case where an Indigenous accused was wanted in the United States for drug offences.[18] Under American law, his Indigenous background would not be considered, and he would face a significantly more severe sentence than in Canada, which also had jurisdiction to try him for the alleged offences. I held that the *Gladue* principle, requiring consideration of an accused's Indigenous background, should be applied in extradition cases and that it had not properly been considered by the Minister of Justice when ordering the accused to be surrendered to the United States.

My most significant decision involving Indigenous issues concerned Steve Powley and his son, Roddy, who had shot and killed a moose near Sault Ste. Marie.[19] They were charged with hunting without a licence, and their defence was that, as Métis people, they had a constitutional right to hunt for food without a licence. I sat with Chief Justice Roy McMurtry and my former classmate and future Supreme Court Justice

Rosalie Abella to decide the first case on the constitutional rights of the Métis to reach an appellate court. The case was brilliantly argued by my former student Jean Teillet.

The Powley case engaged my interest in legal history. There was extensive and fascinating historical evidence about the emergence of the Métis people from the seventeenth to nineteenth centuries. Faced with rejection by both Indigenous groups and European settlers, through a process of "ethnogenesis," the Métis evolved their own distinctive culture and practices.

The case presented a significant challenge. Supreme Court of Canada decisions established a test for determining Indigenous hunting and gathering rights largely based on prior occupation and the situation that existed at the point of contact between European settlers and Indigenous Peoples. But the Métis were a product of that contact, and they evolved their distinctive ways long after contact. I rejected the argument that Métis rights were derivative of the rights of other Indigenous people: "The rights of one people should not be subsumed under the rights of another. To make Métis rights entirely derivative of and dependent upon the precise pre-contact activities of their Indian ancestors would, in my view, ignore the distinctive history and culture of the Métis and the explicit recognition of distinct 'Métis peoples' in s. 35 of the Constitution Act."[20] The evidence established that hunting was an essential part of the Métis culture and way of life. While conservation was an important consideration, other Indigenous groups enjoyed hunting rights, and total exclusion of Métis from those rights could not be justified. I concluded that the Powleys had a significant link with and were members of the historic Métis community of Sault Ste. Marie and that they were entitled to exercise an Indigenous right to hunt for food within the hunting territory of that community.

We were invited by several intervenors to make broad pronouncements on Métis rights. I thought that it would be a mistake to say more than we had to say to resolve the case before us: "At such an early stage of development in this area, a provincial appellate court must approach its task with due regard to the importance and complexity of aboriginal rights. It is impossible to define the rights of an entire people within the confines of one case."[21] It seemed to me that cases of Indigenous rights were very fact specific and that there was a risk that we would either not go far enough or go too far if we tried to pronounce more broadly on the rights of the Métis people. Those rights would "unfold over time in the usual incremental fashion of the common law."[22]

Reaching Just Decisions and Following the Law

Judges have a duty to reach just decisions, but they also have a duty to follow the law. Judges may be inclined to decide a case out of sympathy for an injured party, but the law may stand in the way. I encountered this problem in many cases.

Now, of course, I aspired to reach just decisions. When I encountered a case where the law seemed to take me in a direction I did not like, I felt duty bound to probe and prod the existing legal sources to see if there was not a flaw in the legal argument that produced what seemed to me to be an unjust result.

I encountered that phenomenon in a criminal case involving spontaneous statements made by accused persons upon arrest.[23] Out-of-court statements are generally considered to be inadmissible hearsay, subject to certain exceptions. One exception applies to admissions. That meant that if the statement made upon arrest was incriminating, it could be admitted in evidence at trial. However, if the statement was exculpatory – "I did not do anything wrong" – the admission exception to the hearsay rule did not apply. The accused could take the stand and deny having committed the offence, but the accepted view was that a statement made upon arrest was inadmissible as a prior consistent statement.

This rule struck me as being very unfair to the accused. Incriminating statements were admitted, and the jury would expect an immediate denial from anyone wrongly confronted with a criminal accusation. But my view as to what was or was not fair was not enough to depart from what seemed to be the accepted wisdom.

Assisted by Defence Counsel James Lockyer's thorough argument, I engaged in a careful review of the academic writing and case law, both Canadian and English. I concluded that the law was not nearly as clear as the accepted wisdom and that there was a respectable view favouring the admission of such statements in some circumstances. Admissibility was also supported by two relatively recent general developments in the law of evidence. First was the modern "principled approach" that was more receptive to the admission of hearsay evidence.[24] Second was the departure from hard and fast exclusionary rules to favour the admission of probative evidence unless outweighed by prejudicial effect or some clear ground of law or policy.[25] The judge conducting an inquiry into the wrongful conviction of Guy Paul Morin had argued for admissibility.[26] With the concurrence of my two colleagues,[27] neither of whom were criminal law specialists, we broke fresh ground, ruling that, provided accused persons did not use the statement as a way to avoid being cross-examined on their denial, the spontaneous statement made upon arrest could be admitted.

But finding a way around an apparently unjust result was not always possible. I frequently decided cases involving statutory limitation periods under which an injured party had to bring a claim forward within a specified period. Limitation statutes promote the timely resolution of disputes and protect defendants from stale claims. So do procedural rules imposing time limits for moving the case along. Limitation periods and procedural time limits sometimes operate unjustly in individual cases. Delay might not have deprived the defendant of the opportunity to prepare a full defence. Where there is no other defence to the claim except for the failure to comply with a specified time limit, it seems unjust to deprive the injured party of the right to sue. Some judges are reluctant to enforce limitation periods and time limits. I felt that if there was no proper explanation for the delay or no exception to the statutory limitation period, I had no choice but to apply the statute despite the apparent injustice to the injured party. The very idea behind a limitation statute is to define a general standard that must be applied across the board. Similarly, if procedural rules are not enforced, they cease to have any meaning. If I were to make exceptions for one injured party, I would have to do the same for another, and that would defeat the purpose of the rule or statute. Sometimes the price to be paid for maintaining a general standard is that judges have to make a decision they regard as unjust in the particular case at hand.

At times, I felt that I was prevented by the law from reaching a just result because of what is called the standard of review, which defines when a court of appeal can interfere with a trial decision. I sat on several cases involving wrongful convictions of individuals who had served many years in prison. These cases raised many of the issues that are frequently encountered in wrongful conviction cases[28] and that I would explore in my case study of a nineteenth-century murder conviction in Prince Edward County.[29] They made me aware of the frailties of our criminal process. We strive to make the process as fair as we can, but we sometimes deliver distressingly faulty results.

The experience of sitting on these cases made me worry that the Supreme Court of Canada may have gone too far with its insistence that intermediate appellate courts defer to the results reached by trial courts. Absent a clear legal error or fresh evidence not available at trial, criminal convictions are virtually impossible to appeal. Sentencing decisions can only be appealed where the sentencing judge makes an error of law or an error in principle that has an impact on the sentence, unless it is demonstrably unfit.[30] There were many cases in which I would not have convicted the accused or in which I thought the sentence was unnecessarily harsh, yet I was prevented by the authority of the Supreme Court of Canada decisions from interfering. The deference pendulum may have swung too far in the direction of protecting trial verdicts and sentences and limiting the role of intermediate appellate courts to correct what they perceive to be unjust results.

Compassion and Wisdom

The issues I faced as an appellate judge were intellectually demanding, but the legal process is also an intensely human one. Judging is not a mechanical or abstract process, and being a good judge requires both head and heart. One of my former colleagues, John Morden, widely regarded as a model judge, described the good judge as "a person who has a passion to do justice combined with the knowledge and skills necessary to give effect to this passion."[31] It is crucial for judges to understand the human dimension of the cases they decide. They must do their best to understand and empathise with the litigants at a very human level.

Given Canada's diversity, issues of equality and racial justice are ever-present in our courtrooms. Sometimes these issues are at the legal centre of the case, but more often they are unspoken issues that loom in the background and are not specifically addressed. That does not mean they can be ignored. It is very important for judges to do their best to fully understand the litigants before them. I always tried to remember that I came from a socially and economically privileged class and to recognize that understanding the very different experience of litigants takes real effort. I participated in many judicial education programs, teaching judges the importance of paying attention to the social context of the cases they decide and to be sensitive to the situation of racialized and disadvantaged litigants. Judges must be ever conscious of the fact that the way things seem to be from their perspective will not be shared by all who come before the court.

Compassion in judging overlaps with wisdom, which involves a combination of knowledge, intelligence, and practical common sense. The wise judge is one who is capable of marrying faithfulness to the law with a rich understanding of the human complexities the case presents.

My "Favourite Decision"

When asked "what is your favourite decision?" I am unable to answer for two reasons. The first is that I do not have a favourite decision, and the second is that, even if I did, I would not want to single it out. One cannot sit on the bench without realizing how important every case is for the litigants. For that reason, I would not want to suggest that one case was more important or interesting than all the others. Every decision I had to make was notable for someone.

Despite the intense effort I put into writing my decisions, they faded quickly in my memory as soon as they were released. My approach was to focus on the case I was writing, let it go without looking back, and then move on to the next decision. Rarely did I receive any reaction to what I had written, apart from seeing that leave to appeal to the Supreme Court had been granted or denied. When I come across one of my decisions, I often have to reread it to get it back into my head. I guess this is the product of a "bathtub mind": fill it up when you need a bath and then let it drain away when you get out of the tub.

My decisions, both civil and criminal, cover a wide range of issues, and I loved the variety. This is not the place for me to review a long list of my decisions. They are there to be read, and they will stand or fall on their own. I will, however, mention two of my decisions to illustrate my approach to judging: *Cusson v Quan* and *Jones v Tsige*.

Making Law

Most of the cases I faced as a Court of Appeal judge could be decided on established legal principles. But there were times when I found that it was appropriate to move the law along to meet new problems or old problems that called for reassessment.

I decided a significant appeal on defamation law in 2007, *Cusson v Quan*.[32] This was an issue I had encountered when writing my book on the Currie libel trial[33] and in my advocacy before the Supreme Court of Canada on behalf of the CCLA.[34] The traditional law of defamation was strongly pro-plaintiff: if the story put the plaintiff in a bad light, the plaintiff would win unless the journalist could prove the truth of the facts reported according to the exacting standards of a court of law. Was the rule requiring journalists to prove the truth of everything they wrote to avoid liability consistent with the *Charter* guarantees of freedom of expression and freedom of the press? If not, should we adopt the American rule that, if the matter is of public interest, the person claiming damages must prove that the journalist acted with malice, in other words, knew that the story was false?

A careful reading of the case law revealed that Canadian defamation law was in a state of flux. There was a serious rift between two lines of authority. A series of cases decided by the Supreme Court in the 1950s[35] held that the media should be treated exactly the same as any other defamation defendant. Reporting on public issues gave the media no licence to defame, and unless they could prove their story was true, they were liable. Despite these precedents, some more recent lower court decisions had allowed media defendants to raise the defence of qualified privilege if they were reporting on a matter of public interest.[36] If that plea was allowed, the media would succeed unless the plaintiff could prove that the media had acted with malice, that is, published a story that they knew to be false. If allowed to expand, that line of authority would bring Canadian law very close to the American *New York Times v Sullivan*[37] decision, making proof of malice necessary to support a plaintiff's claim.

That development seemed to be inconsistent with the Supreme Court's 1950s rulings, but the 1950s rulings seemed far more restrictive of freedom of expression and freedom of the press than was tolerable in the age of the *Charter.* I thought that the need to develop the common law in a manner consistent with *Charter* values justified departing from the 1950s decisions, but no more than necessary. It seemed to me that we needed to find a middle ground that would achieve an appropriate balance between protecting reputation and protecting freedom of expression and freedom of the press. To go as far as the media wanted us to go – adopting the malice requirement – seemed to me to be more of a leap than would be consistent with the idea that the common law should develop incrementally.

Developments in other common law jurisdictions supported the argument that the traditional, pro-plaintiff law of defamation had to change to accommodate open public exchange on publicly important issues but not abandon protection of reputation to the extent of American law. The solution I settled on was presented by the intervenors, namely the defence of responsible journalism.[38] Journalists have a defence if they can prove that their story concerned a matter of public interest and that they had taken reasonable steps to ensure both that the story was fair and that its contents were true and accurate. This seemed to me to reconcile the two sides of the debate between protecting reputation and protecting freedom of the press. Journalists had to be given some leeway to allow them to report on important public issues. The threat of a lawsuit requiring proof of the facts had a significant chilling effect on investigative reporting. On the other hand, protecting freedom of the press did not require open season on reputation. Adopting the fault-based responsible journalism doctrine reconciled the competing rights and interests in a legally principled way.

My great-grandparents Jane Millar and Daniel Sutherland.

My parents at their wedding, September 1942.

My father's brothers and sisters and his mother (back row, second from right) with her hand on my father's shoulder.

With Grandmother Sharpe at her farm, 1946.

14 Sept '68

Wedding day, September 1968. (Frederick Bull)

Magdalen College Hockey Club 1971–72. (Gillman and Soame, Oxford)

At Magdalen College with baby Anne, 1972. (Frederick Bull)

Back row: Geraldine, sister-in-law Beverly; Middle row: me, my father, my grandmother Annie Cooper, my mother, brother Ernie; Front row: Claire, Anne, and nephew Robbie, 1976. (Frederick Bull)

Faculty of Law, University of Toronto, 1985.
I am in the second row, second from left.

With Brian Dickson, Ottawa, 1990.

With Bertha and John Wilson, early 1990s.

Law School Dean, 1990.

Marty Friedland's honorary degree, University of Toronto, 2001.

At my swearing in as a trial judge with Brian Dickson
and Jim MacPherson, 1995.

Court of Appeal for Ontario, 2002. I am in the back row, third from the left. (Court of Appeal for Ontario)

Justice of the Court of Appeal. (Court of Appeal for Ontario)

Family gathering for our 50th wedding anniversary, September 2018.
Front row: Anne, Geraldine, me. Back row: Megan, Claire,
Stephen, Kasia, Matthew, Sean. (Kate Shebaz)

With my granddaughter Audrey, 2022. (Claire Sharpe)

My decision was appealed to the Supreme Court, and while the Court essentially adopted my approach, it did so in another case[39] with only a passing reference to my decision. The Court overruled my decision on the ground that I had refused to order a new trial.[40] I had reasoned that, since the defendant had not asked the trial judge to apply the responsible journalism standard, they were not entitled to a new trial. I was more disappointed with not being given credit than with the reversal, but I later received a note from Chief Justice McLachlin saying, "We are indebted to you for the fine work you did in *Cusson*."

My best-known decision is probably *Jones v Tsige*,[41] the case I decided in 2012 that established the right to sue for damages for "intrusion upon seclusion." It is the case that perhaps best reflects my judicial method for deciding a difficult case and I use it in my book *Good Judgment: Making Judicial Decisions* as a case study on judicial law-making in the common law tradition.

The case involved a bank employee who snooped on a fellow employee's banking records. Those records contained highly sensitive personal information. The person snooped on was very upset and sued the snooper for damages. The problem she faced was that the common law of Ontario did not recognize a tort, or civil claim for damages, for invasion of privacy. The question presented to the Court was whether it was time for Ontario to recognize a right to do so.

I decided that the answer to that question was yes. The law recognized and protected privacy in other situations, privacy had been accepted as a *Charter* value, and legal scholars had long advocated the recognition of a tort of privacy. Other common law jurisdictions recognized the right of individuals to sue for breach of privacy, and the advance of technology and the mass storage of private information called for a fresh legal response.

I knew that recognizing a new right to sue for invasion of privacy was a bold step. But one of the great strengths of the common law tradition is its capacity to evolve and change with social change. Modern technology had greatly expanded the capacity to collect sensitive personal information, and that strengthened the case for recognizing a new claim. I found that it was "appropriate for this court to confirm the existence of a right of action for intrusion upon seclusion" and that to do so "would amount to an incremental step that is consistent with the role of this court to develop the common law in a manner consistent with the changing needs of society."[42]

I accept that my decisions "made law" in the libel and privacy cases, but I insist that I did not "make up law." There was something in the law, albeit below the surface, before my decision crystallized from already existing legal sources a new common law rule in keeping with the evolving needs of society.

Had I been appointed to the Supreme Court of Canada, the opportunity to "make law" would undoubtedly have been greater. I was considered as a candidate for the Supreme Court twice, first in 2004 when Justices Rosealie Abella and Louise Charon were appointed and then again in 2011 when Justices Michael Moldaver and Andromache Karakatsanis were chosen. In 2004, there was no application process, but I have been told by a reliable source that I was seriously considered as a candidate. By 2011, an application process had been initiated and I was asked by the Minister of Justice's judicial appointments adviser to apply. I sent in my application but did nothing more to lobby or campaign for the position.

I was certainly disappointed not to move on to the Supreme Court but far from devastated when it did not happen. The selection of some Court of Appeal colleagues over others is bound to cause disappointment but it did not disrupt our collegiality. I remained a happy member of the Court of Appeal. The work was important, varied, interesting, and less stressful than at the Supreme Court. It is much easier to work on a court with revolving panels of three than on a court that routinely sits with the same nine judges for every case. While I enjoyed living in Ottawa during my time as Executive Legal Officer, for personal and family reasons, a move to Ottawa in either 2004 or 2011 would have been a sacrifice. I was fortunate to be a member of a very strong appellate court for over twenty years. The pleasure of working with my beloved Court of Appeal colleagues exceeded my disappointment that I never made it to the top.

13
More Scholarly Adventures

During my time on the Court of Appeal, I managed to maintain my scholarly interests. I spoke at conferences, returned to Oxford as a visiting professor, and wrote four more books. It was one of the most productive and rewarding periods of my legal life. I drew on my judicial experience and perspective when engaged in these scholarly ventures and I think that they made me a better judge.

The Cambridge Lectures

Every two years, with one or two interruptions, I attended and usually made presentations at the Cambridge Lectures at Queens' College Cambridge, organized by the Canadian Institute of Advanced Legal Studies. My association with this series started while I was an academic and continued during my time on the bench.

The Cambridge Lectures were the inspiration of Paul Martin Sr., who studied at Cambridge, had a distinguished political career, and served as Canada's High Commissioner to the United Kingdom from 1974 to 1979. Martin promoted the idea of a regular conference for Canadian judges and lawyers at Cambridge to nurture the roots of our common law heritage. The Lectures were launched through the heroic efforts of Justice Douglas Carruthers, later assisted by Frank McArdle. The Institute later added a parallel French language conference in Strasbourg, France.

My colleague Bob Armstrong served as President from 2003 to 2013, and I succeeded him in 2014 and organized the conference for 2015, 2017, and 2019. The concept was to bring together the three branches of the legal profession – the bar, the bench, and the academy – in the wonderfully collegial setting of Queen's College Cambridge. We did not deal with "how to do it" or with typical professional continuing education issues. Instead, we tried to transcend the day-to-day concerns of practising law or judging by arranging presentations, both legal and non-legal, on a broad range of contemporary issues by leading scholars, lawyers, and judges. Professors, lawyers, and judges, wearing name tags that bore no titles, ate their meals together in the College Hall, attended lectures and slept in student rooms. And there were the added attractions of Cambridge after lectures: tennis on grass courts, choral music at King's College, and after-dinner strolls along the Cam River to a pub in Grantchester.

Return to Oxford

My Oxbridge ties were further strengthened in 2011, when I was appointed as a visiting professor at Oxford to teach as part of the graduate course in civil procedure. I continued in that capacity for ten years, until after my retirement from the bench. My appointment was the initiative of Timothy Endicott, a legal philosopher, now the Vinerian Professor of English Law, who was the Oxford faculty's first Dean and who had been a student in my first-year civil procedure course at U of T. My duties were not onerous. I thoroughly enjoyed going back to Oxford for a few weeks in the spring for Trinity term. I taught with Professor Adrian Zuckerman, or AZ, as he is called by his friends. AZ had persuaded the Oxford Faculty of Law that civil procedure was an intellectually respectable subject and not just the nuts and bolts of practice. I gave a few lectures and participated in the weekly seminars where visiting scholars, judges, and lawyers made presentations. AZ was demanding of his students, but they loved him. He was also very tough on me or anyone else who presented views he did not agree with. But he always did this in the best Oxford tradition of insisting on rigorous reasoning and forceful but respectful intellectual exchange. I was pleased to contribute to the festschrift in his honour[1] when he retired, and Andrew Higgins assumed responsibility for the course. As a visiting professor, I was welcomed back to Magdalen College as an Honorary Member of the Senior Common Room, which gave me lunch and dinner privileges and allowed me to renew my connection with the college law fellows.

Writing Extra-Judicially

I have been asked how I managed to write four books while also handling the full workload of an appellate judge. The answer is the lessons Ian Brownlie taught me as an Oxford graduate student – the "fifteen-minute rule" and the "one brick at a time" approach. I managed to break each project down into manageable pieces and make use of every available bit of time. I knew I could never hope to have an extended period when I could quietly work away on my writing. I had to make use of every available moment to pick away at my project: write a sentence or a paragraph, complete a footnote, or look up a point that required investigation. It also meant working away steadily in the evening and on weekends and not spending much time on the golf course. I was under no obligation to write, but I enjoyed it. Working on these projects was simply a habit I had brought with me from academe, a habit I found impossible to break.

Few judges write extra-judicially. Some fear that it is inconsistent with the judicial role, but there was ample precedent to support its propriety in Canada, England, and the United States. I did not think that being a judge disqualified me from writing. I continued to produce annual updates of my *Injunctions* book, and Kent Roach and I produced new editions of our book on the *Charter of Rights*. I never felt that these writing projects interfered with my ability to come to every case with an open mind. I used to joke that, since my *Injunctions* book was a loose-leaf, I could change anything in it in a flash.

I did, however, avoid writing on controversial issues likely to come before the courts, and I especially enjoyed historical research. I was happy to focus my efforts on exploring interesting aspects of Canada's legal past.

Biography of Brian Dickson

Like so many other events in my life, writing a biography of Brian Dickson[2] happened almost by accident. The project had a modest beginning when I was still Dean at U of T. Peter Oliver, a York University history professor who served as Editor-in-Chief of the Osgoode Society for Canadian Legal History, was looking for someone to interview Dickson for an oral history. I had worked closely with Peter when I published *The Last Day, The Last Hour: The Currie Libel Trial* with the Osgoode Society in 1988. Peter knew that Dickson would likely be reluctant to be interviewed but thought that he might agree if I did the oral history given my prior association with him as Executive Legal Officer. After some gentle persuasion, Dickson agreed to do an oral history, as did I.

As I worked away on the project, making frequent trips to Dickson's farm to conduct the interviews, Peter encouraged me to think about turning the project into a full biography. I knew that Dickson was depositing his papers in the national archives and that his papers would provide a rich resource and likely unprecedented insights into judicial decision making and the work of the Supreme Court of Canada. Despite being fully occupied with my duties as Dean, I could not resist the challenge and the opportunity. I took on the project, and Dickson gave me access to his papers, which were otherwise restricted from public view for twenty-five years from the date of deposit in 1993.

The demands of the Dean's office considerably slowed my progress, as did the demands of judicial office after my appointment to the bench. Fortunately, in 1999, I was able to interest my former student, colleague, and friend Kent Roach in the project. The combination of Kent's prodigious work habits and our coincident periods of sabbatical and judicial study leave in 2002–3 allowed us to complete the book for publication in 2003. Peter Oliver skilfully guided Kent and me through the publication process.

Kent and I worked very well together. We did our best to produce a seamless text. We exchanged countless drafts, and made suggestions, deletions, and additions to each other's work to such an extent that I cannot always remember who wrote what. It was a genuine and rewarding collaboration.

I found the biography to be the most challenging writing project I had ever undertaken. Part of the challenge was the responsibility of trying to explain the career of a man I admired in a fair and dispassionate way. I worried that I might be too close to Dickson to write a proper biography. I consulted U of T colleagues, including Marty Friedland, an accomplished legal historian, and other historians I knew at U of T. They all told me I should do it. Peter Oliver was of the same view. Writing a biography, they said, necessarily entails a relationship with one's subject, sometimes positive and sometimes negative. No biographer can maintain a dispassionate view of the subject. The fact that I had worked for Dickson would be obvious to the reader. It was unlikely that anyone else would have access to Dickson for interviews or to his papers that would be sealed for twenty-five years, and his judicial contribution deserved more immediate treatment.

Dickson cooperated with the interviews. Although we knew each other well, he was a very private man and not the easiest person to interview. He clearly thought that I should be focusing on his legal career, and he was not particularly forthcoming on personal matters. But I did manage to get him to tell me about his wartime experience and about his life as a lawyer and judge in Manitoba, as well as his time on the Supreme Court. As the work proceeded, Kent and I conducted many other interviews of family members, judicial colleagues, former law clerks, and others who had worked with Dickson.

Dickson was conscious of his place in Canadian legal history, and he was pleased that Kent and I were working on his biography. He fully respected our independence as authors. Although I am sure he was itching to see what we were writing, he never asked to see a draft. On the other hand, he did not hesitate to call me on a regular basis for a report on my progress. It was as if I were still on his to-do list to be checked on from time to time.

The Dickson Papers

The most significant part of the Dickson archive is that he preserved a file for nearly all the cases he decided during his seventeen years on the Supreme Court. These files contained documents providing rare insight into the Supreme Court's decision-making process. There were the factums (written arguments) and often some of the record, annotated with Dickson's handwritten notes. Dickson always asked his law clerks to prepare a bench memo summarizing the case, analysing the issues, and usually suggesting the proper result. Perhaps most intriguing were the "conference memos" that Dickson dictated at the end of the Court's sitting day summarizing the judges' post-hearing discussion around the conference table. The files also contained draft judgments and memos to and from members of the Court commenting on drafts. The Dickson papers opened a unique window on how Dickson and his colleagues worked during his seventeen years on the Court.

It is relatively common for American judges to provide researchers and biographers with access to their papers, but this does not happen in Canada. When he deposited his papers in the national archives, Dickson stipulated that they would be closed from public view for twenty-five years, but he reserved to right to grant access, which he did to me and anyone working with me on the biography.

We had access, but the papers still posed a challenge.[3] Out-of-court discussions and deliberations among judges are confidential for good reason. Confidentiality provides judges with a zone of privacy, allowing them to engage in free and open discussion. Exposing those discussions to public view could inhibit frank discussion of cases and adversely affect judicial decision making. Judges might hesitate to explore ideas or test views if the discussion was not kept confidential. Exposure of the twists and turns of judicial decision making could impair the integrity and finality of the judicial process.

On the other hand, in law, confidentiality is rarely, if ever, absolute.[4] I have referred to the American practice in which judicial papers are routinely deposited and open to public view after a judge's retirement or death. We accepted that a more restrictive approach should apply in Canada. But we argued that, as time passes, the interest of secrecy fades, and the public interest in knowing how an important institution that plays a pivotal role in Canada's governance prevails. Dickson had certainly thought about the issue, and he had given me access to his papers. I once asked him how he expected me to use the sensitive material in his papers. His response was: "I expect you to exercise your good judgment." So that is what Kent and I did.

We decided that we could use the papers without harming judicial confidentiality. The book was appearing thirteen years after Dickson's last case and thirty years since his first case. There was only one judge left on the Court who sat with him, Justice Beverley McLachlin, who overlapped for a period of about two years. We respected her right to confidentiality and relied upon only what she had told us in an interview. Another factor was that Dickson had been careful about what he deposited and had removed some material from his files. We were confident that nothing in our book discredited the Court or the judicial process. What the papers revealed was a group of dedicated and hard-working judges attempting to decide cases according to the law and to the best of their ability. We stated in our preface: "We believe that by looking through the window [opened by the papers] as Brian Dickson said we could, we are fostering a better understanding of the decision-making process at our highest court and thereby enhancing public confidence in the judicial process."

After the book was published, Chief Justice Beverley McLachlin wrote to inform me of the Court's newly adopted policy on judicial papers. A master file of all memoranda between judges would be created and deposited in the Archives with a thirty-five-year embargo. She explained the importance of maintaining confidential collegial discussions for thirty-five years and the fear that, if those discussions were revealed, free discussion would be inhibited. She recognized that this policy was not in place during Dickson's time on the Court but stressed that she had always taken it as understood that what was said in the conference room would remain confidential in the same way that Cabinet discussions are confidential. Chief Justice McLachlin's letter concluded with a generous comment: "Let me conclude by saying that the members of the Court applaud your work in preserving and expounding on the work of the Supreme Court and other justice institutions," adding that the Court's concern was that such work "does not undermine the full and free exchange of ideas that is essential to fulfilling the Court's responsibility in Canadian Society."

I certainly understood Chief Justice McLachlin's concern. It was the very issue that Kent and I had struggled with before the book was published. I stand by the conclusion we reached about the propriety of using the Dickson papers in the way we did, but I was not entirely surprised to learn that the Court was uncomfortable with our decision. My own view is that the twenty-five-year embargo imposed by Dickson was long enough and that thirty-five years, or the subsequently announced fifty-year limit imposed by the Court,[5] are unnecessarily long. I hope that our book demonstrates that Dickson was not wrong to have trusted Kent and me to have earlier access to his papers.

A Judge's Journey

As Kent and I worked our way through the Dickson papers in the National Archives, we saw the broad outline of the book and settled on the title: *Brian Dickson: A Judge's Journey*. We traced Brian Dickson's personal journey and unlikely rise as a great judge. He was the child of Irish immigrants and his childhood in Saskatchewan was marked by the Depression. His legal education was decidedly uninspiring and, although he graduated with the gold medal, he could not find a legal job upon graduation in 1938 in post-Depression Manitoba. He did not practise law until seven years later, after a shattering near-death experience in World War II. The gold medallist who was now a wounded war veteran rapidly rose to the heights of corporate Canada. Then, to the astonishment of his corporate law colleagues, and despite never having argued a case in court, he accepted an appointment to Manitoba's trial court, claiming even after his appointment as Canada's Chief Justice that it was the best job he ever had. Within four years, he had been appointed to the Manitoba Court of Appeal and then, six years later, to the Supreme Court of Canada.

How did this conservative corporate lawyer and bank director become a leading exponent of the *Charter*, a judge very sympathetic to the disadvantages experienced by women, Indigenous people in Canada, linguistic minorities, persons accused of crime, and prisoners? We traced the formative influence of growing up in the Depression and Dickson's military service, which left him with a painful disability. Dickson combined the relentless organization and discipline he learned from the army, which allowed him to rise in the profession, with the compassion he felt for those who had suffered death and injury. Similarly, he managed to transfer the skills of a corporate solicitor, rigorously looking at every angle and every possibility, to the task of writing clear decisions in all areas of law, including *Charter* rights.

As we worked on the book, we saw that Brian Dickson had not been on a journey of his own. Although there were occasional flashes of the creative judicial role[6] he would play as an early judicial architect of the

Charter of Rights and Freedoms, we found a distinctly cautious and at times formalistic approach in his early judicial work,[7] That caution and formalism was a product of the times. Brian Dickson's transformation from a careful corporate solicitor to a leading exponent of the *Charter of Rights and Freedoms* paralleled the transformation of Canadian law in the second half of the twentieth century. As one of his former law clerks observed, Dickson "experienced conflict in resolving the rule-oriented cast of his character with a conception of justice as progressive and as an instrument of compassion."[8]

Dickson's intellectual path fascinated me. As a law student in the late 1960s, I had been taught to focus mostly on English cases. We learned that Canadian law was steeped in the tradition of legal formalism, the idea that the law consists of a body of neutral rules that are to be mechanically applied with reference to their normative underpinnings or to context. Our professors did their best to criticize this dominant model of legal reasoning, but it persisted in the courts and in the profession.

Dickson and Bora Laskin were two judicial leaders who guided Canadian law from the shadow of this stifling tradition. Dickson called it "blind and empty formalism"[9] and urged judges to develop a "distinctively Canadian jurisprudence"[10] that did not slavishly follow either English or American law. Departing from formalism meant focusing on underlying legal principles, rather than black letter legal rules, and being open to considering the relevant social context.

What made him such a compelling figure was the way he was able to combine his determination to remain faithful to the rule of law with his willingness to expand his legal horizons to deal with the novel challenges posed by the *Charter*. That was the story of Canadian law in the second half of the twentieth century, the story that I had witnessed and participated in as a lawyer, scholar, and judge. My own journey as a lawyer, scholar, and judge was greatly enriched by my experience working for Brian Dickson and writing his biography.

The book was well received with several positive reviews.[11] The sting of one negative review[12] was soothed by the award of the John Wesley Dafoe Prize, given "to the best book on Canada, Canadians, and/or Canada's place in the world published in the previous calendar year."

The Persons Case

Every first-year law student learns the memorable phase "the Constitution is a living tree, capable of growth and expansion within its natural limits." This metaphor has always intrigued me. It delights those of liberal inclinations, and it infuriates those of a more conservative bent. It is frequently used to distinguish Canadian legal discourse from the originalism that has emerged as a powerful force in the United States.

As I completed the Dickson biography, I started to cast about, looking for my next project. I decided to examine the case that coined the living tree metaphor, the *Persons Case*, decided in 1928,[13] to see if it would be a suitable project. It did not take long to decide that the answer to that question was yes. My U of T Law colleague Jim Phillips, Peter Oliver's successor as Editor-in-Chief at the Osgoode Society, gave me the encouragement and support I needed to take on the project.[14]

The issue in the case was whether a woman could be appointed to the Canadian Senate. Canada's 1867 Constitution provided that "qualified persons" could be appointed to the Senate.[15] In 1867, it was accepted that women could not hold public office and, therefore, that a woman could not be appointed to the Senate. Did that disability hold sixty years later, in 1928? By then, women had been given the vote and elected to Parliament. The Supreme Court of Canada, supported by a long line of English cases holding that women were not persons in the legal sense, held that it would take a constitutional amendment to allow for a female senator. Chief Justice Frank Anglin wrote that the words "qualified persons" had to "bear to-day the same construction which the courts would, if then required to pass upon them, have given to them when they were first enacted."[16] The Judicial Committee of the Privy Council, then Canada's final court of appeal, gave a very different answer. John Sankey, the Lord Chancellor, held: "The exclusion of women from all public offices is a relic of days more barbarous than ours"[17] and declared Canada's Constitution to be a "living tree."

I was eager to explore this case and its background. Who were the people behind it? And what were the legal, social, and political forces that produced this remarkable decision?

It did not take me long to find that an unusual woman was the key figure. The Privy Council's decision in the *Persons Case* was the result of the untiring efforts of Emily Murphy, a much-published author and social crusader, who claimed to be the first woman to be appointed as a magistrate in the British Empire when she was named to the newly created Women's Court in Edmonton, Alberta, in 1916. Although she was a judge, Murphy was not legally trained. She did not conduct herself, either in or out or court, as a traditional judge. She saw her role as being that of a social worker, and she never surrendered her mantle as a social reformer, continuing to speak out on social issues affecting women and children and to advocate legal reforms.

Archival sources were essential for the kind of book I wanted to write. I needed to find out what motivated the principal actors, and I had to gain a flavour of the social climate of the day. I found that there was a Department of Justice file on the case in the National Archives that provided the government's side of the case. In addition, Emily Murphy's papers were deposited in archives in Edmonton and the University of Waterloo. Murphy had enlisted the support of four prominent women who together with Murphy, became known as "the Famous Five." They were leaders of the early feminist movement in Canada: Nellie McClung, Henrietta Edwards, Irene Parlby, and Louise McKinney. Their papers were to be found in various archives across Canada. Murphy was well represented in the case. Newton Rowell, a leading counsel with experience arguing constitutional cases, accepted the brief. His papers were deposited in the National Archives, as were the papers of Mackenzie King, whom Murphy lobbied (unsuccessfully) for a Senate appointment. I also travelled to Oxford to consult the papers of John Sankey, the Lord Chancellor who decided the case in Murphy's favour. I examined these and as many other archival sources as I could find that would shed light on the story. I also made extensive use of contemporary newspaper accounts both in Canada and in England.

As I conducted the archival research, I realized that, as with the Dickson biography, I was taking on a major project that would benefit from the assistance of a co-author. Patricia McMahon, a history PhD as well as a qualified lawyer (and now an Osgoode Hall law professor), had done some excellent work for Kent Roach and me on the Dickson biography. Trish agreed to come on board, and together we wrote the book.

I discovered through my archival research that Murphy's brother, William Ferguson, an Ontario appellate judge, came up with the idea of how to place the issue before the courts. With her brother's assistance, Murphy persuaded Mackenzie King to direct a reference on the question of whether a woman could be appointed to the Senate. That appealed to King, who was fond of shuffling difficult problems off to the courts, and Emily Murphy was becoming a difficult problem. For Murphy, it solved an otherwise insuperable problem. A disappointed Senate candidate had no legal recourse. The other advantage was that, on a reference, the government would pay for Murphy's lawyer, and Newton Rowell was a pricey choice as her counsel.

Murphy regarded the Supreme Court's decision, which was ridiculed in the press, as a temporary setback. She decided to take the case to the Privy Council. There, the response to her plea was considerably more receptive for two reasons.

First, to the dismay of some Canadian constitutional scholars and lawyers, the Privy Council had refused to be bound by the intentions of the framers of the 1867 Constitution to create a strong central government. That meant that the "original meaning" argument would hold less sway at the Privy Council that it had at the Supreme Court of Canada.

Second, the judge who would preside at the Privy Council was the recently appointed Lord Chancellor, John Sankey, a man of liberal and reformist leanings. I was interested to learn more about the person who had coined not only the living tree metaphor but also the description of the presumption of innocence as the "golden thread" that runs "throughout the web of the English criminal law."[18] He frequented Fabian socialist circles after presiding over an inquiry into the coal mining business, where his "sense of justice was outraged by the descriptions of the living conditions of the miners; and his sense of decency was shocked by the cynical and selfish attitude of the owners."[19]

Sankey reviewed the legal authorities excluding women from public office but refused to view the law in static terms or to be bound by the past. The word "persons," he wrote, was "ambiguous, and in its original meaning would undoubtedly embrace members of either sex." If the original meaning of the word could include women, it was social tradition and custom, not the law, that excluded women. Sankey concluded: "The appeal to history therefore in this particular matter is not conclusive."[20] Because the word "persons" could include both genders, Sankey wrote, "to those who ask why the word should include females, the obvious answer is why should it not?"[21]

Sankey emphasized the importance of context, social tradition, and custom in legal development. As the final court of appeal for "the Britannic system," which includes "countries and peoples in every stage of social, political and economic development and undergoing a continuous process of evolution," the Privy Council "must take great care not to interpret legislation meant to apply to one community by a rigid adherence to the customs and traditions of another."[22] Ironically, the voice of supreme colonial power was insisting upon the very independence and legal maturity that Canada's own judges had refused to claim for themselves.

Murphy was never appointed to the Senate. Her legacy is as a crusader for women's legal rights in the courts. Modern feminists applaud Murphy's success in the *Persons Case* but are troubled by many of her views, which were very much the product of her age. Like the other members of the Famous Five, she was a "maternal feminist," espousing a distinctive role of women as mothers and wives, not the obliteration of traditional gender roles. All five women were strong Christians, were adherents of the social gospel movement, and believed in societal improvement through the application of Christian morality in public life. Temperance and the prohibition of alcohol were central to the maternal feminist agenda. Alcohol was blamed for poisoning private, domestic life and was thought to have a corrupting influence on politics. Maternal feminists, in short, were only distantly related to modern feminists. They were overwhelmingly middle-class, white, heterosexual, Anglo-Saxon Christians with an elitist sense of their own virtue and moral superiority. They viewed women as "naturally the guardians of the race,"[23] and that race was decidedly white, British, and Protestant. Maternal feminists shared the racist and xenophobic attitudes that prevailed in the society in which they lived. For example, Murphy's early writing on the drug problem exhibits overtly anti-Asian racist attitudes,[24]and Murphy and her group also promoted eugenics as a way to improve public health.[25]

How should these attitudes, now properly regarded as deplorable, affect our view of Emily Murphy and the Famous Five? In our book, Patricia McMahon and I wrote that, when assessing their actions, we must remember that equality is an evolving concept. It takes different shape in different times. Champions of equality in one era may fail to live up to the ideals that emerge later. As an American judge stated when upholding the right of same sex couples to marry: "The nature of injustice is that we may not always see it in our own times."[26] I believe that by fighting the *Persons Case* to the end and securing a victory few would have predicted, Murphy and the Famous Five created a legacy that transcends their own shortcomings.

The Lazier Murder

When the *Persons Case* project was completed, I turned to a very different case study that took me back to my roots in Prince Edward County.[27] I had always been intrigued by the fact that local memory of an 1884 murder case had not entirely faded. I heard about the case growing up in the County, and I decided to see if it offered an interesting story for my fourth case study.

The case involved the murder of a man named Peter Lazier in a botched robbery at a farmhouse that still stands very close to the property Geraldine and I acquired shortly after I was appointed as a trial judge. Lazier was an overnight visitor at the home of a Quaker couple. The farmer, Gilbert Jones, had sold a crop of hops at the Bloomfield train station earlier in the day and returned to the farm with the proceeds, $555, a substantial sum at the time. Later that evening, two disguised men pounded on the door and entered the house. Lazier emerged from the guest bedroom. Mrs. Jones yelled to her husband to get his gun. One of the intruders was carrying a pistol and the other a gun. Alarmed by Mrs. Jones yelling to her husband to get his gun, one of the intruders fired the fatal pistol shot that struck Peter Lazier in the heart.

A hue and cry was raised. Those who answered were led by the local constables to do their best to trace the tracks in the snow left by the intruders as they ran off. By early morning, George and David Lowder and Joseph Thomset had been arrested. A coroner's jury was immediately assembled to investigate Lazier's death. The accused men were tried at the Picton Courthouse four months after the murder. Justice Christopher Patterson, who started his legal career as a lawyer in Picton and ended it as Justice of the Supreme Court of Canada, presided. David Lowder was acquitted, but George Lowder and Joseph Thomset were convicted and sentenced to hang. Despite pleas for clemency, they were both hanged less than six months after the murder.

Case studies are only possible to write if there are reliable sources and only worth undertaking if they shed light on the law and its evolution. I found that there was a reasonably thick Capital Cases file in the national archives. It contained a full transcript of the trial, the trial judge's written report to the Minister of Justice, other correspondence and letters and petitions from the local community pleading for clemency in favour of the two convicted men. I could see there was enough in that file to get started, and I was confident that I could find other sources, especially contemporary newspaper sources, which would allow me to tell the story.

As I worked away on my project, with Jim Phillips's expert guidance, I started to identify several themes that made this case interesting from a legal history perspective.

The first theme was that of wrongful conviction. The case lingered in local memory because many thought that one, if not both, of the two men had been wrongfully convicted. I was able to identify several features of the case typical of wrongful convictions. It seemed to me that there had been a rush to judgment. The investigation was led by a roguish police detective anxious to build his reputation as a relentless crime buster and willing to use dubious tactics in the process. There was every indication of a "tunnel vision" investigation. The detective saw his task not as conducting a thorough and impartial investigation, but rather as finding or, if necessary, fabricating the evidence needed to convict the accused men. The prosecution presented suspect "expert" evidence and, without disclosure, sprang questionable surprise evidence that the defence was not prepared to meet. The local community was out for blood, and it was hard to see how the local jury could not have been affected by the atmosphere of hostility towards the accused in the courtroom during the trial.

The second theme was that of capital punishment. If the risk of putting to death an innocent person was not enough, Lowder and Thomset suffered a bungled hanging and took several minutes to die by strangulation at the end of the hangman's rope.

The third theme was the evolving nature of the criminal process. Under the law as it stood at the time, Lowder and Thomset were not permitted to testify at their trial. I explored why the law precluded an accused person from testifying and what led to that rule being changed several years later. Another striking difference that I explored was that a convicted person did not have a right of appeal. The only recourse was to petition the cabinet for clemency. That process was fascinating to explore, evaluate, and assess. The final word in the Lazier murder was left to Prime Minister Sir John A. Macdonald and his cabinet.

These features of the case were significant. They showed how the law is in a state of constant evolution. Rules thought necessary to ensure justice in one age seem out of place in another. Complacency with things as they are can be very dangerous.

The fourth theme – and, from a legal history perspective, perhaps the most interesting one – is what Jim Phillips identified as "community justice." In Prince Edward County in the 1880s, the model of community justice prevailed. There was no organized police force, and the law was enforced by amateur local constables and justices of the peace. The local coroner played a major role in the investigation. The detective, brought in from Belleville, represented a shift towards a more professional approach to law enforcement that was coming.

The other aspect of community justice was the force of local public opinion on how the case unfolded. During the trial, the local community was out for blood and wanted the accused men to hang. But after the verdict and before the hanging, another side of public opinion surfaced. Edwards Merrill, a prominent Picton lawyer and later County Court judge, wrote to Prime Minister Macdonald to report that he had attended the trial and had been alarmed by the hostile mood that prevailed in the courtroom. The verdict, he said, was an "echo … of the excited public opinion."[28]

Merrill's letter failed to persuade the Prime Minister to commute the sentence, but it did signal a shift in public opinion. Many local people joined Merrill in their concern for what they perceived to be a miscarriage of justice. That sentiment came too late to save Lowder and Thomset, but gradually the community's lust for a hanging was replaced by a community's sense of guilt and regret. I uncovered two other murder cases tried over the next twenty years in which Picton juries refused to convict despite a strong prosecution case. The local Crown attorney attributed the acquittals to local opposition to capital punishment and the feeling that at least one of the men hanged for the Lazier murder was innocent.

When I was working on the book, I went to the local archives at the Picton courthouse. The local jail was closed, and the archived files were stored in the cells where Lowder and Thomset were held after the trial. The gallows constructed for the double hanging still stand. I wrote in the concluding pages of the book: "The gallows remain as a chilling reminder of the fragility of the criminal trial process, and the brutality and the terrible finality of the capital sentence that was carried out … to a community's profound regret."[29]

14
International Assignments

During my time on the Court of Appeal, I was involved in three international assignments dealing with the state of the judiciary in troubled circumstances. These missions took me to very different places with very different histories and cultures, but they had a common theme: how to deal with threats to the integrity and independence of the judiciary.

Kenya, 2002

When I was Dean, Professor Yash Pal Ghai came to the faculty as a short-term visitor. Yash is a Kenyan, and in the 1960s, he taught at the University of Dar es Salaam in Tanzania, which played a foundational role in the development of the post-colonial legal order in East Africa. After returning to Kenya, he was a victim of racist Kenyan attitudes towards those of Asian descent and was effectively exiled from Kenya for a period, when he held appointments in the United Kingdom, Sweden, the United States, and Hong Kong. Educated at Oxford, Yash is an extraordinary constitutional scholar who has drafted new constitutions for a long list of postcolonial countries in the South Pacific.[1] He returned to Kenya in 2000 to chair Kenya's Constitutional Review Commission, reluctantly established by the two-decades-old and faltering government of Daniel arap Moi.

In 2002, Yash invited me to be a member of a "Panel of Eminent Commonwealth Judicial Experts," established through the auspices of the International Commission of Jurists, to make recommendations on what the new Constitution should say about the judiciary. I joined three senior African judges: Justice Yvonne Mokgoro, Constitutional Court of South Africa; Justice George Kanyeihamba, Supreme Court of Uganda; and Justice Damian Lubuva, Court of Appeal of Tanzania. We were later joined by Professor Ed Ratushny, University of Ottawa, who had extensive experience with the Canadian judicial appointment and discipline processes and who was the President of the Canadian Branch of the International Commission of Jurists.

The project for constitutional change was strongly supported by the Kenyan population. One day, Yash was driving us to a meeting and stopped to buy the three daily newspapers. The street vendor was delighted with the sale and, partway through the transaction, realized who the buyer was. "Yash Pal Ghai!" he cried out. The vendor's excitement showed us that Yash had become a folk hero with his project of constitutional renewal and quest for a government and judiciary free of corruption.

We quickly found that the central problem confronting the Kenyan judiciary was widespread corruption. The judiciary was perceived to be one of the most corrupt institutions in Kenya. The complaints ranged from the relatively petty – such as inducing court officials to lose or misplace files – to the very serious – such as paying money to judges to influence their decisions.

We met with the Chief Justice and senior members of the Kenyan judiciary. The Kenyan judges were very guarded and appeared to be suspicious and resentful of our presence. When asked about the problem of corruption in the Kenyan judiciary, they refused to engage and essentially walked out of the meeting, apparently insulted that we would dare to ask such a question.

The Kenyan experience changed my attitude about the significance of international standards for ideals like judicial independence. I had been sceptical of the value of these standards as empty promises with no teeth when it came to enforcement. Kenya taught me that, when basic rule of law principles are under threat, internationally recognized standards can be crucially important. It is easy for those accused of wrongdoing to brush aside the argument that "this is how we do it in Canada (or South Africa or Uganda or Tanzania)." Internationally established standards carry significantly more persuasive weight. Our report and our recommendations were based on the *U.N. Basic Principles for the Independence of the Judiciary* (1985). I could see how well-articulated international standards can serve as models for reform. Ideals are important, and universally recognized standards of justice can serve to tame raw political forces.

Our team had robust discussions about how to frame the report and our recommendations. I favoured general statements of principle, but my African colleagues told me that my style might be fine for "good guys" but that what Kenya needed was clear and firm rules to discipline some very "bad guys." The more I learned about the situation in Kenya, the more I realized that they had a point, although I still believe that it is dangerous to assume that a specific set of rules will capture every eventuality.

We concluded that, as presently constituted, the Kenyan judicial system suffered from a serious lack of public confidence and was generally perceived as needing fundamental structural reform. Our report[2] delivered a severe criticism of the Kenyan judiciary. As a complete outsider, I worried about delivering such a negative message after only two weeks on the ground. But I was not alone. My African colleagues, especially the judges from Uganda and Tanzania, were close neighbours and, as members of the East African legal community, they were not complete outsiders. I was also bolstered by the depth of the concerns expressed by the Kenyan lawyers, judges, and non-governmental organization (NGO) representatives that we met. The problem of corruption was undeniable and, in the end, I had no hesitation in saying what we said in our report.

We concluded that strong measures are necessary for Kenya to achieve an independent and accountable judiciary, capable of serving the needs of the people of Kenya by securing equal justice and the maintenance of the rule of law under a new constitutional order.

On the positive side, we found that there is a commitment on the part of key members of the Kenyan legal community to undertake the reforms required. Many of those who came before us were young lawyers, full of energy, ideas, integrity, and the willingness to work for a reformed judiciary. I was very impressed by the determination of these young lawyers not to be defeated by the deplorable state of the Kenyan judiciary. In our report, we described these men and women as being "of the highest integrity, well educated, articulate, and determined to achieve a just society." We were "deeply moved by their passionate belief in the rule of law and their commitment to the highest ideals of justice … [and] by their courage in speaking so frankly to us and in confronting the serious problems that bedevil the judicial system in which they work."

Influenced by a meeting with Court of Appeal Justice Kwach and his earlier report on corruption in the judiciary, we rejected the suggestion that all Kenyan judges should be required to resign their positions and reapply under a reformed appointments process. We thought that would be an unfair insult to the conscientious judges who carried out their work with integrity. We recommended strong measures to ensure a more expeditious and independent complaint and removal process, together with a reformed appointments process to restore public confidence. Sadly, not long after our report, Kwach himself was the subject of a disciplinary proceeding for corruption. Our rejection of the suggestion to require all judges to reapply might have been unwise.

Chief Justice Chunga reacted very negatively to our report, as did President Moi. They claimed it was the product of bad manners from outsiders based on rumours and hearsay. Press reports indicated that these reactions were perceived by Kenyans to be petulant and unfortunate and that the problems with the judiciary were well known. A few months after our report, newly elected President Kibaki, who ran on an anti-corruption platform, established a tribunal to deal with allegations of corruption against Chief Justice Chunga and, rather than face the tribunal, the Chief Justice resigned.

I did not think it proper for me as a judge to accept the honorarium that I was to be paid for my work. I asked Yash and his wife, Jill Cottrell Ghai – an accomplished legal scholar in her own right, who was heavily involved in our mission – what I should do with the money. They suggested I donate it to a school they supported. I was surprised to learn that all schools in Kenya charged fees. My honorarium would pay the fees for 100 students. One afternoon, Jill took me to the school, which was located in a large slum. We could only drive to the edge of the slum, and we then walked quite a distance through the worst poverty I have ever seen. I was appalled by the destitution of the children who attended the school. They were mostly AIDS orphans. They greeted their strange white visitor with a spirit and enthusiasm that moved me to tears. The teachers had also been hit by the AIDS pandemic. They complained about the violence of the slum. Inadequate and corrupt police compounded the problem. I could not comprehend how they were able to continue their work in the circumstances they faced.

Kenya's constitutional reform process struggled forward. A draft Constitution was rejected in a 2005 referendum, but a second proposal was adopted after another referendum in 2010. The problem of corruption continued to plague the judiciary and, in 2011, legislation established a scheme to vet all judges who had been appointed prior to the promulgation of the new Constitution. That process resulted in several judges being removed as unfit for judicial office.

The Kenyan experience was exhausting and depressing but at the same time fascinating and exhilarating. It was depressing to see that judges had fallen prey to the temptations of bribery and corruption but inspiring to witness the idealism of young Kenyan lawyers and to see the importance of internationally recognized standards of judicial independence. I was fascinated to work closely with my co-panellist judicial colleagues, whose experience was so different from mine, but who brought a common judicial perspective to bear on the problems we confronted.

I was emotionally drained when I returned from Kenya. It is a beautiful country, rich in resources and human potential, but the harm wrought by colonialism remains. Poverty, corruption, tribalism, and poor governance were obstacles that had not been overcome. I was persuaded that the Kenyan people deserved better, and I was pleased to have been able to play a modest role in their project of constitutional renewal.

Russia, 2005

My next international venture occurred in the spring of 2005, when I was a member of an International Bar Association (IBA) Rapid Response Mission to Russia.[3]

The Russia mission comprised four members: Philip Tahmindjis, Judge William Birtles, Anne McMillan, and me. Philip, Program Lawyer with the IBA, was our leader and had led several similar missions. Philip is an Australian legal scholar. I first met him when he spent some time at the University of Toronto working on a graduate degree. Judge Birtles was from the United Kingdom and had a longstanding interest in Russia and Russian affairs. Anne is an English barrister with extensive international human rights and humanitarian law experience, having served with UN missions in Cambodia, former Yugoslavia, Iraq, and the Middle East.

Our mission was to examine proposals to "reform" the judiciary put forth during a period of national security concern arising from the Chechen situation. We found that there was widespread concern with proposals to change the composition of the Supreme and Judicial Qualification Collegia, the bodies that appoint, promote, discipline, and dismiss members of the judiciary.

Vladimir Putin had just been elected to his second term as President in a landslide, but independent election observers reported irregularities. Many positive judicial reforms had been introduced during the Yeltsin era, and newly elected President Putin had promised to continue and enhance those reforms. While some progress had been made, the response to the Chechen rebel attack on a school had prompted problematic changes, which we were asked to investigate.

Proponents claimed that the changes were necessary to root out judicial corruption. Opponents asserted that they were an attack on judicial independence. We heard conflicting accounts of the work of the Collegia. Some said it protected judges; others claimed it failed to do so and illegally removed judges; still others said it prevented the removal of a judge who should have been removed.

We recommended strengthening the appointments process by ensuring that the judiciary made up two thirds of the membership of the Qualification Collegia and that those bodies include representation from the private bar and NGOs. We also recommended measures to ensure that cases were not transferred from one judge or court to another for nefarious reasons and that the discipline process for removing judges be improved to safeguard judicial independence. Other recommendations included improving the publication of judicial decisions, ensuring that judges were adequately paid, and improving judicial education and training.

Our conclusion was that while the ideal of judicial independence was alive in Russia, it was not well understood by the public, and there was a serious struggle to uphold judicial independence in practice. The debate over the changes to the Qualification Collegia was a side story to a more profound concern about the state of the judiciary in Russia. The conviction rate in criminal cases was worryingly high. We heard a great deal about political control of the judiciary – not only the appointment and discipline of judges but actual interference in judicial decision making. The concept of judicial independence had gained some traction as an ideal in post-Communist Russia, but the reality was that judges were perceived to be subject to political pressure and control. The judiciary was not an institution respected by the public. The problems were more profound than the changes our mission had been asked to investigate.

I observed enormous change since my visit to the Soviet Union with Chief Justice Dickson in 1989. There was a bit of the "wild west" in the air as Russians had gone from the extreme of Communist control to a state of semi-anarchy.

I offer three mundane examples. First, at our hotel, the lounge in the lobby was often frequented by groups of well-dressed but suspicious-looking men huddled in negotiations and surrounded by bodyguards. I could only guess what kind of deals were being made, but the hushed discussions and the gangster-like appearance of the participants made me very suspicious.

Second, one day, we had some time and decided to visit the Kremlin. We were rebuffed at the ticket wicket with a gruff "Kremlin closed." As we retreated, we were approached by a private "guide," who informed us that, for a substantial but manageable sum in roubles, she could get us in. Private enterprise had triumphed even at the Kremlin.

My third example is the "taxi" system. I saw very few licensed taxis, and we were in the pre-Uber era. The surest, although not the safest, way to get somewhere was to stand at the side of the road holding your arm to one side. Within seconds, a driver eager to earn some cash would stop to offer a lift at a price to be negotiated. Needless to say, when I used this method of conveyance, I am sure I paid double or triple the going rate.

I left Russia convinced that Winston Churchill's famous observation that Russia is "a riddle wrapped in a mystery inside an enigma" could be applied to the Russian legal system. The ideal of judicial independence was present but it was competing with a long tradition that gave priority to politics and the pursuit of power.

Pakistan, 2007

I was a member of the IBA's Rapid Response Mission to Pakistan in May 2007, to investigate the circumstances of President's Musharraf's March 2007 attempt to remove Chief Justice Chaudhry from office, and its implications for judicial independence and the rule of law in Pakistan.[4] Our team was small: me; Philip Tahmindjis from the IBA; and Michelle Bradfield, an Australian lawyer who was then a research Fellow at Lauterpacht Centre for International Law in the University of Cambridge. The IBA had invited a prominent Malaysian lawyer to be part of the mission, but he was denied entry.

For unknown reasons, the three of us were not denied entry. It was a mystery why the Pakistan government gave us permission to enter the country. The authorities were clearly suspicious of what we were up to. We were followed everywhere we went during our time in the country. Many of those we met during our investigation were taking a risk by assisting us in a mission that was likely to cast the President in a poor light.

We met a minister who bore the lofty title of "Minister of Law, Justice and Human Rights." His demeanour and behaviour were hardly that of a person dedicated to law, justice, and human rights. He was a thuggish character who glowered at me and said that, as a foreign judge, I had no business being there. We left the ministry just at the time for the Muslim afternoon prayers. All the offices emptied, and the entire ministry filed into the corridors and knelt on the floor to pray. It was apparent that I had entered a very different legal world.

Chief Justice Iftikhar Muhammad Chaudhry was an unlikely hero. He had been a member of Pakistan's judiciary for eighteen years, a judge on the Supreme Court for twelve years and Chief Justice for seven years. Until he became Chief Justice, he appears to have been a rather conventional and unremarkable judge. In 1999, after General Musharraf's coup, he meekly swore a new oath pledging to uphold the coup's Provisional Constitutional Order suspending the Constitution.

However, once he became Chief Justice of Pakistan in 2005, Chaudhry struck a strikingly independent course. He introduced systemic changes to reduce the court's serious backlog of cases. He made frequent use of his "*suo moto*" power to initiate on his own motion proceedings to investigate a wide variety of what he perceived to be abuses of power. Particularly notable and irritating to the Musharraf regime were the "missing persons" cases. Chief Justice Chaudhry regularly summonsed the security forces to court to explain the whereabouts of individuals they had detained and required them to offer legal justification for the detentions. Chief Justice Chaudhry was fast becoming something of a hero to the masses and a serious thorn in the regime's side.

By March 2007, Musharraf was gravely concerned about the implications of Chief Justice Chaudhry's unexpected staunch assertion of judicial independence. Cases were expected to come before the Supreme Court that would test the legality of General Musharraf's hold on the office of President while retaining his position as Chief of the Army Staff in the face of the constitutional provision precluding the President from holding any other public office.[5] An independent-minded Chief Justice determined to uphold the rule of law posed a serious threat to Musharraf's continued retention of power.

There was little doubt about what had happened in March 2007. On the morning of 9 March, Chief Justice Chaudhry was summoned by Pakistan's President, General Pervez Musharraf, to army headquarters in Rawalpindi. In the presence of the Prime Minister and several senior army officers, Musharraf, in full army uniform, confronted the Chief Justice with allegations of misconduct. Musharraf threatened to institute proceedings to remove Chief Justice Chaudhry from office and demanded his resignation. When Chief Justice Chaudhry refused to resign, he was held incommunicado for several hours by senior army officers, who continued to pressure him to resign. Chief Justice Chaudhry held his ground, resisting threats, offers, and enticements, no doubt to the astonishment of the generals, who are used to having their way.

Musharraf's officials launched a rapid series of actions aimed at eliminating Chief Justice Chaudhry as Pakistan's Chief Justice. Musharraf issued an order restraining the Chief Justice from carrying out his functions.[6] No legal authority was offered for this order. In addition, a reference reciting allegations of misconduct against Chief Justice Chaudhry was addressed to the Supreme Judicial Council, the body constituted under Pakistan's Constitution to deal with allegations of judicial incapacity or misconduct.[7] Chief Justice Chaudhry denied the allegations, and members of the legal community doubted their sufficiency to warrant removal proceedings.

An *ex parte* hearing of the Supreme Judicial Council was convened for that same evening of 9 March, and an order was made suspending the Chief Justice from office pending its decision on the reference. Chief Justice Chaudhry and his family were held incommunicado under house arrest. President Musharraf then issued an order placing Chief Justice Chaudhry on "compulsory leave," the legality of which was open to serious question.

Musharraf's attempt to unseat Chief Justice Chaudhry provoked an unusual and unexpected outcry from the legal profession. Lawyers boycotted the courts and held public demonstrations demanding Chief Justice Chaudhry's restoration to office and insisting upon respect for the Constitution and the rule of law. These protests were met with police harassment and violence and resulted in many deaths.

The implications of the Musharraf-Chaudhry showdown transcended immediate personal and political interests and the day-to-day manipulations of Pakistan's volatile political climate. The essential link between democracy, judicial independence and the rule of law ceased to be an abstract subject of theoretical philosophizing. I found myself involved in a compelling tale of judicial independence and judicial courage. The importance of an independent judiciary to secure the rule of law and the conditions necessary for democratic government emerged as a popular rallying cry. We met many senior lawyers and respected members of civil society who had gone into the streets in protest, risking life and limb, determined to restore Chief Justice Chaudhry to office, to repudiate the Musharraf regime's authoritarian disregard for the rule of law, and to lay claim to a democratic future for Pakistan.

We concluded that Musharraf's actions represented a direct assault on the independence of the judiciary. After we delivered our report, Chief Justice Chaudhry and several other prominent lawyers launched proceedings in the Supreme Court of Pakistan to challenge the legality of the proceedings taken against him before the Supreme Judicial Council.[8] Chief Justice Chaudhry was represented by Aitzaz Ahsan, an opposition member in the National Assembly and one of Pakistan's leading counsels. When we met him, he reminded me of Ontario's Ian Scott, a gifted advocate and successful politician. The Supreme Court's judgment, restoring Chief Justice Chaudhry to office, marked the transformation from a docile institution, repeatedly willing to bow to and validate military rule, into an independent court, determined to uphold the Constitution and the rule of law.

Days before a panel of the Supreme Court was expected to rule on Musharraf's eligibility to run for President, Musharraf declared emergency rule. The Supreme Court declared the Declaration of Emergency to be unconstitutional and enjoined all judges from submitting to any change to the constitutional order.[9] Musharraf responded with a Provisional Constitutional Order, giving him near-absolute powers and removing all judges on the Supreme Court. Chief Justice Chaudhry was again placed under house arrest. Regime-friendly replacement judges were appointed.

Bowing to international and internal pressure, Musharraf lifted the Declaration of Emergency on 15 December 2007 and announced that parliamentary elections would proceed and that he would resign his position as Chief of the Army Staff. A coalition of opposition parties formed a government. Musharraf's declaration of emergency and attack on judicial independence figured prominently in the impeachment proceedings that led to his resignation on 18 August 2008.

The clumsy attempt to depose Chief Justice Chaudhry roused Pakistan's legal community into action. Prominent well-to-do lawyers, convinced that Pakistan's fragile legal system would collapse if they did not act, courageously went into the streets in protest wearing their barristers' gowns, where they faced police brutality, arbitrary arrest, and detention. A relatively obscure judge suddenly became a national hero and a symbol of resistance to arbitrary rule. The ideals of the independence of the judiciary and the rule of law became the rallying cry of those opposed to Musharraf's regime of military rule. The lawyers' movement captured media attention and inspired prominent members of Pakistan's civil society and the opposition political parties to stand up to the generals and insist on a return to constitutional democracy.

A seemingly impervious military ruler was swept from office, at least in part because the public reacted with indignation against his cynical disrespect for the ideals of judicial independence and the rule of law that underpin constitutional democracy – ideals that were successfully defended by the Pakistani lawyers who courageously raised their voices and ultimately took to the streets in response to a grave threat to the constitutional order.

I was impressed and inspired by the Pakistani lawyers we met, who so strongly stood up to defend the ideal of judicial independence. As with the Kenyan experience, I learned how important internationally recognized and universally applicable standards can be. They provide an objective standard that authoritarian rulers ignore at their peril.

My experience was completely at odds with the argument that such standards are Western values inapplicable in countries with different histories, traditions, and cultures. I found myself in a decidedly non-Western state, an Islamic Republic, and the Islamic lawyers of Pakistan demonstrated the power of the universal ideals of judicial independence and the rule of law.

Conclusion

My international assignments were rewarding and enriching experiences. They reinforced my belief in the ideals of judicial independence and judicial integrity. I was moved by the power of those ideals to effect change, even in the dire situations of corruption and political interference with the rule of law.

15
Conclusion

Canadian judges must retire when they reach the age of seventy-five. While this rule deprives the justice system of many talented and experienced judges, I believe it is sound policy. Most of us have reached our "best before" date by seventy-five and, even if we have not, it is important for any public institution to have a regular injection of new blood to keep pace with the changing needs of society.

Electing Supernumerary Status

In 2013, when I was sixty-seven, I decided to elect part-time status as a supernumerary judge. That allowed me to continue as a judge of the Court of Appeal with a reduced sitting load until I reached the mandatory retirement age of seventy-five. Supernumerary judges are eligible for the judicial retirement annuity (as the judicial pension is called) but continue to be paid the usual judicial salary. They are called "supernumerary" because another full-time judge can be appointed in their place. When confronted with the suggestion that this is a sweet deal for the judge, my response is that it is also a good deal for the taxpayer. The judge could retire, do nothing, and draw the retirement annuity, fixed at two-thirds of the judicial salary. By topping up the annuity by one-third, the public retains an experienced judge, assuming a fifty per cent workload. I cannot say that I usually win that argument, but I certainly enjoyed supernumerary status. I was able to continue my judicial work, continue my writing, and start to think about what I might want to do in retirement.

Good Judgment

I decided that, rather than take on another legal history project, I would try to write a book about judging. I wanted to explore the art and craft of effective and responsible judging from my perspective – an experienced judge of an intermediate appellate court with an academic background. The result was *Good Judgment: Making Judicial Decisions*, published in 2018.

I trace the origins of *Good Judgment* to a paper I wrote for the CIAJ on judicial discretion[1] and papers I presented at two NJI conferences that bore the title "Good Judgment." I was greatly assisted in my thinking for the book by an intensive seminar I taught at the U of T Faculty of Law for three years. I used the seminar as a workshop for my draft chapters. I involved several of my judicial colleagues, asking them and the students to comment on my drafts. One of my students, Scarlett Smith, took a strong interest in my project. She volunteered to do some editing, which led me to hire her as a research assistant, a task she performed brilliantly.

The first part of the book is a prequel to this memoir. I describe how I came to the law and what has fascinated me about it. I also describe the day-to-day work of both trial and appellate judges. The rest of the book deals with issues that confront judges when they make decisions.

I hoped that, by writing the book, I could work out in my own mind an understanding and reconciliation of two fundamental features of judging: judicial choice or discretion and judicial discipline. How should judges reconcile the tension between the considerable choice and discretion they exercise when deciding cases with their duty to follow the law in a disciplined manner?

The law does not always point judges unambiguously in the direction of the right answer. That means that judges make difficult choices, often with only very general guidance from the formal legal rules. This element of uncertainty may seem at first blush to be a flaw in the legal regime, but the more I read and thought about it, the more I became convinced that it was an inevitable and desirable feature of law.

Law is, by its very nature, general and universal, intended to apply across the board to all situations. A law that applies equally to all will necessarily be general in nature. Generality gives law its objective, rational, and systemic quality. That is what distinguishes the law from the judicial decisions applying the law. It is not possible to achieve universality of application and at the same time provide immediate answers to all cases that might arise. The immediate answers applying the general legal norms in particular cases are provided by courts and judges.

The law's generality and flexibility give judges the discretion to make sensible decisions, tailored to the facts of each case. My task as a judge was to interpret and apply the law's general norms or standards to the specific context of the case I was deciding. As a trial judge, I had to find the facts – who did what to whom? Every case presented different facts, and different facts call for different decisions. And, as my book on the *Persons Case* had shown, the interpretation of general legal principles – in that case, whether a woman is a "person" – changes over time as society evolves. It was unthinkable when Canada became a nation in 1867 that a woman could hold public office. By 1928, women were in the workplace, and they could vote and sit in the House of Commons. Nineteenth-century misogynistic views could no longer be legitimized by law.

As a judge, I welcomed the fact that the law was sufficiently flexible to allow me and my colleagues to decide individual cases justly. But how far could I go? Did I not have to constrain my judicial choice and judicial discretion to remain faithful to my oath to uphold the rule of law?

As a judge, I understood that I had to make choices. But I certainly did not feel that my choices were unlimited or that I could decide cases according to my personal sense of right and wrong. I had to come up with a decision that respected my obligation to follow the law. The judicial choice I exercised to reach just results had to be reconciled with the judicial discipline required to maintain the rule of law.

The importance of reconciling judicial choice with judicial discipline had become more evident by the time I was a judge than it had been when I started my legal journey fifty years earlier. When I was a law student, a legalistic version of formalism reigned. The law was seen as a set of rules that were to be applied more or less mechanically. English decisions were accorded dominant precedential weight. Academic writing was sparse and rarely cited by the courts. Judges were discouraged, if not forbidden, from considering the normative underpinnings of the laws they interpreted and applied. There was very little consideration of the broader social context from which the case arose. While most of my professors were critical of legalistic formalism, there could be little doubt that it represented the way most lawyers and judges thought about the law.

As I reached the end of my time in the law, the era Brian Dickson described as "blind and empty formalism"[2] was history. The pretence that cases were to be decided by a mechanical application of clear rules had been abandoned. Judges were expected to consider the law's normative underpinnings when deciding how to apply legal rules. As a lawyer, I had argued *Charter* cases, urging judges to interpret *Charter* rights generously. As a scholar, I had done my best to identify a principled basis for deciding a wide range of issues. I had written about how legal history reveals the contingency of law. As a judge, I had become an active participant in judicial education programs that emphasized the importance of considering the social context to ensure just decision making.

I welcomed this liberation of law from its rigid past. It presented a more accurate picture of the law and judicial decision making, and it gave judges the liberty to decide cases justly. But I also worried that accepting the inevitable uncertainty of the law posed a danger. Could the liberty to decide cases justly disintegrate into an unconstrained liberty to decide according to the judge's personal sense of right and wrong? Where would that leave the rule of law?

I wanted to see if I could describe what I felt instinctively as a judge: namely, that there must be an acceptable middle ground between the pretence of blind legal formalism and the risk that recognizing judicial choice and discretion might lead to judges deciding on the basis of their personal views of right and wrong.

I do not think that judges can solve this conundrum by refusing to accept the element of legal uncertainty. I think it important that judges be honest with themselves and with the public they serve. When deciding cases, they do not just "call balls and strikes," as Chief Justice John Roberts famously claimed during his confirmation hearing.[3] I believe that the conscientious judge should not hide behind a façade of judicial neutrality but rather engage in the self-reflection necessary to ensure that personal views and attitudes are placed in proper perspective. I recognized that the decisions I made were value laden and influenced by my background and my life experience. I did my best to consciously reflect on the values I brought to my task. It is easy for a judge to say they are simply applying common sense in deciding a case. There is nothing wrong with common sense decisions if the common sense is supported by the law and general social attitudes. The problem is that what seems to me to be common sense may be the product of a host of factors that have nothing to do with the law and that are not shared by the litigants. Common sense will often be a shield for personal views and biases that should be set aside when deciding cases.

My bedrock principle was not surprising. I saw my role as a judge as being to apply the law faithfully. My job was to render justice under the law, not justice according to my personal beliefs. I recognized that the law did not always provide me with clear answers and that there were what are known as "hard cases," in which there will be a legitimate and likely unresolvable debate in legal circles about what is the "right answer."

Several of the cases that I have discussed in earlier chapters fell into that category. Is there a right of action for invasion of privacy? How should the law resolve the conflict between freedom of the press and the protection of reputation? When should a court assert jurisdiction against a foreign defendant? When faced with deciding these cases, I could not throw up my hands and say, "I don't know." Nor could I say, "the law is unclear, so I am entitled to decide this case as I please." I had to work with existing legal sources, however imperfect or incomplete, and decide the case in a legally principled way. I thought long and hard about each case, I read as much as I could about the issue it presented, and I did my best to decide the case in a way that fit with the existing legal sources and made the law a more coherent whole. I tried to follow a cardinal judicial virtue – namely, to deploy some accepted general principle as a reasoned basis for my decisions.[4]

In a "hard case," I had to accept that my answer was not legally inevitable and that another judge might decide the case differently. I did my best to persuade my colleagues, the litigants, and the public at large that I had reached the right answer. I did not think that the fact that there was no way to be sure that I had reached the right answer relieved me of my duty to aspire to achieve that goal.

In *Good Judgment*, I described the factors that discipline judicial decision making, in particular the obligation to support every judicial decision with a reasoned explanation. The discipline of which I speak was a form of self-discipline. I faced no sanction, apart from professional embarrassment, for failure to adhere to what I saw as the principles of good judgment. Judges are subject to being reversed on appeal if they err, but the principle of judicial independence protects them from discipline for simply being wrong. But judges are also members of a legal community that aspires to uphold the rule of law. I was proud to be a member of that community, and I had taken an oath to uphold the law. That meant that I had to give priority to the law over my personal beliefs.

I have said that blind and empty formalism is dead, but there is an important element of formalism that remains. I was expected to base my decisions on a limited, albeit ill-defined, set of accepted or recognized legal sources. I felt that I had to accept that the law, however incomplete or imprecise, set parameters for my decisions. I saw my role as a judge as being different from that of a scientist, a philosopher, a social scientist, or a law professor. They were engaged in an unconstrained search for the truth. I was doing my best to come up with just results, but I had to respect the limits the law imposed. They were expected to arrive at the best result, all things considered. I was not allowed to consider all things. I had to accept that if I did my job conscientiously to achieve justice under the law and not according to my own beliefs, there would be times when I had to render a decision with which I did not agree, if that was the decision the law expected me to make.

I am sure that, for some, the views I expressed in *Good Judgment* seem too liberal. I reject the "I just call balls and strikes" approach. I recognize that judicial decisions could be influenced by a judge's beliefs and background. I accept that there is a legitimate law-making role for judges in the common law tradition. I welcome the role conferred on judges by the *Charter* to advance our fundamental rights and freedoms.

Others will think that I take an unduly conservative view of the judicial role by insisting that disciplined judicial decision making limits the capacity of a judge to make the world a better place. I accept that sometimes judges must make decisions they personally regard as unjust.

My objective in writing the book was to explore these controversial issues about judging, to develop and explain my own views, and to contribute to what will inevitably be an ongoing debate about judicial decision making. I wanted to promote and contribute to that debate, fully realizing that my book would not end it. If I was able to stimulate thought and discussion, my objective has been achieved, even if not everyone agrees with my views.

Leaving the Judiciary

I am not sure how long I would have continued as a judge had I not faced mandatory retirement at age seventy-five. But faced with that prospect, I decided to leave on my own terms. I did not want to stop working, and I looked forward to undertaking some arbitration work and returning to the U of T Faculty of Law as Distinguished Jurist in Residence to do some writing.

I retired from the judiciary on 28 February 2020, the twenty-fifth anniversary of my appointment to the trial court, nine months before my seventy-fifth birthday. I was very pleased that my last significant judgment[5] was co-authored with my close friend, judicial colleague, and regular golf and tennis partner Russell Juriansz. On my last day in Court, I sat with two wonderful colleagues, one an old friend, Jim MacPherson, and the other a rising judicial star, future Supreme Court Justice Mahmud Jamal.

Arbitration and Mediation

After I left the bench, I joined Arbitration Place in downtown Toronto, home to a long list of arbitrators and mediators that includes several retired judges. My entry into the alternative dispute resolution world was slow, since it coincided with the COVID-19 pandemic and lockdown. But gradually I got rolling, doing an interesting mix of commercial arbitrations and a few mediations and being consulted by lawyers on forthcoming trials and appeals. The arbitration work took me back to my days as a trial judge, while the consultations drew more on my experience as an appellate judge. In most cases, I have usually acted as a sole arbitrator, but I have also sat on panels of three, at times with some of my former judicial colleagues. The cases have been interesting and, since the stakes are typically high, they are well presented by highly skilled advocates.

Throughout the COVID-19 lockdown, proceedings were conducted over the Zoom platform. I much prefer in-person proceedings, but I was surprised at how well virtual hearings worked. It certainly would have been better to have counsel and the witnesses in the hearing room, but I felt I was able to assess credibility and reliability fairly and properly. Despite my lack of experience and the disadvantage of not having the parties present, I was able to settle a few cases in mediation including a complex dispute after an exhausting seven days of discussion over Zoom.

The major difference between sitting in court and sitting as an arbitrator is that, in arbitration, the proceedings are private and confidential. Hearing the witnesses and the arguments is familiar, as is the task of writing reasons. But when I was a judge, every decision I wrote was public and available for all to see, whereas my arbitral awards will never be seen by anyone other than the immediate parties.

The other difference is that arbitration allows the parties considerable latitude in designing a process that is tailor-made to meet the demands of their dispute. As a judge, I followed the standard rules of procedure, while as an arbitrator I find that I am spending time and effort on assisting the parties in developing a process that meets the needs of their case.

Distinguished Jurist in Residence

As I was leaving the bench, Dean Edward Iacobucci invited me to return to the Faculty of Law at the University of Toronto with the lofty title of Distinguished Jurist in Residence. That welcome was extended by Ed's successor, Dean Jutta Brunnée. I have been warmly welcomed back to the faculty by my old colleagues and by many new ones. My duties are light, and I am happy to be able to return to the rich intellectual life of the faculty.

Final Reflections

When I started to write this book, I was not sure that I would finish it. I kept going because I became fully engaged with the exercise of recollecting and recording my thoughts about the various aspects of my life and my professional career. I ceased caring whether what I was writing would ever be published or if it was, whether anyone would read it. The experience of reliving my past was enough to justify carrying on.

Reflecting on my past, I realize how fortunate I was to find the law and to have the support of my family, friends, and colleagues. As I moved from student to lawyer, professor, scholar, dean, and judge, I saw many sides of the law and encountered many remarkable people who have been with me on my journey. My relatively short time in practice at MacKinnon McTaggart helped shape my career as a lawyer, scholar, and judge. Arthur Stone's view on the lawyer's role and the importance of professional integrity and excellence left an indelible mark. Working with two brilliant litigators, Bert MacKinnon and Ian Binnie, exposed me to the qualities of superb advocates. I opted for a different career but what I learned from them made me a better teacher and scholar and allowed me to make the occasional foray back to the courts to argue public law cases while I was a professor.

The U of T's Faculty of Law was my intellectual home as a student and as a professor and has welcomed me back in retirement. Marty Friedland has been a friend and role model from the time I was a student in his first-year criminal law class. Marty and Deans Iacobucci and Prichard worked hard to provide faculty members with a stimulating and collegial environment. The privilege of working on projects with Stephen Waddams, Kent Roach, Katherine Swinton, and Jim Phillips made me a better scholar. It has been a joy to participate in the rich intellectual life of the faculty led by people like Michael Trebilcock, Ernie Weinrib, Brian Langille, and others too numerous to mention.

My two years studying at Oxford were formative. Guided by H.W.R. Wade and Ian Brownlie, I learned how to tackle and complete a major writing project. I have faithfully followed the Brownlie "one brick at a time" and "fifteen-minute" rules with all my writing projects. I have adhered to Professor Wade's view that the important thing is to start writing as soon as possible and to let your ideas develop as part of the writing process. Both my supervisors instilled in me the idea that the task of a legal scholar is to dig beneath the surface of legal rules to identify and develop fundamental principles upon which a coherent legal structure can rest. I followed that direction as a teacher, scholar, and judge. When I shifted my legal writing from legal doctrine to legal history, I enjoyed the challenge of seeing law from a different perspective.

My three years working for Brian Dickson at the Supreme Court of Canada was one of the greatest privileges of my life. I doubt that I would ever have become a judge without that experience. Dickson's wisdom, humanity, and long list of outstanding decisions mark him as my judicial hero. To work with him was a unique experience and to relive that experience when writing his biography and tracing his path to the bench and to judicial greatness was enormously enriching.

Being a judge brings with it a huge responsibility. For me, the weight of the responsibility of sitting in judgment of one's fellow citizens was bearable for two reasons. First, knowing that society had trusted me to perform my role diligently and faithfully was itself a reward that spurred me on to do my very best. Second, I shared the responsibility with a group of dedicated and hard-working colleagues. It was a privilege to come together with my colleagues to solve difficult legal problems. Even when I disagreed with my colleagues, I had no doubt that our work was stronger than had I been left to my own devices.

I do not think of myself as a risk taker, but at several points in my career, I was prepared to change course and take a direction others thought unwise. Each time, my change from what most people would regard as an orthodox career path enriched my personal and professional life. The story of my legal life reflects a line in a John Lennon song: "Life is what happens to you while you're busy making other plans."[6]

My year away in France after first year law school surprised my family and my classmates. It turned out to be one of the best experiences of my life, opening my mind to a different culture and language and teaching me what it is like to live as an outsider in a different society.

I enjoyed the cut and thrust of law practice and litigation, but I was diverted from that career path first by taking two years to study at Oxford and then by deciding to give academic life a try. My time in Oxford was one of the most enjoyable periods of my life. My "temporary" diversion from practice to try teaching for a year unexpectedly became permanent when I found how much I enjoyed being a legal scholar and teacher. Many colleagues doubted the wisdom of my next diversion from the law school to serve as Executive Legal Officer at the Supreme Court of Canada. Why leave the post of professor to be a glorified law clerk? But those three years working with one of Canada's greatest judges were transformative.

I came to the law at an ideal time. I entered law before the field became competitive and money-driven. I did not have to have outstanding grades and an impressive resume to get into law school, and I stumbled upon an amazing group of lawyers when I articled and practised law. In today's intensely competitive world of law, most aspiring young lawyers plan every move to ensure professional success and satisfaction. I did not have to do that. I always felt that I had the freedom to pursue unexpected opportunities when they arose. I know that my experience is dated, but I still think it is important for aspiring lawyers not to commit too early on a path from which they are not prepared to deviate. Instead, I think they should be prepared to seize opportunities when they arise. I have found that doing what I found interesting and challenging served me better than trying to follow some preconceived path. When things fell my way, as they frequently did, I followed my instincts, accepted the challenge, and worked hard to make the most of the opportunity that had been presented.

I had the good fortune to be a lawyer, a scholar, and a judge during an unusually dynamic period in Canadian law. Law never stands still, but my time in the law coincided with an era when more and more attention has been focused on law and more and more has been expected from lawyers and judges.

When I entered law school, Canadian law was still emerging from its colonial past. We read many English decisions and relied on English textbooks. Legal formalism – the idea that the law was a fixed set of rules that could be mechanically applied to solve all problems – prevailed. Law was seen in essentially static terms. Only the brave dared to suggest that courts and judges could make law if that was what was needed to achieve just outcomes. Canadian constitutional law focused on resolving jurisdictional disputes between the federal government and the provinces. Provincial human rights codes had been enacted, as had the *Canadian Bill of Rights*, but the courts seemed determined to interpret these tools narrowly and were reluctant to make use of them to advance human rights and basic freedoms.

I argued cases, taught students, and wrote about law as all of that was changing. Judges like Bora Laskin and Brian Dickson started to lead Canada out of the era of "blind and empty formalism."[7] Understanding the law in terms of its underlying purposes and values was liberating. Twelve years after I graduated from law school, Canada entered the era of the *Charter of Rights and Freedoms*. Lawyers, judges, and law professors took up the challenge of breathing life into that document. For the next four decades, I found myself engaged as a lawyer, as a scholar, and as a judge in Canada's attempt to make something of the *Charter* and, more generally, to shape the law in the post-formalist era.

I could never have imagined that I would be afforded these opportunities when I was growing up in Prince Edward County. It has been an amazing and unexpected ride.

I have said a great deal about the lawyers, professors, and judges with whom I have worked. But at the end of the day, there is nothing quite like the reality check at the family dinner table. My wife, Geraldine and my three children, Anne, Claire, and Stephen, listened patiently when I explained what I was working on. They regularly offered me sage advice, but most of all, they kept me grounded in the things that really matter in life.

Notes

1. Beginnings

1 I am indebted to Roger Timms for his genealogical sleuthing to trace the Sharp(e) family lineage.

2 Eric Brown & Tim Cook, "The 1936 Vimy Pilgrimage" (2011) 20:2 Canadian Military History 37.

2. Early Education

1 The leading US case was *McGowan v Maryland* 366 US 420 (1960) and the Canadian decision is *R v Big M Drug Mart Ltd*, [1985] 1 SCR 295.

2 I am indebted to Diane Mills, Academic Counsellor at Western's Faculty of Music, and to Janet Stubbs, my law school classmate and singer of many leading mezzo soprano roles, for information about Prof. Rosé.

3. Law School

1 Ian Kyer & Jerome Bickenbach, *The Fiercest Debate: Cecil A. Wright, The Benchers and Legal Education in Ontario, 1923–57* (Toronto: The Osgoode Society, 1987); Philip Girard, *Bora Laskin: Bringing Law to Life* (Toronto: University of Toronto Press and the Osgoode Society for Canadian Legal History, 2005) ch 7.

2 Martin Friedland, *Searching for W.P.M. Kennedy: The Biography of an Enigma* (Toronto: University of Toronto Press, 2020).

3 (Toronto: McClelland and Stuart, 1966).

4 *Reference Re: Steven Murray Truscott*, [1967] SCR 309.

5 *Truscott (Re)*, 2007 ONCA 575.

6 *Fontaine v British Columbia (Official Administrator)*, [1998] 1 SCR 424, citing Cecil A. Wright, "Res Ipsa Loquitur" in *Special Lectures of the Law Society of Upper Canada (1955), Evidence* (Toronto: Richard de Boo, 1979).

7 A restrictive covenant is a term that prevents the owner from using the property in a specified way. Such a term "runs with the land" if the restriction binds a subsequent purchaser who did not agree to the term.

8 Sharpe, *Good Judgment: Making Judicial Decisions* (Toronto: University of Toronto Press, 2018) at 14.

9 *Times* Obituary, 8 October 2004.

10 For Canadian lawyers, *Halsbury's Laws of England* has now been replaced with *Halsbury's Laws of Canada*.

4. MacKinnon McTaggart

1 The firm's story is told by Ian Binnie, "Work Hard and Don't Grumble" (2022) 41:3 Advocates' Journal 27; and by Arthur Stone, "The Ault Firm – A Brief Memoir," unpublished.

2 Binnie, *supra* note 1 at 27.

3 "The Admiralty Court in Colonial Nova Scotia" (1994) 17 Dal LJ 363.

4 *Re Forfar and Township of East Gwillimbury et al*, [1971] 3 OR 337 (CA).

5 *Re Forfar and Township of East Gwillimbury et al* (1972), 28 DLR (3d) 512 (SCC).

6 *Re Baby Duffell Martin v Duffell*, [1950] SCR 737.

7 Unreported.

8 *Banks v the Globe and Mail Ltd et al*, [1961] SCR 474.

9 *Re The Ontario Crime Commission, Ex parte Feeley and McDermott*, [1962] OR 872 (CA); *Re Ontario Crime Commission*, [1963] 1 OR 391 (CA).

10 *The Queen v George*, [1966] SCR 267.

11 *Attorney General of Canada v Lavell*, [1974] SCR 1349.

12 *Jordan House Ltd v Menow*, [1974] SCR 239, recently identified as a "pivotal moment" of change in Canada's tort law system: Rande Kostal & Erica Chamberlain, "The Reinvention of Canadian Tort Law. 1945–95: *Jordan House* as Case Study" (2023) 73 UTLJ 133.

13 *Regina v Ontario Labour Relations Board, Ex parte Trenton Construction Workers Association, Local 52*, [1963] 2 OR 376 (SC).

14 *Howard et al v Parrinton et al*, [1971] 3 OR 659 (SC).

15 Binnie, *supra* note 1 at 28.

16 John Omstead, "Plan for Pickering Airport Dead after More Than 50 Years of Debate, Ottawa Says," *CBC News*, 27 January 2025, online: <www.cbc.ca/news/canada/toronto/ont-pickering-airport-lands-1.7442457>.

17 Philip Girard, *Bora Laskin: Bringing Law to Life* (Toronto: University of Toronto Press and the Osgoode Society for Canadian Legal History, 2005) at 368.

18 Binnie, *supra* note 1 at 31.
19 [1959] SCR 121.
20 *MacLean et al v Liquor Licence Board of Ontario et al*, 1974 CanLII 856 (ONSC), affirmed by the Divisional Court (1975), 9 OR (2d) 597.
21 [1978] 1 SCR 369.
22 See John Olthius, "Project North Defends Indigenous Rights – The Mackenzie Valley Pipeline Proposal" in Joe Gunn, ed, *Journeys to Justice: Reflections on Canadian Christian Activism* (Toronto: Novalis Publishing Inc, 2018).
23 *Re Canadian Arctic Gas Pipeline Ltd et al* (1975), 65 DLR (3d) 660 (FC).
24 *Ibid* at 667.
25 *Ibid*.
26 [1978] 1 SCR 369 at 394.

5. Oxford

1 Peter Cane & Jane Stapleton, eds (Oxford: OUP, 2008).
2 *Somerset v Stewart* (1772), 98 ER 499.
3 S 10(c).
4 Wade's approach has, however, since fallen out of favour as an appropriate framework for judicial review of administrative action in general. The modern approach recognizes and respects the expertise of administrative decision makers and requires the courts to defer to their decisions unless they are unreasonable: see *Canada (Minister of Citizenship and Immigration) v Vavilov*, 2019 SCC 65.
5 Jack Beatson, "Wade, Henry William Rawson, 1918–2004" British Academy, (14 June 2019), online: <www.thebritishacademy.ac.uk/publishing/memoirs/6/wade-henry-william-rawson-1918-2004/>.
6 19 January 2010.
7 *R v Chapman and Currie* (1972) 14 Crim Law Q 399.
8 11 January 2010.
9 *Commissioner of Police for the Metropolis and Others, Ex Parte Pinochet*, [1999] UKHL 17.
10 (London: Duckworth, 1977).
11 Wally Cherwinski, "Blackpool Hockey Night All Oxford," 27 May 1972.
12 *The Politics of the Judiciary* (Fontana: London, 1977) at 82.
13 (1977) 40 Mod L R 239.
14 20 May 1977.
15 "*Habeas Corpus* and the Canadian Charter of Rights and Freedoms" in Guy S Goodwin-Gill and Stefan Talmon, eds, *The Reality of International Law: Essays in Honour of Ian Brownlie* (Oxford: Oxford University Press, 1999).

6. Law Professor

1 (Oxford: Clarendon Press, 1969).
2 I return to this idea in Chapter 7.
3 See Robert Sharpe, *Good Judgment: Making Judicial Decisions* (Toronto: University of Toronto Press, 2018) at 14.
4 Charles Clark, "The Handmaid of Justice" (1938) 23 Wash U L Rev 297.
5 *Jordan House Ltd v Menow*, [1974] SCR 239.
6 Abram Chayes, "The Role of the Judge in Public Law Litigation" (1976) 89 Harvard L Rev 1281.
7 I did eventually write an article on the subject: "Injunctions and the Charter" (1984) 22 Osgoode Hall LJ 473.
8 The next few paragraphs draw freely on my essay "Ethics and Professionalism in Advocacy: Resolute Advocacy and Civility" in Archibald et al eds, *The Trial Book* (Toronto: Thompson Reuters, 2021).
9 W. Bradley Wendel, "The Limits of Positivist Legal Ethics: A Brief History, Critique, and a Return to the Foundations" (2017) 30 Can J L & Juris 443 at 445.
10 For an engaging discussion of this issue by a leading criminal defence lawyer, see Marie Henein, *Nothing but the Truth: A Memoir* (Toronto: Penguin Random House, 2021).
11 Kent Roach, *Wrongfully Convicted: Guilty Pleas, Imagined Crimes and What Canada Must Do to Safeguard Justice* (Toronto: Simon and Schuster, 2023).
12 The Bar Council, "Cab Rank Rule: Statement of the Four Bars" (26 May 2023), online: <www.barcouncil.org.uk/resource/cab-rank-rule-statement-of-the-four-bars.html>.
13 CP Curtis, "The Ethics of Advocacy" (1951) 4 Stan L R 3; Monroe Freedman, *Legal Ethics in an Adversary System* (Indianapolis: Bobbs-Merrill, 1975).
14 *Code of Professional Conduct*, Rule 5.1–1.
15 *Ashby v White*, (1703) 92 ER 126.
16 For a recent attempt, see Stephen Smith, *Rights, Wrongs, and Injustices* (Oxford: OUP, 2019).
17 (1985) 43 U Toronto Fac L Rev.
18 "Strict Liability and Due Diligence in Public Welfare Offences: *R v City of Sault Ste. Marie*" (1979) 4 Canadian Business LJ 453.
19 "Claiming Privilege in the Discovery Process" (1984) Law Society of Upper Canada Special Lectures, 163.
20 *Blank v Canada (Minister of Justice)*, 2006 SCC 39; *Lizotte v Aviva Insurance Company of Canada*, 2016 SCC 52.
21 "Constricting Federal Court Jurisdiction: A Comment on *The Queen v Fuller Construction*" (1980) 30 UTLJ 283.

22 *Canadian Civil Procedure*, 3rd ed (Toronto: Emond Montgomery, 1988).
23 "Bora Laskin and Civil Liberties" (1985) 35 UTLJ 632.
24 "Commercial Expression and the Charter" (1987) 37 UTLJ 229.
25 For example, "The Charter of Rights and Freedoms and the Supreme Court of Canada: The First Four Years" (1987) Public Law 48.
26 *Interprovincial Product Liability Litigation: Jurisdiction, Enforcement and Choice of Law* (Ottawa: Consumer and Corporate Affairs Canada, 1981).
27 *Interprovincial Product Liability Litigation* (Toronto: Butterworths, 1982).
28 *Morguard Investments Ltd v De Savoye*, [1990] 3 SCR 1077.
29 (1982) 60 Can Bar Rev 541 at 546.
30 See Chapter 12.
31 "Damages for Lost Opportunity to Bargain" (1982) 2 Oxf J Leg Stud 290.
32 Future UK Supreme Court Justice Andrew Burrows described the article as "groundbreaking" while disagreeing with applying it generally. "One Step Forward?" (2018) 134 LQR 515.
33 Courts of Law and Equity were fused in the 1850s in Nova Scotia and New Brunswick and were never separate in Western Canada: Phillips, Girard & Brown, *A History of Law in Canada, Volume Two: Law for a New Dominion* (Toronto: University of Toronto Press and the Osgoode Society, 2022) at 90–94.
34 Canadian Foundation for Legal Research, "Walter Owen Book Prize," online: <https://cflr-fcrj.ca/walter-owen-book-prize>.
35 See, e.g. Jeff Berryman, "Injunctions and Specific Performance, Second Edition" (1994) 73 Can Bar Rev 105; Anthony Ogus, "Injunctions and Specific Performance by Robert Sharpe" (1985) 5 Legal Studies 112; D.R. Harris, "Remedies: A Canadian Perspective" (1987) 7 Oxford J Leg Stud 465; Beverley McLachlin, "Injunctions and Specific Performance" (1984) 18 UBCLR 412; Charles Harpum, "The Law of Damages and Injunctions and Specific Performance" (1985) Cambridge LJ 495;
36 Christine Boyle, "Injunctions and Specific Performance; The Law of Damages" (1985) 63:2 Can Bar Rev 427.
37 Published as "Injunctions and the Charter" (1984) 22 Osgoode Hall LJ 473.
38 One of my favourite articles is Calabresi and Melamed, "Property Rules, Liability Rules and Inalienability: One View of the Cathedral" (1975), 85 Harvard L Rev 1089, an article that strongly influenced my treatment of injunctions as a remedy for nuisance as well as my views on how to approach different legal theories: see *Good Judgment* at 15.
39 *Law and Learning: Report to the Social Sciences and Humanities Research Council of Canada* (1983).
40 *Ibid* at 65–66.
41 See Mark Weisberg, "On the Relationship of 'Law and Learning' to Law and Learning" (1983) 29 McGill LJ 155.

42 Tom Cromwell, "In the Matter of an Arbitration Between the Union of Doctrinal and Theoretical Scholars and the Consultative Group on Legal Research and Education in Law" (1984) Osgoode Hall LJ 761.
43 For examples, see *Good Judgment, supra* note 3 at 179–86.

7. My First Adventures in Legal History

1 Jim Phillips, "The Importance of Legal History" (2010) 41 Victoria University at Wellington Law Rev.
2 "*Habeas Corpus*, Extradition and the Burden of Proof: The Case of the Man Who Escaped from Devil's Island" (1990) 49 Cambridge Law Rev 422, commenced and largely written before but published after *The Last Day, the Last Hour: The Currie Libel Trial*.
3 (1907) 51 Sol J 571.
4 (1888) 60 LT 538; (1888) 5 TLR 160; (1888) 5 TLR 188.
5 For technical reasons, a judgment in a *habeas corpus* case does not have binding effect if the same issue arises again: Robert Sharpe, *The Law of Habeas Corpus* (Oxford: Clarendon Press, 1976) at 201–12.
6 (Murray, 1928).
7 (Doubleday, 1929).
8 5 TLR at 190.
9 *I Was a Bandit* at 248.
10 5 December 1940.
11 *The Last Day, the Last Hour: The Currie Libel Trial* (Toronto: Osgoode Society and Carswell, 1988) and (Toronto: Osgoode Society and University of Toronto Press, 2009).
12 *Cusson v Quan* 2007 ONCA 771, discussed in Chapter 12.
13 Canadian juries must be unanimous in criminal cases, but most jurisdictions, including Ontario, allow for majority verdicts in civil cases.
14 *The Last Day, the Last Hour, supra* note 11 at 244.

8. Constitutional Litigation

1 *Charter Litigation* (Toronto: Butterworths, 1987).
2 *Re Warwick and Minister of Community and Social Services* (1978), 21 OR (2d) 528 (CA).
3 See A Alan Borovoy, *At the Barricades* (Toronto: Irwin Law, 2014).
4 See Kent Roach, "The Impact of the Charter and the Judicial Activism Debate" in *Acting for Freedom: Fifty Years of Civil Liberties in Canada* (Toronto: Second Story Press, 2014).
5 *Re Klein and Law Society of Upper Canada* (1985), 50 OR (2d) 118 (SCDC).

6 A Alan Borovoy, *When Freedoms Collide: The Case for Our Civil Liberties* (Toronto: Lester Orpen and Dennys, 1988)
7 The CCLA's intervention application failed but the Alberta Court of Appeal held that the *Criminal Code* provision should be stuck down as a violation of freedom of expression: *R v Keegstra*, 1988 ABCA 234. The CCLA intervened when the case was appealed to the Supreme Court of Canada where the hate late law provision was upheld as a reasonable limit on freedom of expression: *R v Keegstra*, [1990] 3 SCR 697
8 *R v Keegstra*, [1990] 3 SCR 697.
9 *R v Zundel*, [1992] 2 SCR 731.
10 *Re Ontario Film & Video Appreciation Society and Ontario Film Review Board et al; Canadian Civil Liberties Association, Intervenor* (1986), 57 OR (2d) 339 (SC).
11 *Re Zylberberg et al. and Director of Education of Sudbury Board of Education; League for Human Rights of B'Nai Brith Canada et al., Intervenors* (1986), 55 OR (2d) 749 (Div. Ct.)
12 S 28(1) of RRO 1980, Reg 262, enacted under the *Education Act*, RSO 1980, c 129.
13 *R v Big M Drug Mart Ltd*, [1985] 1 SCR 295.
14 *Zylberberg v Sudbury Board of Education*, 1988 CanLII 189 (ONCA), 65 OR (2d) 641.
15 *Corporation of the Canadian Civil Liberties Assn v Ontario (Minister of Education* (1988), 64 OR (2d) 577 (SC).
16 *Canadian Civil Liberties Assn v Ontario (Minister of Education)* (1990), 71 OR (2d) 341 (CA).
17 *War Veterans Allowance Act*, RSC 1970, c W-5.
18 *Bregman et al v Attorney-General of Canada*, 1986 CanLII 2485 (ONCA).
19 1987 1 SCR vi.
20 *Andrews v Law Society of British Columbia*, [1989] 1 SCR 143.
21 *Lavigne v Ontario Public Service Employees Union*, [1991] 2 SCR 211.
22 *R v Edwards Books and Art Ltd*, [1986] 2 SCR 713.
23 *R v Swain*, [1991] 1 SCR 933.
24 *Remedies for Violations of Human Rights; A Two-Track Approach to Supra-National and National Law* (Cambridge: Cambridge University Press, 2021).
25 *Schachter v Canada*, [1992] 2 SCR 679.
26 *The Constitution Act, 1867*, s 93(1).
27 *Tiny Separate School Trustees v The King* [1928] AC 363.
28 *Reference re an Act to Amend the Education Act*, 1986 CanLII 2863 (ONCA).
29 [1987] 1 SCR 1148.
30 [1995] 2 SCR 1130.
31 376 US 254 (1964).
32 *Grant v Torstar* 2009 SCC 61. See Chapter 12 for further discussion.

9. Executive Legal Officer at the Supreme Court of Canada

1 *R v Sault Ste Marie*, [1978] 2 SCR 1299; "Strict Liability and Due Diligence in Public Welfare Offences: *R. v. City of Sault Ste. Marie*" (1979), 4 Canadian Business LJ 453.
2 [1979] 2 SCR 373.
3 "Antonio Lamer and Section 7 of the Charter: A Law Reformer's Ambition, a Judge's Restraint" in Adam Dodek & Daniel Jutras, eds, *The Sacred Fire: The Legacy of Antonio Lamer* (Toronto: Lexis-Nexis, 2009).
4 *R v Miller* (1975), 63 DLR (3d) 193 (BCCA). At the Supreme Court, Chief Justice Laskin and Justice Dickson joined the majority in affirming the majority decision and rejecting Justice of Appeal McIntrye's dissent: [1977] 2 SCR 680.
5 Beverley McLachlin, (1984) 18 UBCLR 412.
6 "The La Forest Years: The Vocation of Judging – A Judge's Perspective" in R Johnson & JP McEvoy, eds, *Gerard V. La Forest at the Supreme Court of Canada 1985–1997* (Winnipeg: Supreme Court of Canada Historical Society, Canadian Legal History Project, Faculty of Law, University of Manitoba, 2000).
7 "A Comment on David Beatty's 'The Politicization of Law'" (1991) 41 University of Toronto LJ 469.
8 Quoted in Robert Sharpe & Kent Roach, *Brian Dickson: A Judge's Journey* (Toronto: University of Toronto Press and the Osgoode Society, 2003) at 206–7.
9 *Ibid* at 213–14.
10 I described the role in "The Tasks and Role of a Media Spokesperson for the Courts" (1991) 1 Media and Communications Law Rev 271.
11 [1988] 2 SCR 712.
12 *R v Morgentaler*, [1988] 1 SCR 30.
13 *Tremblay v Daigle*, [1989] 2 SCR 530.
14 *Brain Dickson: A Judge's Journey* at 393–394.
15 *Andrews v Law Society of British Columbia*, [1989] 1 SCR 143.
16 *Edmonton Journal v Alberta (Attorney General)*, [1989] 2 SCR 1326.
17 *Ford v Quebec (AG)*, [1988] 2 SCR 712.
18 *Irwin Toy Ltd v Quebec (Attorney General)*, [1989] 1 SCR 927.
19 *R v Crown Zellerbach Canada Ltd*, [1988] 1 SCR 401.
20 *Janzen v Platy Enterprises Ltd*, [1989] 1 SCR 1252.
21 *R v Bernard*, [1988] 2 SCR 833.
22 *R v Corbett*, [1988] 1 SCR 670.
23 *R v Mack*, [1988] 2 SCR 903.
24 [1989] 2 SCR 1228.
25 [1989] 2 SCR 1181.
26 [1989] 1 SCR 426.

27 [1989] 2 SCR 574.
28 *Judges Act*, RSC, 1985, c J-1, s 60(1).
29 Quoted in *Brian Dickson: A Judge's Journey* at 320.

10. Law School Dean

1 Published (1991), UTLJ 295.
2 *Re: Resolution to amend the Constitution*, [1981] 1 SCR 753.
3 Quoted in Robert Sharpe & Kent Roach, *Brian Dickson: A Judge's Journey* (Toronto: University of Toronto Press and the Osgoode Society, 2003) at 269.
4 *Supra* note 2 at 884.
5 *The Charter of Rights and Freedoms* (Toronto: Irwin Law, 1998).
6 "La Carta canadese dei diritti e delle liberta" [1992] Quaderni Costituzionali 363.
7 "The Impact of a Bill of Rights on the Role of the Judiciary," 16 July 1992, Australian National University, later published in Philip Alston, ed, *Promoting Human Rights Through Bills of Rights: Comparative Perspectives* (Oxford: Oxford University Press, 1999).
8 See e.g. Michael Mandel, *The Charter of Rights and Freedoms and the Legalization of Politics in Canada*, 2nd ed (Toronto: Thompson Educational Publishers, 1994); Andrew Petter "The Politics of the Charter" (1986) 8 SCLR 473.
9 See e.g. David Beatty, *Talking Heads and the Supremes: The Canadian Production of Constitutional Review* (Toronto: Carswell, 1990).

11. Trial Judge

1 The *Courts of Justice Amendment Act, 1989 (No. 1)* SO 1989, c 55.
2 "Courtroom to Classroom: Two Perspectives on the Law," Yves Pratte Lecture, Faculty of Law, University of Toronto, 6 November 1996 (unpublished).
3 I discuss my most significant reversal, the *Dunmore* decision, below.
4 A pilot project on judicial evaluation in Nova Scotia was successful: Dale Poel, "What Do Lawyers Think About Judicial Evaluation? Responses to the Nova Scotia Judicial Development Project" (2005) 10 The Innovation Journal: The Public Sector Innovation Journal, article 5.
5 *Aguonie v Galion Solid Waste Material Inc.* (1998), 38 OR (3d) 161 (CA).
6 *Hryniak v Mauldin*, 2014 SCC 7. I was a member of the five-judge panel in the Court of Appeal in that case that overruled *Aguonie*, 2011 ONCA 764. The Supreme Court's decision took an even more pro-summary judgment position.

7 *Mahar v Rogers Cablesystems Ltd*, 1995 CanLII 7428.
8 *United States of America v Friedland* (1996), 30 OR (3d) 568 (SC).
9 *Transamerica Life Insurance Co. of Canada v Canada Life Assurance Co.* (1996), 28 OR (3d) 423 (SC).
10 For example, *Dabbs v Sun Life Assurance Co of Canada* (1998), 40 OR (3d) 429 (SC), dealing with the test to approve proposed settlements.
11 *Windisman v Toronto College Park Ltd.* (1996), 28 OR (3d) 29 (SC).
12 *Lloyd's London, Non-Marine Underwriters v National Armoured Ltd* (1996), 142 DLR (4th) 506 (SC).
13 *Scintilore Explorations Ltd v Larche*, [1999] OJ No 2847 (SC).
14 *Dunmore v Ontario (Attorney General)* (1997), 37 OR (3d) 287 (SC).
15 (1999) 182 DLR (4th) 471 (ONCA).
16 2001 SCC 94.
17 *Daly v Ontario (Attorney General)* (1997), 38 OR (3d) 37, affd 44 OR (3d) 349 (ONCA).
18 See Chapter 7.
19 *Pizza Pizza Ltd v Toronto Star Newspapers Ltd* (1998), 42 OR (3d) 36, affd 49 OR (3d) 254 (ONCA).
20 *Ibid* at para 20.
21 "The Application and Impact of Judicial Discretion in Commercial Litigation" (1998) 17:1 Advocates' Journal 4 (also published in ML Pilkington, JM Spence & H Dumont, eds, *The Administration of Justice in Commercial Disputes* (Montreal: Edition Themis, 1997).
22 As discussed in Chapter 14, I returned to Kenya in 2002.
23 "The La Forest Years: The Vocation of Judging – A Judge's Perspective" in R Johnson & JP McEvoy, eds., *Gerard V. La Forest at the Supreme Court of Canada 1985–1997* (Winnipeg: Supreme Court of Canada Historical Society, Canadian Legal History Project, Faculty of Law, University of Manitoba, 2000).
24 All trial judges are appointed as "ex officio" judges of the Court of Appeal and, when the need arises, are able to sit as a judge of that Court.
25 *Mutual Life v Sun Life* Nov 17, 1998 (unreported) sitting with Finlayson and Austin JJA.

12. Court of Appeal

1 For a full account of Roy McMurtry's career see Roy McMurtry, *Memoirs and Reflections* (Toronto: University of Toronto Press and the Osgoode Society for Canadian Legal History, 2013).
2 As I will explain in Chapter 13, the confidentiality of judicial deliberations posed a problem when Kent Roach and I were writing the Dickson biography.

3 *BD v Halton Region Children's Aid Society* (2006), 79 OR (3d) 45 (CA).
4 *Syl Apps Secure Treatment Centre v BD*, 2007 SCC 38.
5 *R v Sheppard*, 2002 SCC 26.
6 *Muscutt v Courcelles* (2002), 60 OR (3d) 20 (CA).
7 *Van Breda v Village Resorts Ltd*, 2010 ONCA 84.
8 *Currie v McDonald's Restaurants of Canada Ltd* (2005), 74 OR (3d) 321 (CA).
9 *Club Resorts Ltd v Van Breda*, 2012 SCC 17.
10 Chapter 6.
11 In a review of my book *Good Judgment: Making Judicial Decisions*, University Club Newsletter June 2019, Peter Griffin, one of our leading advocates, observed: "Judicial decision-making spans a broad spectrum from the Justice Sharpes to others who may be more visceral in their decision-making process."
12 Standard of review is discussed further below.
13 Richard Posner, *How Judges Think* (Cambridge MA: Harvard University Press, 2010) at 221.
14 Emmett Macfarlane, *Governing from the Bench: The Supreme Court of Canada and the Judicial Role* (Vancouver: UBC Press, 2013) at 106–7.
15 *Good Judgment*, *supra* note 11 at 47.
16 *R v Omar* 2007 ONCA 117.
17 *Ibid* at para 32.
18 *United States v Leonard*, 2012 ONCA 622.
19 *R v Powley* (2001), 53 OR (3d) 35 (CA).
20 *Ibid* at para 101.
21 *Ibid* at para 75.
22 *Ibid*.
23 *R v Edgar*, 2010 ONCA 529.
24 *R v Khan*, [1990] 2 SCR 531.
25 *R v Seaboyer; R v Gayme*, [1991] 2 SCR 577.
26 *The Commission on Proceedings Involving Guy Paul Morin: Report* (Toronto: Ontario Ministry of the Attorney General, 1998).
27 Justices of Appeal Feldman and Gillese.
28 See Kent Roach, *Wrongfully Convicted: Guilty Pleas, Imagined Crimes, and What Canada Must Do to Safeguard Justice* (Toronto: Simon and Shuster, 2023).
29 Chapter 13.
30 *R v Lacasse*, 2015 SCC 64.
31 "The Good Judge" (2005) 23 Advocates' J 13.
32 *Cusson v Quan*, 2007 ONCA 771.
33 Chapter 7.
34 Chapter 8.
35 Especially *Douglas v Tucker*, [1952] 1 SCR 275.

36 *Cusson, supra* note 32 at paras 59–71.
37 *New York Times Co v Sullivan*, 376 US 254 (1964).
38 As developed by the English courts: see *Reynolds v Times Newspapers Ltd*, [2001] 2 AC 127.
39 *Grant v Torstar Corp*, 2009 SCC 61.
40 *Cusson v Quan*, 2009 SCC 62.
41 2012 ONCA 32.
42 *Ibid* at para 65.

13. More Scholarly Adventures

1 "How Judges Decide" in Assay and Higgins, eds, *Principles, Procedure and Justice: Essays in Honour of Adrian Zuckerman* (Oxford: OUP, 2020).
2 *Brian Dickson: A Judge's Journey* (Toronto: University of Toronto Press and Osgoode Society, 2003).
3 We provided a detailed discussion of this issue and an explanation of how and why we had used the papers in the preface to *Brian Dickson: A Judge's Journey*.
4 For example, there is a twenty-year limit on the confidentiality of Cabinet documents *Privacy Act*, RSC 1985, c P-21, s 70(3). For the situation at common law, see *Attorney General v Jonathan Cape Ltd*, [1975] 3 All ER 484 (the Crossman Diaries case), refusing to enjoin the publication of a cabinet member's dairy disclosing cabinet discussions ten years earlier.
5 Sean Fine, "Supreme Court of Canada to Keep Records of Deliberations Secret for at Least 50 Years," *The Globe and Mail* (13 May 2018), online: <www.theglobeandmail.com/canada/article-supreme-court-of-canada-places-50-year-embargo-on-public-access-to/>.
6 See *R v Sault Ste Marie*, [1978] 2 SCR 1299.
7 Perhaps most notably his decision in *Harrison v Carswell*, [1976] 2 SCR 200.
8 Jamie Cameron, "Dickson's Law: Manifestly One of the Humanities" (2005) 55 UTLJ 93 at 103.
9 *Vetrrovec v R*, [1982] 1 SCR 811 at 823.
10 *Judge's Journey, supra* note 2 at p 216.
11 Richard Pound, "A judge's journey well detailed; his inner life only partially revealed" Policy Options, December 2004–January 2005; Ellen Anderson, (2004–5) 74 U of T Quarterly 575; Jamie Cameron, *supra* note 8; Brian Crane, (2004–2005) 36 Ottawa LR 362; Roland Penner "Defender of the Charter: Portrait of a Supreme Court justice as humanist and innovator" (May 2004) Literary Review of Canada 25.
12 RW Kostal, "Shilling for Judges: Brian Dickson and His Biographers" (2006) 51 McGill LR 199.
13 *Edwards v Attorney General*, [1930] AC 128.

14 Patricia I McMahon & Robert J Sharpe, *The Persons Case: The Origins and Legacy of the Fight for Legal Personhood* (Toronto: University of Toronto Press and Osgoode Society, 2007).

15 S 24.

16 *Reference Re the Meaning of the Word 'Persons' in Section 24 of the British North America Act*, [1928] SCR 276 at 282.

17 *Supra* note 13.

18 *Woolmington v DPP*, [1935] AC 462.

19 RFV Heuston, *Lives of the Lord Chancellors, 1885–1940* (Oxford: Clarendon Press, 1964) at 505.

20 *Edwards*, *supra* note 13 at 134.

21 *Edwards*, *supra* note 13 at 138.

22 *Ibid.*

23 Nellie McClung, *In Times Like These* (1915; reprint, Toronto: University of Toronto Press, 1972) at 22.

24 *The Black Candle* (Thomas Allen: Toronto, 1922).

25 *Sterilization Act*, SA 1928, c 37. See Timothy Christian, *The Mentally Ill and Human Rights in Alberta: A Study of the Alberta Sexual Sterilization Act* (Edmonton: Alberta Law Foundation, 1974).

26 *Obergefell v Hodges* 135 S Ct 2584 (2015), per Kennedy J.

27 *The Lazier Murder, Prince Edward County, 1884* (Toronto: Osgoode Society and University of Toronto Press, 2011).

28 *Ibid* at 154.

29 *Ibid* at 15.

14. International Assignments

1 Coel Kirkby, "Commonwealth Constitution-Maker: The Life of Yash Ghai" in Richard Drayton & Saul Dubow, eds, *Commonwealth History in the Twenty-First Century* (London: Palgrave Macmillan, 2020), SSRN-id3802980(1).pdf.

2 *Report of the Advisory Panel of Eminent Commonwealth Judicial Experts*, Nairobi Kenya, 17 May 2002.

3 International Bar Association, *Striving for Judicial Independence: A Report into Proposed Changes to the Judiciary in Russia* (London: IBS, 2005), online (pdf): <www.ibanet.org/images/downloads/2005_06_June_Report_Russia_Striving%20for%20Judicial%20Independence_Final_English.pdf=.

4 International Bar Association, *The Struggle to Maintain an Independent Judiciary: A Report on the Attempt to Remove the Chief Justice of Pakistan* (London: IBA, 2007). This part draws on Robert Sharpe & Michelle Bradfield, "Crisis in Pakistan" in Adam Dodek & Lorne Sossin, eds, *Judicial Independence in Context* (Toronto: Irwin Law, 2010).

5 *Constitution of the Islamic Republic of Pakistan*, art 43.
6 IBA Report, Appendix D.
7 *Constitution of the Islamic Republic of Pakistan*, art 209.
8 In the Supreme Court of Pakistan, Constitutional Original Petition No. 21 of 2007.
9 "Emergency to End Judicial Activism," *Dawn* (4 November 2007), online: <www.dawn.com/news/274266/>.

15. Conclusion

1 "The Application and Impact of Judicial Discretion in Commercial Litigation" (1998) 17:1 Advocates' Journal 4 (also published in ML Pilkington, JM Spence & H Dumont, eds, *The Administration of Justice in Commercial Disputes*, Edition Themis, 1997).
2 *Vetrovec v R*, [1982] 1 SCR 811 at 823.
3 *Confirmation Hearing on the Nomination of Chief Justice John G Roberts Jr to be Chief Justice of the United States*, 12 September 2005, Serial No J-109–37 (Washington: US Government Printing Office, 2005).
4 HLA Hart, *The Concept of Law*, 3rd ed (Oxford: Oxford University Press, 2012) at 273.
5 *Brazeau v Canada (Attorney General)*, 2020 ONCA 184.
6 Beautiful Boy (Darling Boy).
7 *Supra* note 2 at 823.

Index

PUBLICATIONS OF THE OSGOODE SOCIETY FOR CANADIAN LEGAL HISTORY

2025 Robert Sharpe, *My Life in the Law: Lawyer, Scholar, Judge*
Eric Adams and Jordan Stanger-Ross, *Challenging Exile: Japanese Canadians and the Wartime Constitution*
Carolyn Strange, *Fatal Confession: A Girl's Murder, a Man's Execution, and the Fitton Case*
Jim Phillips, *I Did Not Commit Adultery: Marital Conflict and the Law in Ontario in the 1870s*

2024 Adam Dodek, *Heenan Blaikie: The Making and Unmaking of a Great Canadian Law Firm*
Colin Campbell and Robert Raizenne, *A History of Canadian Income Tax Volume II, 1948–71*
Wayne Sumner, *Prairie Justice: The Hanging of Mike Huck*
Ian Radforth, *Deadly Swindle: An 1890 Murder in Backwoods Ontario That Gripped the World*

2023 Lori Chambers and Joan Sangster, eds., *Essays in the History of Canadian Law Volume XII: New Perspectives on Gender and the Law*
C. Ian Kyer, *The Ontario Bond Scandal of 1924 Re-examined*
Jonathan Swainger, *The Notorious Georges: Crime and Community in British Columbia's Northern Interior, 1909–25*

2022 Jim Phillips, Philip Girard, and R. Blake Brown, *A History of Law in Canada Volume II: Law for the New Dominion, 1867–1914*
J. Barry Wright, Susan Binnie, and Eric Tucker, eds., *Canadian State Trials Volume V: World War, Cold War and Challenges to Sovereignty, 1939–1990*
Constance Backhouse, *Reckoning with Racism: Police, Judges and the RDS Case*

2021 Daniel Rück *The Laws and the Land: The Settler Colonial Invasion of Kahnawà:ke in Nineteenth-Century Canada*
Lyndsay Campbell, *Truth and Privilege: Libel Law in Massachusetts and Nova Scotia, 1820–1840*
Martine Valois, Ian Greene, Craig Forcese, and Peter McCormick, eds. *The Federal Court of Appeal and the Federal Court: Fifty Years of History*
Colin Campbell and Robert Raizenne, *A History of Canadian Income Tax Volume I: The Income War Tax Act 1917–1948*

2020 Heidi Bohaker, *Doodem and Council Fire: Anishinaabe Governance through Alliance*
Carolyn Strange, *The Death Penalty and Sex Murder in Canadian History*

2019 Harry Arthurs, *Connecting the Dots: The Life of an Academic Lawyer*
Eric Reiter, *Wounded Feelings: Litigating Emotions in Quebec, 1870–1950*

2018 Philip Girard, Jim Phillips, and Blake Brown, *A History of Law in Canada Volume 1: Beginnings to 1866*
Suzanne Chiodo, *The Class Actions Controversy: The Origins and Development of the Ontario Class Proceedings Act*

2017 Constance Backhouse, *Claire L'Heureux-Dube: A Life*
Dennis G. Molinaro, *An Exceptional Law: Section 98 and the Emergency State, 1919–1936*

2016 Lori Chambers, *A Legal History of Adoption in Ontario, 1921–2015*
Bradley Miller, *Boarderline Crime: Fugitive Criminals and the Challenge of the Boarder, 1819–1914*
James Muir, *Law, Debt, and Merchant Power: The Civil Courts of Eighteenth-Century Halifax*

2015 Barry Wright, Eric Tucker, and Susan Binnie, eds., *Canadian State Trails Volume IV: Security, Dissent and the Limits of Toleration in War and Peace, 1914–1939*
David Fraser, *"Honorary Protestants": The Jewish School Question in Montreal, 1867–1997*
C. Ian Kyer, *A Thirty Years' War: The Failed Public /Private Partnership that Spurred the Creation of The Toronto Transit Commission, 1891–1921*

2014 Christopher Moore, *The Court of Appeal for Ontario: Defining the Right of Appeal, 1792–2013*
Dominique Clément, *Equality Deferred: Sex Discrimination and British Columbia's Human Rights State, 1953–84*
Paul Craven, *Petty Justice: Low Law and the Sessions System in Charlotte County, New Brunswick, 1785–1867*
Thomas Telfer, *Ruin and Redemption: The Struggle for a Canadian Bankruptcy Law, 1867–1919*

2013 Roy McMurtry, *Memoirs and Reflections*
Charlotte Gray, *The Massey Murder: A Maid, Her Master and the Trial That Shocked a Nation*
C. Ian Kyer, *Lawyers, Families, and Businesses: The Shaping of a Bay Street Law Firm, Faskens 1863–1963*
G. Blaine Baker and Donald Fyson, eds., *Essays in the History of Canadian Law Volume 11: Quebec and the Canadas*

2012 R. Blake Brown, *Arming and Disarming: A History of Gun Control in Canada*
Eric Tucker, James Muir, and Bruce Ziff, eds., *Property on Trial: Canadian Cases in Context*
Shelley A.M. Gavigan, *Hunger, Horses, and Government Men: Criminal Law on the Aboriginal Plains, 1870–1905*
Barrington Walker, ed., *The African Canadian Legal Odyssey: Historical Essays*

2011 Robert J. Sharpe, *The Lazier Murder: Prince Edward County, 1884*
Philip Girard, *Lawyers and Legal Culture in British North America: Beamish Murdoch of Halifax*
John McLaren, *Dewigged, Bothered, and Bewildered: British Colonial Judges on Trial*
Lesley Erickson, *Westward Bound: Sex, Violence, the Law, and the Making of a Settler Society*

2010 Judy Fudge and Eric Tucker, eds., *Work on Trial: Canadian Labour Law Struggles*
Christopher Moore, *The British Columbia Court of Appeal: The First Hundred Years*
Frederick Vaughan, *Viscount Haldane: The Wicked Step-father of the Canadian Constitution*
Barrington Walker, *Race on Trial: Black Defendants in Ontario's Criminal Courts, 1850–1950*

2009 William Kaplan, *Canadian Maverick: The Life and Times of Ivan C. Rand*
R. Blake Brown, *A Trying Question: The Jury in Nineteenth-Century Canada*
Barry Wright and Susan Binnie, eds., *Canadian State Trials Volume 3: Political Trials and Security Measures, 1840–1914*
Robert J. Sharpe, *The Last Day, the Last Hour: The Currie Libel Trial*

2008 Constance Backhouse, *Carnal Crimes: Sexual Assault Law in Canada, 1900–1975*
Jim Phillips, R. Roy McMurtry, and John Saywell, eds., *Essays in the History of Canadian Law. Volume 10: A Tribute to Peter N. Oliver*
Gregory Taylor, *The Law of the Land: Canada's Receptions of the Torrens System*
Hamar Foster, Benjamin Berger, and A.R. Buck, eds., *The Grand Experiment: Law and Legal Culture in British Settler Societies*

2007 Robert Sharpe and Patricia McMahon, *The Persons Case: The Origins and Legacy of the Fight for Legal Personhood*
Lori Chambers, *Misconceptions: Unmarried Motherhood and the Ontario Children of Unmarried Parents Act, 1921–1969*
Jonathan Swainger, ed., *The Alberta Supreme Court at 100: History and Authority*
Martin Friedland, *My Life in Crime and Other Academic Adventures*

2006 Donald Fyson, *Magistrates, Police and People: Everyday Criminal Justice in Quebec and Lower Canada, 1764–1837*
Dale Brawn, *The Court of Queen's Bench of Manitoba 1870–1950: A Biographical History*
R.C.B. Risk, *A History of Canadian Legal Thought: Collected Essays*, edited and introduced by G. Blaine Baker and Jim Phillips

2005 Philip Girard, *Bora Laskin: Bringing Law to Life*
Christopher English, ed., *Essays in the History of Canadian Law Volume 9: Two Islands, Newfoundland and Prince Edward Island*
Fred Kaufman, *Searching for Justice: An Autobiography*

2004 John D. Honsberger, *Osgoode Hall: An Illustrated History*
Frederick Vaughan, *Aggressive in Pursuit: The Life of Justice Emmett Hall*
Constance Backhouse and Nancy Backhouse, *The Heiress versus the Establishment: Mrs. Campbell's Campaign for Legal Justice*
Philip Girard, Jim Phillips, and Barry Cahill, eds., *The Supreme Court of Nova Scotia, 1754–2004: From Imperial Bastion to Provincial Oracle*

2003 Robert Sharpe and Kent Roach, *Brian Dickson: A Judge's Journey*
George Finlayson, *John J. Robinette: Peerless Mentor*
Peter Oliver, *The Conventional Man: The Diaries of Ontario Chief Justice Robert A. Harrison, 1856–1878*
Jerry Bannister, *The Rule of the Admirals: Law, Custom and Naval Government in Newfoundland, 1699–1832*

2002 John T. Saywell, *The Law Makers: Judicial Power and the Shaping of Canadian Federalism*
David Murray, *Colonial Justice: Justice, Morality and Crime in the Niagara District, 1791–1849*
F. Murray Greenwood and Barry Wright, eds., *Canadian State Trials Volume 2: Rebellion and Invasion in the Canadas, 1837–1839*
Patrick Brode, *Courted and Abandoned: Seduction in Canadian Law*

2001 Ellen Anderson, *Judging Bertha Wilson: Law as Large as Life*
Judy Fudge and Eric Tucker, *Labour before the Law: Collective Action in Canada, 1900–1948*
Laurel Sefton MacDowell, *Renegade Lawyer: The Life of J.L. Cohen*

2000 Barry Cahill, *"The Thousandth Man": A Biography of James McGregor Stewart*
A.B. McKillop, *The Spinster and the Prophet: Florence Deeks, H.G. Wells, and the Mystery of the Purloined Past*
Beverley Boissery and F. Murray Greenwood, *Uncertain Justice: Canadian Women and Capital Punishment*
Bruce Ziff, *Unforeseen Legacies: Reuben Wells Leonard and the Leonard Foundation Trust*

1999 Constance Backhouse, *Colour-Coded: A Legal History of Racism in Canada, 1900–1950*
G. Blaine Baker and Jim Phillips, eds., *Essays in the History of Canadian Law Volume 8: In Honour of R.C.B. Risk*
Richard W. Pound, *Chief Justice W.R. Jackett: By the Law of the Land*
David Vanek, *Fulfilment: Memoirs of a Criminal Court Judge*

1998 Sidney Harring, *White Man's Law: Native People in Nineteenth-Century Canadian Jurisprudence*
Peter Oliver, *"Terror to Evil-Doers": Prisons and Punishments in Nineteenth-Century Ontario*

1997 James W. St. G. Walker, *"Race," Rights and the Law in the Supreme Court of Canada: Historical Case Studies*
Lori Chambers, *Married Women and Property Law in Victorian Ontario*
Patrick Brode, *Casual Slaughters and Accidental Judgments: Canadian War Crimes and Prosecutions, 1944–1948*
Ian Bushnell, *The Federal Court of Canada: A History, 1875–1992*

1996 Carol Wilton, ed., *Essays in the History of Canadian Law Volume 7: Inside the Law – Canadian Law Firms in Historical Perspective*
William Kaplan, *Bad Judgment: The Case of Mr. Justice Leo A. Landreville*
Murray Greenwood and Barry Wright, eds., *Canadian State Trials Volume 1: Law, Politics and Security Measures, 1608–1837*

1995 David Williams, *Just Lawyers: Seven Portraits*
Hamar Foster and John McLaren, eds., *Essays in the History of Canadian Law Volume 6: British Columbia and the Yukon*
W.H. Morrow, ed., *Northern Justice: The Memoirs of Mr. Justice William G. Morrow*
Beverley Boissery, *A Deep Sense of Wrong: The Treason, Trials and Transportation to New South Wales of Lower Canadian Rebels after the 1838 Rebellion*

1994 Patrick Boyer, *A Passion for Justice: The Legacy of James Chalmers McRuer*
Charles Pullen, *The Life and Times of Arthur Maloney: The Last of the Tribunes*
Jim Phillips, Tina Loo, and Susan Lewthwaite, eds., *Essays in the History of Canadian Law Volume 5: Crime and Criminal Justice*
Brian Young, *The Politics of Codification: The Lower Canadian Civil Code of 1866*

1993 Greg Marquis, *Policing Canada's Century: A History of the Canadian Association of Chiefs of Police*
Murray Greenwood, *Legacies of Fear: Law and Politics in Quebec in the Era of the French Revolution*

1992 Brendan O'Brien, *Speedy Justice: The Tragic Last Voyage of His Majesty's Vessel* Speedy
Robert Fraser, ed., *Provincial Justice: Upper Canadian Legal Portraits from the Dictionary of Canadian Biography*

1991 Constance Backhouse, *Petticoats and Prejudice: Women and Law in Nineteenth-Century Canada*

1990 Philip Girard and Jim Phillips, eds., *Essays in the History of Canadian Law Volume 3: Nova Scotia*
Carol Wilton, ed., *Essays in the History of Canadian Law Volume 4: Beyond the Law – Lawyers and Business in Canada 1830–1930*

1989 Desmond Brown, *The Genesis of the Canadian Criminal Code of 1892*
Patrick Brode, *The Odyssey of John Anderson*

1988 Robert Sharpe, *The Last Day, the Last Hour: The Currie Libel Trial*
John D. Arnup, *Middleton: The Beloved Judge*

1987 C. Ian Kyer and Jerome Bickenbach, *The Fiercest Debate: Cecil A. Wright, the Benchers and Legal Education in Ontario, 1923–1957*

1986 Paul Romney, *Mr. Attorney: The Attorney General for Ontario in Court, Cabinet and Legislature, 1791–1899*
Martin Friedland, *The Case of Valentine Shortis: A True Story of Crime and Politics in Canada*

1985 James Snell and Frederick Vaughan, *The Supreme Court of Canada: History of the Institution*

1984 Patrick Brode, *Sir John Beverley Robinson: Bone and Sinew of the Compact*
David Williams, *Duff: A Life in the Law*

1983 David H. Flaherty, ed., *Essays in the History of Canadian Law Volume 2*

1982 Marion MacRae and Anthony Adamson, *Cornerstones of Order: Courthouses and Town Halls of Ontario, 1784–1914*

1981 David H. Flaherty, ed., *Essays in the History of Canadian Law Volume 1*